praise for barry friedman and his books

"No one I know of has honored a father as gallantly as has Barry Friedman, animating 'the oddities and wonders of Jack Friedman' for readers whose misfortune was never to have met him. Jack's enormous success was to have raised a son who loved him so faithfully, so drolly, and—our reward—so memorably."

Mark Singer, author of Funny Money and staff writer for The New Yorker

"You can't go on the road with standup comedian Barry Friedman, which is probably good for your health and sanity. But you can feel what it felt like, through this funny, gritty, wondrously detailed and scarily honest book I really am enjoying it."

Dave Barry, author, recipient of the Pulitzer Prize and the Walter Cronkite Award for Excellence in Journalism (about The Joke Was on Me)

"From the Baby O! Lounge in Hastings, Nebraska to the Elks Lodge in Seminole, Oklahoma, it's Barry Friedman! Let's give him a big hand, folks. He's written a book with all the wisdom and humanity of Alexis de Tocqueville's Democracy in America, but with way better jokes and twice as many clitoral piercings."

John H. Richardson (about The Joke Was On Me)

"This masterpieces would blow away the competition, if there were competition for such a masterpiece, which there is not."

Shane Gericke, bestselling author of *The Fury* (about *Jacob Fishman's Marraiges*)

"Seeing the broken yet still beautiful work through Barry's eyes is cathartic"

Jennifer Taub, author of *Big Dirty Money* (about *Jacob Fishman's Marraiges*)

"I knew this book would be special after reading the first sentence — 'You died today.' I was right. In *Four Days and a Year Later*, every single word counts. Barry Friedman invites readers to bear witness as he opens his heart and soul and pulls no punches in telling a story of loss and survival that is both tragic and inspirational. This book is simply incredible. What a gift Friedman has created for us."

Michael Wallis, author, *The Best Land Under Heaven: The Donner Party in the Age of Manifest Destiny*

"I haven't been able to get five pages in without having to catch my breath. You're a brave writer, my brother."

Charles P. Pierce, *Esquire* (about *Four Days and a Year Later*)

"[*Four Days and a Year Later*] is a shattering memoir about love and parenthood and all the ways you can love too much and still lose everything. For anyone struggling to understand the current drug crisis and anyone trying to imagine the outer edges of family this book will both sear and hold you. Powerful, brutally self aware, Barry Friedman is a flashlight through loss and redemption"

Dahlia Lithwick, Senior Editor, *Slate*

jack sh*t volume two

Wait for the Movie. It's in Color.

Barry Friedman

Copyright © 2024 by Barry Friedman

All rights reserved.

No part of this book may be reproduced in any form or by any electronic or mechanical means, including information storage and retrieval systems, without written permission from the author, except for the use of brief quotations in a book review.

To Leo and Marilyn Friedman (both in blessed memory) for their hospitality, the jelly candies, and the remembrances of Brooklyn, the war, the cousins, and the fur business

acknowledgments

To Thomas Walsh, Melissa Moss, Jerry Izenberg, and LeAnna Loeschen

foreword

Previously, in *Jack Sh*t, Volume One: Voluptuous Bagels and Other Concerns of Jack Friedman* . . .

The miserable bastards at Smith's Food and Drug in Las Vegas (I mistakenly wrote in Volume One it was the people at Von's who perpetrated this horrible, horrible crime. My apologies) had just taken a schmear of $7.44 as a service fee when my father cashed $93 in pennies at its Coinstar® machine that he had been collecting in a three-foot plastic Coca-Cola® bottle. The bottle, near the door that led to the garage, was in his office in the house he owned—a thirty-year mortgage he got when he was eighty-four—on Tumble Brook Drive in Summerlin, Nevada, a community just to the west of Las Vegas. The Coke bottle was under his fake framed CPA diploma that was kept on the wall by a solitary nail that had mostly given up on life.

My father, maybe due to his age, maybe because generations of Friedmans had done so, especially during the Depression, kept money strategically (and not so strategically) placed throughout the house, a trait he had acquired from his mother, my grandmother Riva, who had what are known in Yiddish as *pishkas* (small containers) of money around her apartment at 922 57th Street in Brooklyn. My father stashed money in the zippered compartments of tennis-racket cases in the hall closet, old wallets in desk drawers and nightstands in the guest bedroom, and in a folder in a file cabinet named CORPORATE TAXES. That's where the big bucks, the fives and tens, were kept.

"Don't tell anyone, Ba, the money's here," he'd say, calling me into his office and opening the file CORPORATE TAXES from his desk drawer every time I came to Vegas. "If you need a couple of bucks, here's where it is. Just let me know what you took. Let me know, all right?"

There were three plastic casino cups, lined up from biggest to smallest, on the credenza of his desk, in which he had quarters, dimes, and nickels. Back then, back when casinos were taking quarters—the gaming floors were much noisier then—my father had $383 in quarters and nickels, which we cashed in at one of the casinos before he left town. I don't know where my father got all the dimes, or for that matter the pennies in the plastic Coke bottle, as no casino was using them.

"What's with all the quarters?" I asked him once, finding a plastic bag of them in the guest bedroom. "I thought you didn't play slots."

"I don't, I don't. I just play once in a while. You can't win."

"So why are you playing?"

"I don't."

"But you did play—that's where the quarters came from. And, apparently, you won. And how come you didn't cash them in earlier?"

"They're good to have around. You never know."

"It's not like you need them to do your laundry."

"Why does it bother you?"

"It doesn't bother me. I'm just curious."

"I gamble at the slots when I don't feel like playing crap [his characterization of the game craps], that's all. But I don't play."

With the quarters, dimes, nickels, and pennies cashed in and the buckets tossed—the empty plastic Coca-Cola bottle, however, made the trip to Tulsa, along with other less important household items—his days at 2621 Tumble Brook Drive were over. The Survivors Group gave him a going-away dinner—Jeannette and he did not sit together—and they bought him some nice parting gifts.

He always invited me to dinner when I was in town, which he didn't have to do. This night, this final night, I had an argument with Ivan, a retired cop from California, about gun control.

Ivan mentioned that he didn't want anyone taking away his gun.

"Ivan," I said at dinner, "I don't want to take away your gun. I just don't want my father to have one." At that moment, my dad was across the table trying to turn on his cellphone.

Bill, my father's closest friend—he was taking care of his wife, who was in the throes of Alzheimer's—came up to me and said, "It's good you're taking him to Tulsa with you. He needs to go. I wish my wife's family would take her in. I can't do it anymore. But of course I will."

While packing, my brother Wayne and I found boxes of my father's toupees in suitcases, overnight bags, bigger boxes, and other bags in the garage. These women's hairpieces had metastasized like Tribbles on *Star Trek*, so we knew there were many more around the house. Tossing out your father's hairpieces brings siblings closer together.

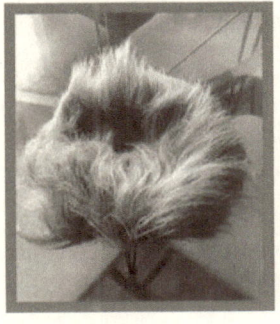

Jack Friedman's hair

"Good Christ, look at this," I said to Wayne about a large shipping container that I figured held ten hairpieces.

"We toss them?" he asked.

"Oh, we toss them."

The plan was that, once he left Vegas, my father would stay a few weeks with Wayne, while the movers took his stuff, including the three-foot plastic Coke bottle, to Tulsa. I had rented a two-bedroom place at the Mansion House Apartments near downtown. When he'd tell his friends about his new place, he'd often leave out the "House" and "Apartments" part and just tell them he was moving to the "Mansion," as if there was only one in Tulsa and he had it.

He was on his way to California with Wayne when I got a call from his real-estate agent, the non-Mustard, non-Schwartz Vicki, to tell me the buyers had pulled out of the sale. She didn't know why but said this had never happened to her so late in the process. The good news was that even though they could have demanded their $5,000 deposit back, the buyers were not going to, which was how I decided I was going to spin the story when I called my father.

"Dad," I said, calling him. I decided to wait until he had arrived in Eagle Rock.

"What's up, sweetheart?"

"You want the good news or you want the bad?"

"Give me the bad news."

"The sale of the house fell through."

"The what?"

"The house sale. It didn't sell."

"What happened?"

"I don't know. Vicki doesn't know either."

"Vicki?"

"Simons—the woman selling you the house."

"Oh, yeah, yeah, I know her. You know, I know two other Vickis—"

"I know."

"So what happens now?" he asked.

"She looks for another buyer."

"So what's the good news?"

"The buyers put down five thousand for a deposit and you get to keep that."

"All right, shouldn't be a total loss."

"Sorry about this, Dad. Nobody saw this coming."

"It's all right, what are you going to do? These things happen."

My father—and this is reason enough to love him—was more upset about a $7.44 fee when he cashed in his pennies at Smith's than he was about the sale of a $179,000 house falling through.

(The buyers pulled out because my father had purchased a new combination air conditioning/heating unit a year or so before he moved—or so he thought. As it turned out, it was just a heating unit, which the buyers decided was reason enough to cancel the sale, as the house was listed as having a new combo heat/AC unit. When I told my dad about this latest development, he said, "Ah, c'mon. I'm supposed to know what they're putting in?")

Jack Friedman is not a man who concerns himself with the particulars of life. Many people, oddly, would care about such a thing.

But let's continue.

("They told me the unit was new. These people don't know what they're talking about.")

My plan was to get my father into the Charles Schusterman Jewish Community Retirement Center in Tulsa. (The name was eventually changed to Zarrow Pointe. Many religious leaders and those associated with faith-based organizations were dropping their denominational labels on the theory they'd make their facilities more inclusive. My father still referred to the place as "the Hebrew Home" because "it's got a lot of Jews, you know?") It had a nursing wing, of which he was not in need, but it was on property when the time came that he would. The CSJCC complex also included an Independent Living wing, which would have been perfect for him and where I was trying to get him an apartment. The campus also had an indoor and outdoor pool, gym, workout rooms, and tennis courts, held exercise classes, had movies, activities, and field trips, provided housekeeping and security, and, not to put too fine a point on this, was home to many, many Jews. It wasn't exclusively a "Jewish place," as my father called it, but it was founded and run by Jews and Jewish organizations. My father liked the idea of being Jewish. He knew he had Jewish blood—it's how he characterized it—so it wasn't necessary, for instance, to keep kosher or fast on Yom Kippur. But he wouldn't eat ham—that was different. Ham, unlike bacon, unlike shrimp, was really not kosher. Unfortunately, Zarrow Pointe was expensive and had a waiting list, so it was going to have to wait. I knew the CEO of Zarrow, Jim Jakubovitz, and while he said it would be a long process, he promised my father would eventually get into the place. Jim suggested writing a letter to the board of directors petitioning for my father to get in.

Jim said it probably wouldn't happen the first year—and it didn't. Jim said that my father, as a new resident of Tulsa, would have to wait a few years.

So he moved into the Mansion.

My father was eighty-eight when he got to Tulsa. His health was remarkably good. By the time he left Vegas, he was no longer playing tennis (even though he said he still did) but was still bowling twice a week (even though he told people it was three times). He told whoever asked that he played handball (even though this was preposterous) and ran and jogged (which was hilarious). While his blood pressure was elevated, he ate what he wanted and had remarkable recuperative powers. He still had atrial fibrillation, but it somehow got better. He had stenosis in his neck, but it too, seemingly, just gave up and went away. His last few years in Vegas, he shopped, drove, and stayed out late gambling. His toe, for which he received the Purple

Heart and which never bothered him, was still the topic of conversation—his "war wounds," which he didn't suffer—whenever talk of military service kicked in with whoever crossed his path.

* * *

As mentioned, he and Jeanette had broken up before they left. She found him argumentative and loud and unwilling to make an effort for her. And in truth, he was a lousy boyfriend. I was once with him on Easter Sunday at the Orleans Casino when I heard him tell her on the phone he couldn't see her because he was meeting "some tax clients."

On Easter Sunday. At a casino.

"You don't think she really believed that story, do you?" I asked.

"What? I've met clients before."

"Not on Easter Sunday in a casino you haven't."

"She doesn't know that."

"Oh, I think she does."

At that point in his life, Jack Friedman had stopped courting women.

"I got to go all the way there," he said about the twenty-minute drive down Tropicana to her mobile home, "and come all the way back, then drop her off, and then come back. She wants me to come get her and bring her back from the dinners we have with the group—you know, the mob. I got nothing else to do?"

"But you have nothing else to do."

"Ach. It's too much."

"It's not too much."

"And I got to pay for her meal?"

"Does she expect you to?"

"I don't know."

"Then how do you know she wants you to?"

"How do I know? I don't know. But she makes money."

"Dad, you're dating her, though. Shouldn't you *want* to pay for her meal once in a while?"

"What kind of dating? We're seeing each other. There's no sex, Barry."

"Really more than I needed to know. But I think she wants to be treated better."

"Ah, c'mon. What about the way I'm treated? She buried two husbands, you know."

"I'm aware."

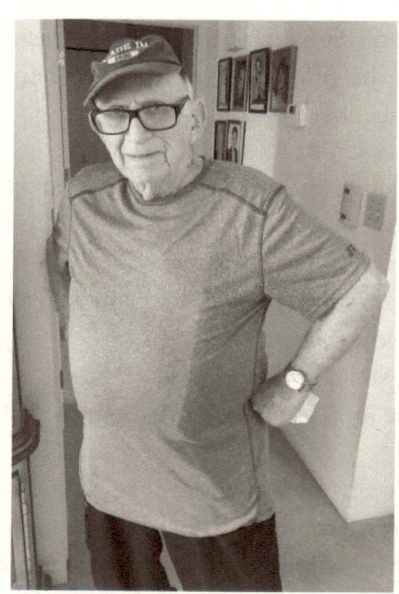

Preening in purple

one
2015

JANUARY

2 JANUARY

In which Jack Friedman, now in Mastic Beach, New York and having breakfast with his daughter, Susan, and his grandkids, calls to ask why nobody thought to ask the jam company's founder about this in 1897.

"Why would a guy keep the name Smucker's? I'm putting the jelly on the, you know, the—"

"—toast?"

"Toast. And it's good, but if he was going to stay in the business of making jelly, didn't he know that people would put a '-ch' sound to it and call it *Schmucker's*?"

"Who would do that? Who would call it *Schmucker's*?"

"That's not my point."

"It sounds like it's your point."

"I'm just wondering."

"Is there an answer I could give you?"

"My question's academic. Goodbye."

* * *

3 January

In which Jack Friedman sees the productivity gains in telecommunications and decides he can harness that power.

"Say, Ba, when I get to Tulsa, and I forgot to tell you about this, but we need to look into getting me a bigger cellphone."

"A bigger one?"

"You know, the longer, thinner ones like you and the kids have, with the big screen. I'm doing a lot more with my phone these days. It's not just calls, but now I'm checking bank balances."

Mastering the phone

* * *

10 January

In which Jack Friedman, hearkening back to the previous post, puts most of the blame for his telecommunications woes on the design of the human body, while not completely exonerating technology.

"Hey, Ba," he says when he calls this morning from Susan's, "you have to change my password on Bank of America."

"Why? What did you do?"

"I didn't do anything. I just can't get to the . . . whatchamacallit. I put in the wrong code a couple of times—I don't know what the hell they want from me—and they shut me out."

"Did you talk to Susan?"

"No, it's not that. My fingers are just too goddamn big for the phone, that's all, but I can't see my money. But why do they do that?"

"Security. And why are you checking your balance so many times?"

"I just want to check."

"If you're worried about the money from the house, it won't hit the account until Tuesday or Wednesday. Nothing is going to happen until then. So stop checking."

"I checked one time."

As it turns out, Vicki Simons, his real estate agent—not to be confused with Vicki Schwartz, his first girlfriend in Vegas, or Vicki Mustard, who was dating someone in "the Mob"—sold the house within a week of the previous buyers pulling out. It went for $181,000, $2,000 more than the original sales price. Considering my father also got to keep the original buyers' $5,000 deposit, he made about $36,000 on the house. Not bad for four years. Between that and his Social Security and the tax work he was still doing for clients—including a longtime friend, Petar, a Serbian internist-landlord—my father had enough to get by. It wasn't "the world," as he liked calling it, but it was enough. He went to stay with Susan, his daughter/my sister (and trust me, as the story progresses, it is a distinction that must be made), after a short trip to see Wayne in California.

"You checked more than once."

"I swear I didn't. Twice because I thought I was doing something wrong."

"Dad."

"I only checked it a couple of times and then, bingo! I can't get in."

"Let me talk to Susan."

"All right, hold on."

Susan comes to the phone. She's already giggling.

"Hi, Sue, so what's—"

"Dad, Dad . . . DAD! The mugs are in the cabinet. Not there. The other . . . the . . . I'll get it, I'll get it. Barry, he's been here a month."

"No. It just feels like a month—he's been there about a week."

"You so owe me."

"Just curious. How many times today has he tried to check his bank balance?"

"About ninety."

* * *

12 January

In which Jack Friedman questions his youngest grandson's career goals.

Noah, let us recall, is Susan's youngest boy. There's Jesse, Chris, and Noah, and Emily, the oldest and the only girl. Jesse and Chris are computer programmers, and Emily works odd jobs in retail and health care. They all live at home with their mother in Mastic Beach, New York, on Long Island, and get along remarkably well. Noah graduated from Farmingdale State College (SUNY) and is now working at JFK Airport in security. I didn't hear the conversation, obviously, between my father and Noah, but Noah told me he tried to tell his grandfather what he did for a living.

"What kind of cockamamie degree is Airport Management? What? You manage the airports or what?"

* * *

20 January

In which Jack Friedman arrives in Reno none the worse for wear—okay, a little worse—and then has fond memories of his grandchildren, whatever their names.

I decided to give Susan a break, so I had my father fly to Reno, Nevada, where I was performing at Catch a Rising Star at the Silver Legacy. Over the previous decade, I'd have him come to my shows here. He enjoyed coming mostly because I got him coupons to Flavors!, the buffet that's one floor up from the casino. He called me while waiting for the courtesy van at Rogue Valley International Airport.

"I ate too many nuts on the plane. I shouldn't do that," he said, sounding like he was off his usual game. "Ach, Barry."

"Why did you do that?"

"'Cause they give you nothing to eat on these goddamn planes."

"Susan packed you snacks and cookies and cheese and crackers."

"She did, but, remember, I had to fly from Long Island to wherever the hell it was first."

"Denver?"

"No, not Denver. No, yeah—Denver. And then to Vegas."

"Reno."

"What'd I say?"

"Doesn't matter. Susan didn't give you enough snacks for the whole trip? What kind of daughter makes her father starve like that? Take her out of the will."

"Nah, she's all right, your sister. We had a great steak dinner last night. Don't start making headaches. And the kids, they were all, you know, good. There was Noah and, uh, uh, you know, all of 'em—and Louie."

"Louie? Who's Louie?"

"Louie."

"Louie? You don't have a grandkid named Louie."

"You know . . ."

"You mean Chris, Jesse, and Emily?"

"Yeah, I was going to say that, but I forgot. Anyway, they were wonderful—no joke, all of them. They held my hand when I was walking up and down the stairs at the airport. Good kids! And the boys are making big bucks, too."

Later...

As discussed in *Jack Sh*t Volume One: Voluptuous Bagels and Other Concerns Of Jack Friedman*, my father often orders his fashion from Haband, an online haberdashery that specializes, according to its website, "in style, comfort, AND value." Additionally, the company on rare occasions offers free gifts, like watches, when an order reaches $50. Today at dinner, at Flavors!—did we use coupons? You have to ask?—he presented me with a Haband brown quartz watch with a faux diving meter.

"Can you use?" he asked, handing it to me at dinner.

"Of course."

I can't.

After dinner, and after my show, where he sat in the back and drank a mixture of orange juice and 7-Up, and after watching him play crap, the watch, I shouldn't have to tell you, stopped working. Not that it matters. I'm still going diving. And it was still sweet of him.

* * *

22 January

In which Jack Friedman doesn't ask for much.

"Ba, what the hell's going on with this remote?" he says in a call from his room. "What does it want from my life?"

"What's going on?"

"They give me a hundred million buttons. I got a button for full mute, half mute, go forward, go back, one to do this, one to do that. I don't know what the hell's going on. I don't know what they're talking about! I want to watch television, *nu*? I want four buttons: on, loud, soft, and one to change the channels. That's all."

"You want me to come over?"

"No, no, it's working now. I fixed it."

"So why'd you call?"

Later . . .

"How goes your life, Miss America?" my father asks Marte, our server this morning at the coffee shop. She is wearing a button on her lapel that reads EL SALVADOR. Her English is rough.

"You behaving yourself? If not, take my number," my father tells her, as he points to the coffee cup, his finger like a gun, pointing and pumping his thumb, meaning he wants it refilled.

Marte seems perplexed.

"I no understand," she says.

"I'm just joking," he says. "You're all right? Okay, you ready, Barry?"

"Yeah, I'll have—"

"Okay," my father interrupts, "I want two sunny-side eggs, leave them up, don't turn them, and then lie them intimately on well-done white toast. Don't butter the bread. I want them stark naked."

I can't tell for sure, but Marte smiles in a way that suggests that at this moment she misses her homeland very much.

Later . . .

Before the show tonight, my father and I were at the register at Flavors! when I notice Cynthia, a waitress at the buffet whom I've known for years, walking by.

"Cynthia, how are you?" I ask.

"Good, Barry. Is this your dad? I remember him."

"It is. Jack Friedman, Cynthia. Cynthia, Jack Friedman."

"Nice to see you, Jack."

"What's your name again, dear?"

"Cynthia."

"Cynthia?"

"Cynthia."

"I have a cousin named Cynthia."

"Niece," I say.
"What?"
"Niece."
"What'd I say?"
"Cousin."
"Cousin? No, she's my niece," he says to me.
"I know."
"She's not my cousin. She's my niece."
"I know. I just told you that."
"I know who she is. You don't have to tell me."
"She died, you know?"
"Vivian's daughter, really? Cynthia died? How'd she die?"
"I don't know."
"Wait, you're right. I was at the cemetery. I saw. You know Vivian died, too—that's my sister."
"I know. It was, like, fifty years ago. And Normie, Cynthia's husband, died too."
"He died? You know he went blind first."
"And their son, Cliff."
"Cliff I haven't talked to in years. He's a doctor."
"He was. He died."
"Cliff died? Funny how the whole family died."
Funny?
This Cynthia appears to be getting a migraine.

* * *

24 January

In which Jack Friedman reviews last night's show and the very nature of the performing arts.

"I think that Indian guy's going to be good," he says of the middle act. I'm headlining the show this week. "He reminds me of you with his delivery and material. And you were good, too, by the way. Sometimes you're very hot onstage. Why is that?"

"If I knew that, Dad . . . Wait—I remind you of the Indian comic?"

"You know what I mean."

Later . . .

My father is at a full blackjack table, killing with my material. I walk up behind him and hear him say, "These two Irish guys walk out of a bar—hey, could happen." It's a silly joke I do onstage when I feel like telling joke-jokes.

The crowd at the table erupted.

"You're stealing my jokes," I said.

"Ah, c'mon, what do you know about comedy? I tell them better."

* * *

25 January

In which Jack Friedman tries to unravel the mysteries of the weather.

Took my father to Lake Tahoe today.

"What kind of weather do they have in Idaho?" he wanted to know on the way there.

"Idaho? I don't know. We're not in Idaho."

"I know, but is this the same snow we saw earlier? And what do they have in Idaho?"

"Why are you asking about Idaho?"

"I want to know."

"I don't know about Idaho. We're in Nevada. I think, though, this is the same snow as the snow in Reno, but there's probably snow here we haven't seen before. There's a lot of snow."

We saw where *Bonanza* was filmed, specifically the Ponderosa Ranch, and where the boathouse scenes in *The Godfather, Part Two* were shot, then gambled at Harrah's, had lunch, and took a drive around Lake Tahoe.

"Why is the lake so goddamn big?" he asked. "Wow-wee-wow! Who made it this big?"

"God."

"I'm going to rap you right in the mouth."

Later...

To the waitress at Olive Garden in Carson City, Nevada, after not enjoying his wait to get a table: "Does it cost extra to have someone feed me?"

* * *

26 January

In which we leave Reno, but not before Jack Friedman dispenses nutritional advice.

We're at Flavors! for a change.

"What are you eating that for?" he asks of my French toast. "You can't eat that. You're aging yourself."

"Huh?"

"No good. Look at you. All you need is cereal and coffee in the morning," he says, as his Frosted Flakes arrive. He tears open the individual box. He then proceeds to put the contents of two packs of Equal, three packs of Sweet'N Low, and four tiny containers of Half & Half into his decaf.

"And that's healthy?" I ask, pointing at his coffee.

"I do this to sweeten the coffee, that's all."

Later...

As we board the plane back to Tulsa—he'll stay with Melissa, my girlfriend, and me until his stuff arrives from Vegas—my father starts complaining about how windy it was in Reno, to which Sharon, the Southwest flight attendant, with whom he had been flirting, replies, "It was windy. It could blow your hair off."

"Not that hair," I say. "Glue."

* * *

29 January

In which Jack Friedman reminds us of the power of a father's love.

"Barry, I couldn't have done this without you," he says. "You know, the moving and whatnot and all you do. Good thing you don't work and have the time to do this."

Later...

At IHOP tonight—we're now in Tulsa—he tells the waitress at various points in the meal: "Behave yourself. And if you can't, take my number," and "Behave yourself. It's a public place," and "Behave yourself. And if you can't, get a friend for me."

* * *

31 January

In which Jack Friedman reminds us to watch out for difficult women.

"So, Ba, Melissa's been married twice?"

"Yeah."

"I don't mean anything bad by this, but is she tough to live with?"

Later...

Upon returning from her ex-husband's memorial service a few hours later—he had died after a two-year pummeling by cancer—Melissa was exhausted and drained.

"What's the matter?" my father asks her, noticing her sadness. "It didn't go well?"

Later...

"Dad, we're going to Ed's tomorrow for the Super Bowl," I tell him at dinner.

"Who?"

"Ed. Your wife's, my mother's, brother, remember?"

"Oh, I know, I know. I always confuse him with Mendel, Max and Dora's son."

"Who are they, again? Have I met these people?"

"You don't know Max?"

"Why would I know Max?"

"What do you mean, you don't know Max?"

"Who really knows Max? Besides, he was your cousin growing up."

"Right. This was before your time."

"Okay, the Super Bowl tomorrow—you wanna go, right?"

"Yeah, yeah. Who's playing?"

"Seattle and New England."

"Seattle? What kind of team is that?"

"What kind of . . . I don't know. The Seahawks. They won last year."

"Okay. And New England, huh? How long have they been good?"

"Many years."

"You know, I grew up with Max."

FEBRUARY

1 February

In which Jack Friedman reminds us that man can live by bread alone, provided it's toasted properly.

Last night, my father ordered well-done white toast at Village Inn (imagine IHOP with better pies but not as clean). You wouldn't think a man would be so particular about white bread, whatever its form, but you, alas, would be wrong. When it was served to him, it was not as well-done as he imagined everyone in the universe knew that's how he preferred his toast. He was simply not happy with Village Inn's commitment to the entire toasting process. Now, a man approaching ninety, you might think, would have learned by this point in life to not sweat the small stuff, which this certainly would be, but you, alas, would be wrong again.

Jack Friedman is not such a man.

"What's the matter? They don't know how to toast bread in Oklahoma? Every time I order well-done toast here, it comes—

what should I call it?—lacking, soft, nowhere. You're uncivilized in this state."

"How many times have you ordered toast in Oklahoma?"

"Many times."

"It was one waitress, one order of toast. Give the state a break."

"No, it's happened before."

"You just got here. How has it happened before? How many pieces of toast have you had in the state that have disappointed you?"

"You don't know what you're talking about."

* * *

2 February

In which, hand to God, it happened again. This morning at breakfast—this time at IHOP—he picked up what should have been well-done, toasted white bread, waved it, and plopped it back down before calling the waitress and sending it back.

"What kind of fakakta state you got here? They don't have toasters?"

Later...

"I didn't like how either team played," he said about yesterday's Super Bowl, on the way to his apartment to meet the movers. "That stupid call at the end by Seattle. Run it, dummies!" As for the defense New England played, "You let 'em run up and down the field. I wouldn't give the trophy to either of them."

Later...

There is no earthly reason to believe this, but the first item the movers carried into the apartment at the Mansion (House Apartments, if you're just joining us) is this . . .

We're in the apartment and my father is talking to the man assembling his desk, telling him about the women he's known, the tax clients he's had, his huge home in Las Vegas (1,100 square feet, two bedrooms), and the "stag films" he owns. The man, putting the desk together, is clearly wearing headphones and just as clearly is unable to hear my father, a fact that does not deter him in the slightest. Then, because you knew he would, he tells the man the joke about the woman walking into the bar with a parrot on her shoulder.

In case you're new to these parts:

A woman walks into a bar with a parrot on her shoulder and the bartender screams, "Get out. We don't serve animals here."

"Animal?" says the woman. "This is not an animal. This is a parrot, a rare, expensive parrot. It is no animal."

"I was talking to the bird," says the bartender.

Later . . .

"I know why you don't like these toupees, Barry," he says to me in the Target parking lot.

It's been a long day. This is how I want to end it: with a conversation about what passes for the hair atop his head.

"This should be good. Go ahead."

"Because you think they make me look younger than you."

At the time, I was drinking a can of Diet Pepsi, the contents of which came out my nose. "That's what you think?"

"You betcha sweet ass, baby. Many times I tell people my age, they don't believe it. I tell them your age, they tell me I look younger than you."

"Many times? That has never happened."

"Once it happened."

"You are making this up. It never happened."

"It happened years ago—you weren't around."

I think it's actually impressive he's doubling down on this preposterous story.

"This never happened. Nobody told you that, ever."

"All right, I'll tell you the truth. I'm thinking of going without the hairpieces. I am thinking about it, but I need hats. Really cool hats."

"Cool hats you shall have. We're going to Target, after all."

"They got hats here if I decide to get one?"
"If there's a God, they do."

* * *

3 February

In which Jack Friedman comments on the mendacity of Oral Roberts as we drive by the sixty-foot-tall supplicant-hands statue at Oral Roberts University, all while stipulating he's got nothing against the man personally.

"What a farce this guy was! What a farce! And the place is crooked. Did he want it that way? Oh, oh, the hands. He built this shit with his members' money. And they let him get away with it? Don't get me wrong. I'm not knocking the guy."

Later...

"Hello," I say to the Cox Communications representative, now that we're back at my father's apartment. "Was supposed to have installation between three and five p.m., and it's five thirty."

I give the rep my father's address, phone, Social Security number.

"I don't have you in the system," says the rep.

"Do they know who I am, or what?" my father asks from the sofa.

"They know. Hold on, Dad."

"What?"

"Hold on!"

"I'm holding. I'm holding."

"How is that possible?" I say to the woman on the phone. "Got a call last night confirming you had me, uh, my father in the system."

"What city are you in?"

"Tulsa."

"Tulsa?" my father asks, laughing. "Who would go to Tulsa?"

"I was looking in Oklahoma City," says the woman.

"What kind of Tulsa?" asks my father.

"Dad, please."

"Tulsa? They don't know I'm in Tulsa. Where do they think I am?"

"They know—Dad!"

"What?"

"I'm on the phone. Let me talk!"

"Talk. Who's stopping you?"

"I thought you said Oklahoma City," says the woman.

"I didn't say that."

"Yes, sir, I have you. You're in Tulsa, not Oklahoma City, and we have you scheduled between three and five and it's . . . oh, five thirty."

"My point, yeah."

"Are they coming, or what?" asks my father.

"They're coming."

"When? Next Tuesday?"

"Maybe he got stuck in traffic," says the woman.

"Wouldn't he have called someone—you, me?"

"I'll have him call you if he calls in. Watch your phone for me, okay?"

"Watch my phone?"

"Can I help you with anything else today?"

"You mean other than the installation? No, that pretty much covers the reason for the call."

"Thank you for choosing Cox."

I then repeat to my father the very conversation he'd just heard me having.

* * *

4 February

In which my good friend Charlie Pierce of Esquire *announces the arrival of Jack Friedman to Oklahoma in his blog "Politics With Charles P. Pierce."*

"Friedman père is now in Tulsa. The ladies are helpless. Plan accordingly."

* * *

5 February
In which Jack Friedman experiences TV caller-ID for the first time.
"Barry, it's Dad," he says to me as he answers the phone. "You're on television."
"What do you mean?"
"On television. I'm watching *King Kong* and it says 'Barry Friedman calling.' Were you in that movie?"
"No."
"You sure?"
"Yeah, sure. That's a feature Cox gives you."
"Who?"
"It's your cable comp—never mind. It's part of the phone package. It lets you know who's calling and flashes it on the screen."
"So it knew you were calling? Wow-wee-wow! Does everyone who's watching this see that you're calling?"
"No, just you, because I'm just calling you."
"I know, I know. I was joking. But I'll be a son of a gun. 'Barry Friedman calling.' What's up, sweetheart?"
"Nothing. I can't even remember why I called."

* * *

6 February
In which Jack Friedman explains how Facebook can bring love to a hurting world.
"Yeah, yeah," I hear him say to Wayne, who called. "Barry sent the picture of me in the hat to his people on, I don't know what it is, the thing—and I already got three marriage proposals."

Jack Friedman in the Navy (which he wasn't)

* * *

7 February

I was going to give you a day off from *Jack Sh*t*—and you all have been wonderful throughout the move—but this was too good. While talking on the phone to one of his many ninety-year-old tax clients, Sonya Lamut ("She's from the old country, Ba"), he tells her, "My son's in show business, and I moved to Tulsa because I have a lot of clients in show business."

* * *

8 February

In which the phone rings. The day begins.

"Barry, this stupid computer. It doesn't print. I tell it to print—nothing. It hums at me. What does it want from my life?"

Later...

My father is disturbed by the Picasso on the wall.

"What the hell is that?" he asks at dinner tonight at our house. He is at the dining room table, facing this Picasso print.

"It's a Picasso," Melissa says.

"He's a two-year-old with a pencil."

"Here we go," I say.

"I think it looks like a crazy guy hugging a guitar," says Gregory, Melisssa's son.

"A what? I mean, really, what the hell is that? It's disjointed. Did he paint it and show it to his mother, who said, 'Eat something. You'll feel better'? He should be arrested."

"He's dead," I say.

"Doesn't matter. It's crap."

"Next time," Melissa says to me, or maybe to God, "he sits facing away from the Picasso."

"No, I'm serious," my father insists. "What is it supposed to be? I see an arm and a toilet face."

* * *

9 February

In which we are reminded why we should all want to be Jack Friedman someday.

My father called this morning and said he couldn't sleep last night, so, apparently, he got up, got dressed, and drove to River Silk or River Stix—his names for the River Spirit Casino—at three thirty in the morning. This is an eighty-nine-year-old man, let us remember. Once at the casino, he had four gin-and-tonics and proceeded to win $345 playing blackjack. ("I didn't feel like standing. I usually play crap.") He then found a bench outside the buffet, sat down, and fell asleep for an hour or so before being awakened by a security guard, who told him the casino frowns on old men napping on benches in the middle of the night.

My father then drove home, half-drunk, dead-tired.

"Hey, Ba," he says, "you wanna go for pancakes?"

"Of course I do. I'll pick you up. No more driving."

"You gotta deal," he says.

"Melissa," I say (she's in bed next to me), "my father's hungover and I'm taking him for pancakes."

"Enjoy."

Later...

"This waitress, she must have been eighteen," he says to me, as I return from the restroom. "Who knows? Looks like she might need some romance. Who the hell knows? She asked for my number."

"Did you give it to her?"

"I don't know what it is. What the hell is it, anyway?"

On a bench

* * *

10 February

In which there were also these moments.

While the hug he gave me in his apartment, seemingly out of nowhere, was sweet and goofy (he smashed his glasses into my chest), it's when he said, "You probably have to get home and do some work, no? I take too much of your time. I'm sorry. I mean, I think you do. You working or what these days?" that made the moment memorable and hilarious.

"Not really, Dad. I got time. Wanna go to the casino?"

"Yeah. Let's eat something. What the hell?"

We arrive at the Hot Rod Casino—his name for Hard Rock Hotel and Casino—and head first to the buffet.

"The vegetables, Ba. The other places, they're plain. But here, they fry them, they grill them, they coat them. They dress them up. And such an enormous variety."

* * *

12 February

In which Jack Friedman goes to the doctor and regales Domonique, one of the medical assistants who works at Dr. Jerry Block's office, with past glories while simultaneously bemoaning the brutality of aging.

"I used to play tennis," he tells her. "Every day! But the legs, the legs! They gave out on me. Ah, what's your name again, dear?" and before she can answer, he asks, "Where did it all go? I was sixteen two weeks ago."

Later...

"Dad, what are you doing for dinner?" I ask in a call. "You wanna go out?"

"Nah, I got undressed, I just crawled into bed, I'm watching a movie set in Ireland with some girl in it, I poured myself a gin, and I think I'm going to have some potato chips. I'm very comfortable."

* * *

14 February

In which, during a drive through South Tulsa, Jack Friedman questions the mindset of those in Oklahoma.

"What kind of name is 'Jenks'?"

"It's the name of a city."

"Jenks? Jenks? Jenks! Nu, Jenks. Who does that?"

"Why does that bother you?"

"It doesn't bother me, but I don't understand what the hell they were thinking."

"I don't know what they were thinking, Dad."

"Is it a guy's name? Did he come to work one day? Were they in a meeting and they said, 'Okay, we'll call it Jenks. Sam Jenks, we'll name it after you. And why J-e-n-k-s? Why not J-i-n-x? That I could understand."

"*That* you could understand?"

"Does it snow in Jenks?"

Transitions, in case you haven't caught on yet, are not things my father finds especially necessary.

"No, oddly enough. Everywhere but Jenks."

"Ah, please. Jenks? Jenks? 'What are you doing?' 'I'm in Jenks.' 'You're in Jenks?' 'Yes, I'm in Jenks.' 'What are you doing in Jenks?' 'What does anyone do in Jenks?'"

"Dad, you okay? Who you talking to?"

"No good, Barry, no good. This is no name . . . Jenks! It's uncivilized."

"It's a name!"

"We have to move, Ba. Oklahoma! This is not a place for humans. It's only for Southerners."

* * *

15 February

In which the greatest name for a bagel place is born.

Ever since my father arrived in Tulsa, we have been going most mornings, when I can talk him out of Panera, to Old School Bagel Cafe, which is run by two good friends of mine, Joe and Aaron.

"Dad, what do you want to do today for breakfast?"

"Let's go to, what is it again? You know . . . uh, Owl Head Bagels."

"'Owl Head Bagels'? Do you mean Old School Bagel Cafe?"

"What? No—yeah, I don't know. The place. Your guys. They got good coffee there."

At "Owl Head" Bagels

* * *

17 February

In which allowances must be made for lunch.

We get to the Hot Rod—the 2-for-1 buffet we discover is applicable to both lunch and dinner—early.

"It's good we're here," he says.

"Why?"

"Don't you remember the place was mobbed last week?"

"I don't."

"Mobbed."

"Mobbed?"

"Mobbed."

"Okay, mobbed."

"What time does lunch start?" he asks.

"Eleven."

"Good."

It's ten thirty.

Later...

Those miserable bastards. There is no 2-for-1 buffet today on account of Mardi Gras.

"You don't tell people?" my father asks the cashier.

"We put signs out," she says. "We tried to let people know."

"Nobody told me! All right, dear, I'm not blaming you. How much will it be, then?"

"About twenty-three dollars, with tax."

"For that kind of money," my father says, "I want someone to feed me."

* * *

19 February

In which we are reminded that Tulsa has so much to learn.

We're at breakfast today at Panera—not Owl Head—and my father is not happy.

"Up to the top they fill it?" he asks, as he sees the coffee in his cup. "There's no room for the cream. What's the matter with you people? And get a bigger cup, for crying out loud!"

"I didn't pour your coffee. There is self-serve over there." I point to coffee pots. "Go do it yourself."

"These people."

"They don't know how much coffee you like in your coffee. You asked her to help you. You can pour the refills. Most people don't want it with all the cream and sugar you put in anyway."

"That's the way I like it!"

"But she didn't know that."

"And toast the goddamn bread! This is limp. It's nowhere."

"You didn't order bread."

"They do the same thing here."

Later . . .

"I need to go to Staples, Ba," he says as we're leaving.

"How come?"

"I need Wite-Out."

* * *

20 February

In which we are reminded you quiz Jack Friedman at your own risk.

This morning at Owl Head, Aaron Quinton, its owner, joins us for breakfast.

"Hey, Jack," he asks, "what's the name here?"

"Uh, let me think," my father responds. "Let's see . . . uh, 'Old Cow Bagels'?"

Aaron drops his head, a beaten man.

* * *

21 February

Today, good friends Sharon and Gary, both in their fifties, came up to Tulsa from Dallas. We're all at Owl Head.

"I don't mean to pry," my father asks them, "but how come neither of you have any kids?"

"That's pretty much the definition of prying, Dad."

"What am I asking? Why don't they have kids? They can't?"

(Years ago, Gary met my father, who asked him, "How many leased cars do you think there are in Texas? You know, generally?")

* * *

22 February

In which Jack Friedman sees the absurdity in current Oklahoma law and asks the question as only he can.

On the drive to the Hot Rod, he sees a flashing message board on I-44 for automatic weapons.

"Nu? You can advertise a machine gun, but you can't advertise liquor? What do I want with a machine gun? What kind of shit is this state?"

* * *

23 February

In which my father lies to an audiologist.

"You know," he says to the doctor, "I lost my hearing in the war."

"No, you didn't," I say.

"You don't know."

"I know."

"You know?"

"I know."

"We were in Okinawa [he wasn't] when a bomb resulted in mayhem and destruction [there may have been, but he wasn't there to experience any of it], and because of that, I got the Purple Heart. I've had ringing in my ears ever since."

"None of that is true, Doctor," I say.

"Some of it," my father says. "I have a Purple Heart, don't I?"

"But your hearing wasn't affected, and that's not why you got it."

"What about my toe?"

* * *

24 February

In which he wonders about Oklahoma gun laws and those left behind.

As happened last week on the way to the 2-for-1 buffet at the Hot Rod, we see the billboard that's advertising machine guns.

"So, you're telling me I can get a machine gun for $395, and if someone breaks into my house, I can shoot them?"

"Yes, but unless you have it in your lap, you'd have to ask him to stand there while you get your glasses and then go get the machine gun out of the closet."

"Then I could shoot him?"

"Yes, if you had the right glasses on. You don't want to put on the reading glasses."

"If I could even find them. And how patient is he going to be?"

"Exactly."

"Okay, so I shoot him with the machine gun. He's dead. Now what?"

"Under Oklahoma law, you're probably okay."

"But what would his widow say?"

"'What would his widow say?' How do you know he has one? Wow! I don't know. Unless he's a prick, she'd probably be pissed."

"I don't know, Ba. I still don't want one. There's no need."

Later . . .

After telling the same buffet hostess for the third time in as many weeks, "Thank you for last night" and telling her—again, for the third time in as many weeks—that she's supposed to respond, "Oh, was that you?" my father dug out a picture of his wife, my mother, and said, pointing to the picture, "Such a beautiful woman, a Liz Taylor lookalike. She went too soon! But she was a brunette here and then became a blonde when she died."

* * *

25 February

In which nobody gives a compliment like Jack Friedman.

My father came over for dinner. After Melissa went to sleep, he said to me, "When Melissa puts on the heels and a dress, she's very attractive . . . A very handsome girl."

* * *

26 February
In which Jack Friedman seems underwhelmed by his progeny.
At dinner tonight, my father said to the waitress, pointing to me, "This is the son of my wife, who died."

* * *

27 February
In which my father's fame comes into focus after an accident.
Sitting at Olive Garden (don't ask, he loves their soups), he says, "Barry, I need to ask you a personal question, okay?"

"What is it?" I ask, curious about his tone, expecting a query about fathers and sons, mortality, his wife (my mother), something.

"Be honest."

"Sure. What is it?"

A long pause ensues. He appears to be searching for the right words.

"Tell me, Ba . . . why are there so many fat girls around? I don't mean just fat, I mean enormous! Do they eat too much, or what?"

Later . . .

We took separate cars, and on the way home, he had an accident. He ran into a woman in a Toyota who had the temerity to want to turn left.

I got a call from the paramedics. It happened five minutes from the house.

"Dad, you okay?" I ask, finding him sitting in the back of an ambulance van.

"Don't you people spend any money? Fix the goddamn roads! A left she's making? Nu."

"She's allowed to make a left. Seems like you ran into her."

"I ran into her?"

"You did. The back of her car is all pushed in."

"Who the hell knows? Ach, I'm going back to Vegas."

"People turn left there, too, you know. By the way, where's your hair?"

He touches his head.

"I don't know."

"Maybe it flew off," I say.

"Would you go look for it?"

I leave the ambulance and go back to his car, which is clearly totaled, looking for his hair. I find it in the backseat. I pick it up.

Why aren't tongs a part of everyday life?

I bring it back, hand it to him.

"Who's your favorite child?"

He puts it on his head, sort of.

The EMT enters.

"He's been cracking me up," he says. "He doesn't want to go to the hospital."

"What? I'm not going to no hospital," my father says.

"We know that."

"He's really fine. Let me ask a question: Is his name Jack Friedman?"

"Yes."

"I've read about him."

"You're kidding."

"He's a celebrity. Are you Barry?"

"This is too weird."

Just then a woman walks to the ambulance.

"Hi," she says. "Is he okay?"

"He's fine," I say. "You're who he hit, I take it. Sorry."

"No, don't worry about it. I'm fine. But we're worried about him—my husband and me."

"That's very nice of you. Looks like he'll be fine."

"We think we know him."

This cannot be happening.

"Really?"

"I love reading about him. You're Barry, right?"

"I am."

"I read about him on Facebook all the time. We know about Bernie and Jeannette and the move. I love him."

"You hear that, Dad?"

"Reads about me? What do you mean? How does she read about me?"

"I write about you."

"What do you say?"

"How you're a terrible driver. Thank you," I say to the woman.

"He's such a sweet guy."

The woman and I exchange insurance cards and she leaves.

"So, Dad, what do you want to do? You want me to take you home?"

"Yeah, let's get out of here."

"Take him tomorrow to his doctor," says the EMT. "But I think he's fine."

We walk past his car.

"Why don' t they fix these cockamamie roads in Tulsa?"

"Yeah, how dare someone make a left in front of you when you're trying to go straight?"

* * *

28 February

In which Jack Friedman is not happy with the doctor's orders.

"I'm not sore," he says to Dr. Block. "It's just a little tender. There's no pain. It just hurts."

And of course he didn't want to go to the doctor. Earlier, when I insisted, he says, "What's he going to do? Look at me and check me out?"

"That's exactly what he's going to do."

"Why?"

"Because you're an old man and you were in an accident."

"Ach!"

"Why did God design a body like this?" he asks Jerry. "It's flawed."

Jerry checks him out. He is indeed fine.

"Now—driving, Jack. I'll make you a deal," says Jerry. "You take a driving test. If you pass, you can keep your license. Otherwise, you have to give it up."

"I'd probably fail."

"Exactly."

"The state's going to tell me if I can drive? No."

"The state can do that, yeah."

"Fine, I'll take one."

On the way out, my dad thanked everyone in the office for their time, and we went for pancakes.

MARCH

For the first time since I kidnapped my father from Vegas and dragged him to Tulsa, I am going out of town—Port Charlotte, Florida, for a weekend gig, then San Antonio, Texas, for a few days for another gig, and then to Oregon to see my daughter, where I'll watch her eat vegan food and yell at me for not being sustainable enough. My father should be fine, as he is now settled in his apartment at the Mansion. The Honda was totaled —how about that woman having the temerity to make a left in front of him?—so he is now in a rental, until we figure what comes next in his automotive life. (Personally, I think taking away his license and shackling him to the sofa should be the next thing.) Melissa will be here, so if he needs anything, she can invite him over and have him sit away from the Picasso, while she doubles up on Klonopin. It's a relief knowing he's not alone. He had friends in Vegas, so he was never truly alone there, either, but they had as many aches and pains as he did and were just as lousy driving a car as he was. Octogenarians and nonagenarians shouldn't be in charge of getting other octogenarians and nonagenarians to the hospital and to Panera—that's what sons are for.

* * *

1 March

In which we learn that when Jack Friedman wants office supplies, price be damned. I'm leaving tomorrow, so this must be done today. And when I say it has to be done, it really doesn't.

I pick him up at the Mansion.

"I need paper clips desperately."

"Desperately?"

"I must have paper clips!"

"Okay, we'll go to Office Depot. Do we need a police escort? You seem concerned."

"Office *Dee Pot?*" he says. He always says it like this, thinking it's hilarious, just as he always calls Bob Dylan "Bobby *Die-Lan*" because that, too, tickles him. Yeah, I don't know, either.

"Office Dee Pot?" he says again. "You know what they get for paper clips?"

"No idea and I'm a little concerned you do."

"We'll go to Walmart instead. They're cheaper. I have gotten them there before."

"You want to drive to Walmart, across town, for paper clips? Office Depot is down the street. How much more could they be?"

"Yeah, you're right. What am I knocking my brains out for? Whatever it costs, it costs. But I must get paper clips!"

* * *

2 March

I headed first to Florida's west coast for a gig at Visani's Italian Steakhouse in Port Charlotte. I told my father for days I was going and this trip was happening, but I call him this morning to remind him one more time.

"You got a gig? Good! You're making money—go, go! I'll be fine. I'm here with Meliss," which is what he calls her. "You think You'll get much in terms of a gate at the club?"

* * *

7 March
In which Jack Friedman and Melissa Moss go drinking.
Melissa filed this report:
"We're at dinner," she says to me this morning in a call, "and your dad had a hamburger and mashed potatoes. And we start drinking. After the second round, he says, 'Let's have another,' and I—*I*—had to be the responsible one. I told him *no*. You owe me—because I needed a drink, many drinks, after eating a meal with your father without you."

"Many girlfriend points. What then?"

"I brought him back to our house and he fell asleep on the sofa for a half hour. I then drove him home."

"Good, you didn't let him drive. What else?"

"He said you don't drink because you don't want to lose control."

"He's not entirely wrong."

"He didn't say it in a bad way."

"So what are you saying? He likes me?"

"Well, I didn't say that. But he didn't say he didn't."

* * *

10 March
In which we learn why airbag manufacturers needed one more day when deciding upon a name for their product.
I'm back in town—at the Mansion, specifically—when my father gets a phone call from the insurance company.

"What? I don't understand," I hear him say. "Who are you again? Could you speak up—"

"Dad, let me talk to them."

"Here, talk to my son," he says, handing me the phone. "I don't know what the hell they want from me."

Among other topics, I'm asked if I was driving the car at the time of the accident.

"No, no. Who told you that?"

"Your father said you were driving, last time we spoke with him."

"He told you that? I was with him *after* he had the accident, I drove him *after* the accident—but not driving during it."

"Oh, okay. We thought that was probably the case. Can we speak to him again?"

"Sure. He's right here."

"Yes, yes, I was driving," I hear him say. "Who told you I wasn't driving? I'm sorry. My son was just . . . well . . . Yeah, yeah. What's that, dear? I guess I'm at fault. Could you speak a little louder? I mean, I don't know. I'm sure you'll determine that. The roads are terrible, though. The driver, a woman, was turning left and I guess I hit her from behind. That's what she says. I tried to stop after I ran into her, but . . . uh . . . uh . . . the balloon came out."

* * *

11 March

In which Jack Friedman, especially if you're a New York state resident, has some tax advice for you.

"In the old days, you could file tax returns any way you wanted," he tells me on the phone. "Then they gave you the choice between electrifying them on the computer or filing them by hand, and now, cockamamie New York requires that you file it by the machine. You following me? Now, they have to be electrified. New York, nu? What do they want from my life?"

* * *

12 March

In which we learn about the cattle industry and why Dennis Miller is dead to him.

"Do you get hot summers here, or what?" he asks, looking up at the sun on the way to Owl Head.

"Pretty hot, Dad."

"Not like Vegas, though. Wow-wee-wow!"

"It gets pretty hot, though, let me tell you."

"Texas, too?"

"Yeah."

"Well, sure, that's why ranches are so big down there. The cows love that kind of weather."

Later...

Driving on Riverside Drive in Tulsa, he asks, "Did Tulsa steal this from New York, because you know there's a Riverside Drive, too, along the Hudson River?"

Later...

We're inside the Hot Rod Casino, passing the will-call window and the VIP booth. We see a line developing.

"Hey, Ba, what's this?"

"Dennis Miller is performing."

"The comedian?"

"You know Dennis Miller?"

"Yeah, he's the guy who does that thing. He's funny."

"Don't get me started."

"No, he was all right before, but then he started picking on Clinton and Obama. Everything they did was wrong."

"I agree. He used 9/11 to bash liberals and boost his career. He's classy like that."

"But Mr. Bush he loved!" my father said. "Nu? Let's go. I'm not going to waste my time with him."

* * *

17 March

In which Jack Friedman searches for (and finds) the sweet spot long after the sweet spot makes itself known.

Here at Owl Head, and I realize I am nobody to talk, what with all the Diet Coke I drink, but my father—in addition to the four packets of Sweet'N Low and multiple containers of flavored Half & Half that usually go into his coffee—added to his decaf one Equal, a bit of cream from the top of a chocolate cream cake he was eating, and two ice cubes from his raspberry iced tea, which he was also drinking intermittently.

"You know, Ba," he said after taking a few sips, "they make good coffee here."

* * *

19 March

In which Jack Friedman is still unhappy with the streets because "they're too goddamn narrow," but now he won't be rushed.

"Let 'em honk!" he says about the guy behind him. "I'm going to turn because he's honking? And you can't make a goddamn left in this town, anyway. You'll have an accident."

"I don't think it's mandatory you'll have an accident. Lots of people do and nothing happens to them."

The guy behind him keeps honking.

"He's got a horn, nu? Good for him. Dummy!"

* * *

26 March

In which Jack Friedman recounts his first-ever experience in a tornado but doesn't dwell on it.

"Nothing, Ba, nothing like a tornado. It didn't even rain. The sky got dark, all the rumbling. Say, what's going on with this stupid computer?"

"Hold it! You were never in a tornado, Dad."

"Yeah, I know. But you know."

APRIL

2 April

In which Jack Friedman issues fair warning to Oklahoma that he's no longer playing around.

I should add that, unlike at casinos in Las Vegas, the Native American tribes that run the gambling joints here in Oklahoma take a fifty-cent fee on every hand of blackjack. My father believes there should be some conflation of issues in Oklahoma—and maybe there should be.

"If you don't fix these goddamn roads," he says on the way back from Hot Rod—like I'm supposed to fix them—"and stop taking fifty cents with every blackjack bet, and start offering orange marmalade at these cockamamie places, I'm going back to Vegas."

I have no idea how marmalade got into the mix, but then again, this is Jack Friedman we're talking about here. I don't have to know. You don't, either.

* * *

5 April

In which we celebrate Easter, at Owl Head Bagels, and its relative importance to Christians.

By this time in life, the routine is pretty simple: We walk into Owl Head, he sits down, and I go to the counter. He blurts, "Don't get me a bagel. They're too—what do I say?—voluptuous. So get me a soft roll [he means a croissant]. The toughness of the bagels is killing me."

A few minutes later, one of the counter guys, who's about fourteen, brings it to him.

"I'm supposed to have this fed to me," my father says to the kid, which both embarrasses and confuses him. "I'm just joking," my father adds, which makes the kid look like he's going to cry.

"Jack, what are you doing?" asks Aaron from behind the serving area before walking out to greet us.

"Don't you wear pants?" my father asks. Aaron is in shorts.

"It's hot back there, Jack."

"What's today? It's mobbed."

"It's Easter Sunday."

"Is that a religious holiday? I mean, is it a church day?"

* * *

7 April

In which Melissa puts the kibosh on joining my father and me at this coming Friday's Milestone Shabbat at B'nai Emunah, which features a dinner honoring many of the synagogue's older members.

"I don't know," she says. "All that lip-smacking, hacking, throat-clearing, and coughing. It'll be like dinner, uh, at four p.m. at Luby's."

"What'd she say?" my father asks. "Why does she mumble?"

"She's not mumbling, Dad. You're going deaf."

"What?"

The timing couldn't have been better.

Later . . .

At tonight's Tuesday Night All-You-Can-Eat 2-for-1 Buffet today at the Hot Rod, my father says to the cashier, who's rather zaftig, let's say, and in her mid-fifties, "Bless you, my dear, may you never know the horrors of stretch marks."

An icy stare comes in return.

"It's a blessing," my father says, sensing a problem. "You shouldn't get stretch marks, that's what I meant."

"Too late," she says, handing him his change.

"Dad, the act just doesn't work for everyone."

"I was just joking."

"I know."

"C'mon, she was enormous."

"Nice."

Minutes later, at a serving station, two tiny Asian women are dishing Asian food—one is holding a bowl of sweet-and-sour chicken, and she's the one my father asks, "How goes your life, Miss America?"

A sweet, clueless smile is the reply.

"Your life, Miss America," he says again. "How goes it?"

You have to love the fact he thought that changing the order of the sentence was going to improve things.

Again, another sweet, clueless smile. The woman clearly does not understand English.

The story might end there for many, but this is Jack Friedman, let's remember.

"Very unfriendly people here, Ba," he says as we bring our Chinese food to the table.

* * *

8 April

In which Jack Friedman understands life's limitations and plans accordingly. And isn't above a little thievery.

Jack Friedman has a cold. I know Gay Talese had success with that opening in his famous *Esquire* article on Frank Sinatra, so thought I'd try it here.

We're at Mondo's, an Italian restaurant in town, my favorite, which my father calls "Moodo's," for reasons all his own. As we get to the car, I see that he has a cloth napkin from the restaurant.

"Yeah, let's go to the casino for an hour," he says, "but afterward, let's stop and get something not to cure the cold, just to dry it out."

"Dad, you stole a napkin?"

"My nose is running. What do you want me to do?"

"Not steal a napkin."

"C'mon, my nose is running."

* * *

10 April

In which Jack Friedman makes allowances for, but doesn't surrender to, the faith.

We, in fact, go to the Shabbat dinner at B'nai Emunah Synagogue. And while he didn't stand for the concluding prayer, he did stop eating his chocolate cake during a particularly touching part of the service. Beforehand at our table, which included Rabbi Fitzerman and his wife, Alice, and the synagogue president and his wife, my father told the joke about attacking a girl in the alley. It didn't work—big surprise—so he went right into the parrot joke; unfortunately, he forgot it was a bird and actually had the woman call the thing on her shoulder an animal, so when the woman started defending the parrot, saying how it wasn't an animal, the joke broke down significantly, as he already gave away the punchline of a pretty terrible joke anyway. There was also this about his life in Las Vegas.

"I played handball, tennis, gambled, and chased sixteen-year-old girls because they come with instructions."

Not to quibble, but he didn't play handball.

* * *

18 April

In which we are reminded that Jack Friedman is a tough love.

My sister, Susan, called today with this story.

"So I called Dad the other day and said, 'Hi, Dad,' and he responded with 'Who's this?' I said 'Dad, how many other women call you and say, "Hi, Dad"?' And, Barry, swear to God, he said, 'I don't have time for this shit,' and hung up on me."

* * *

21 April

In which Jack Friedman thinks ahead to our trip to Boca Raton in May and the people he has known.

"And if he's around, we'll see Carl. Good-looking guy, but conceited. But I think he's dead, so you don't have to worry about him."

* * *

23 April

In which Jack Friedman wonders about Bernie, Part the Infinity

"You know, Ba, in the Family Circle, you get a burial plot. It's free with the membership. You know what those things cost these days? Wow-wee-wow! You can't touch them. But your wife, or husband, has to be Jewish or they can't get in. Remember Bernie? He married that big blonde thing, this zaftig woman with the big lips. He died, you know. I mean I don't know, but somebody told me that. I should call Ida—she'd know. Anyway, she was gorgeous, Bernie's wife! She wasn't Jewish, so she couldn't be buried there. She divorced him twenty-five years later, so it didn't matter. He owned a grocery store on 7th Avenue. You don't remember him?"

25 April

In which we spend the evening at ONEOK Field, watching the Tulsa Drillers, a Texas League affiliate of the Los Angeles Dodgers, and witness Jack Friedman's first experience in a luxury box, thanks to friends Michael Patton and Anna America.

"Ba, how much is the chicken?"

"It's free."

"Free?"

"Free."

"How can it be free?"

"It's free."

"I understand that, but free?"

"Yeah."

"What about the cookies?"

"Also free."

"Get me some, would you? Not too many."

Later...

A ball gets hit into the left-center-field gap, and it doesn't look like the runner is going to try for second base.

"Run, you hockey puck!" my father screams.

* * *

26 April

In which we are reminded how nobody makes introductions quite like my father.

We are supposed to go to lunch and then to the Hot Rod (which we will), but my father shows up with a date.

"Barry, this is Terry. She lives in the building next door, and I met her in the lobby. Her daughter was murdered in Vegas. I told her I lived there."

Later...

Jack, Terry, and I are at lunch.

"Tell you what," he says to Terry, who's about to order, "you order a pasta dish and we'll split it. I just can't eat as much as I used to. I used to play a lot of tennis."

"You want me to order a pasta dish?" she asks.

"Yeah, because I can't finish it."

The waitress comes by. Terry does as she's told.

At one point, I ask Terry how her daughter died.

"She was shot by gang members."

"Shit! Sorry."

"Thank you."

"There are just no words," I say.

"My wife was a costume designer at the Taj Mahal in Atlantic City," my father says, finding a transition where there is none.

*　*　*

27 April

In which Jack Friedman questions the very basis of gambling in Oklahoma and worries about the tribes left out.

"We've been coming to these so-called Indian casinos for months," he says to me at the Creek Nation Casino, "so how come I've never seen an Indian?"

"You're kidding, right?"

"You mean because they're in modern dress now?"

"Yeah."

"And how come the Apaches don't have a casino? They were the big ones."

*　*　*

28 April

In which Jack Friedman reconsiders assisted living and reconnects with his faith and his people's tidiness.

Driving by the Tulsa Jewish Community Retirement Center, he muses, "You know, maybe living in the Hebrew Home won't be so bad. There are Jews. I'm sure they keep the place nice."

MAY

5 May

In which Jack Friedman clears up the matter of whether he, in fact, needs hearing aids. We are at the audiologist because, I can assure you, he needs hearing aids.

"Mr. Friedman, you have seventy percent hearing loss in one ear, fifty percent in the other," says the audiologist.

"What's that, dear?"

"I said you could use hearing aids."

"Well, there's a lot of that going around. I'm just joking. You know, I played tennis every day of my life. Now, the legs—they're gone."

* * *

7 May

In which Jack Friedman, at the end of dinner, realizes that life is just one big black hole of deception and unanswered questions.

"You know," he says to me after the waiter brings him his coffee at Mondo's, "you order decaf, but after you're done putting in the Sweet'N Low and the Half-and-Half you don't know it's decaf. They could give you regular. They could give you anything they want. You don't know what the hell they're giving you. Ach!"

* * *

10 May

Melissa and I took my father on a trip to Ponca City, Oklahoma today, Mother's Day, to see her parents, and Melissa and I couldn't decide at the end of the day which was more exhausting: explaining to my father how it is possible that I am older than Melissa's parents, what a podcast is, or that Amy, Melissa's sister, is married to a woman named Chera and they have two children from a surrogate father.

(Actually, that last one is a little complicated.)

* * *

11 May

In which, thinking about our trip to Boca Raton and Delray Beach tomorrow, Jack Friedman muses about those relatives who have relocated to South Florida and what the melting pot has done to the Big Apple.

"They're all gone, Ba, they're all gone. Nobody left in New York but the Jamaicans and the Hindus."

* * *

12 May

In which we head to Boca Raton and Jack Friedman tests the boundaries (and patience) of the TSA.

In his carry-on, my father has a big pair of scissors, two bottles of Super Glue (for his toupees), hair gel (for his toupees after the pieces are affixed in place), what appears to be a half gallon of body lotion he got from the Dollar Tree, and a small tube of bronzer.

"Sir, you can't take all this onboard," says the TSA rep.

"Never had any problem before," my dad says, reaching for his Super Glue, which is in an open toiletry bag that's still on the conveyor belt.

"Sir, don't touch anything."

"Sorry, dear," he says, "I was just reaching for —"

"I know, sir, but please. Do you want to recheck them or throw them out?"

"What do you think, Ba?"

"Out."

"Are you his traveling companion?" the agent asks me.

"No. I've never seen this man before in my life."

* * *

P.S. One of the supervisors caught up with us after we left security and handed him one of his bottles of Super Glue. "Oh, sir," she said, "here you go. Have a good flight."

Later...

On the flight, a woman sitting in a bulkhead seat is blaming Obama for giving our tax dollars to Public Service Company of

Oklahoma, the electric company, and ordering the firm to change our electric meters from analog to digital.

"And the analog ones were just the best things."

"Ba, what the hell is she talking about?" my father asks.

"I can assure you, Dad, she has no idea."

Later...

We have made it to Delray Beach and Uncle Leo and Aunt Marilyn's condo. It is a condo, my father tells me, for which Hy, Leo, and my father's brother loaned them money to buy. Aunt Marilyn, ninety, is still talking about the stupidity of the Miami Heat getting rid of Mike Miller and is blaming the team's inability to make the playoffs this year not on LeBron James leaving, not on Chris Bosh getting injured, but on Henry Walker's inconsistent play.

"He shoots too many threes. He's good, he's not good. Ach!" she says.

"So, Leo," my father asks, "why did you stop driving? I still drive."

"Any trouble?" Leo asked.

"No, not at all."

I nearly spit out spearmint slices that they always buy for me. "Really, Dad?"

"What do you know?" he says, waving me off.

Uncle Leo, ninety-two, the only liberal Democrat NRA member in South Florida, stopped driving about two years ago.

"Yeah, what happened, Leo?" I ask. "Why'd you give up your license?"

"The thing is this"—Leo usually starts stories that way—"I asked my doctor twenty years ago if I could still drive and he said, 'Sure, on a deserted island with nobody around.'"

* * *

13 May

In which Jack Friedman marvels at the passage of time and the ties (and technologies) that bind us.

"You know, Ba," he says on the way to Leo and Marilyn's this morning, "I'm surprised at my brother. Still has his wits about him at ninety-four. He doesn't rant or rave or carry on. All right, he's prejudiced about a lot of things, but that's not my point. And, oh yeah, how do you work that goddamn coffee maker in my room? What, you add the coffee and pour in the water?"

"That's pretty much it, Dad."

"I tried that. Nothing. And it would kill them to give you a mug in the room? A paper cup they give you. Nu?"

Later...

"So one time, I go by this bum," Leo tells us, reliving his past glories of working for the USPS in Brooklyn, "who I knew, a guy on disability. He was an okay guy, but a bum, and he comes up to me and says, 'Is my money here? Is my money here?' and then reaches into the mailbag. I tell him, 'Take your hand out of the bag!' 'No,' he says, 'I want my money!' and again reaches into the bag. This goes on three or four more times. Finally I tell him, 'Look, you put your hand in the bag one more time, I break your arm.' It was the last time he put his hand in the bag."

And so concludes the story.

After dinner tonight, we're on our way to the Seminole Casino, and it begins to rain—I think. It looks like rain, I know—yes, it's definitely rain. Unless it's not.

"Is that rain coming down," my father asks, "or just drops from above?"

* * *

14 May

I mentioned to Leo that I have posted a picture of Marilyn and him on Facebook and it got 175 "likes."

"That's very nice. I don't know what the hell it is you're talking about. Who are these people you're talking about? Did they send gifts?"

Later . . .

In which Jack Friedman, eighty-eight, puts life and death in perspective and reminds us all how important it is to move on.

We are on our way to see Ida, who married Max. Together, they had Jeffrey, who, according to my father, dropped dead while walking across 5th Avenue in New York. Ida has a new fella because Max also died—my father thinks in his sleep, but he's not happy with that explanation. ("You die in your sleep? How is that possible? You don't thrash around? You don't wake up the person next to you? Wouldn't the act of dying wake you up?") This is the same Ida who wouldn't allow us to get my mother a mauve headstone fifteen years ago. This my mother would not forgive. My father doesn't bring it up.

"You know," he says to me on the way to Leo's to pick them up, "Ida is the only one left down here, besides Marilyn and Leo. Pitsy, Selma, Jerry . . . they all went home to New York, even though they're still here sometimes. All right, Selma had a stroke and Jerry's got something with his foot, but Ida . . . yeah, she's it. She's got a new boyfriend. The old one died. I mean, he was already half dead, I think. The new guy's name is Ernie."

* * *

15 May

In which Jack Friedman thinks of those less fortunate.

At breakfast this morning at the Doubletree, my father is deep in thought.

"What is it, Dad?"

"Why couldn't you come into the buffet in the morning and sit here all day and eat? What, you think they're going to check? How would they stop you? They're not going to check. I mean, if you're homeless and could afford one meal, you could do it. Come in for breakfast and stay, that's all. I'm surprised others haven't thought of it."

"Maybe they have."

"You're probably right."

Later . . .

After my son, Paul, died, I wound up with his favorite glass: a tall, thick highball with the Yuengling logo. That was seven years ago. Today, in Deerfield Beach, Florida, sitting around the pool at the hotel with his grandfather, I am having my first-ever Yuengling. I hear it's the oldest beer company in America.

"What are you drinking, Ba?" my father asks. "I thought you didn't drink beer."

"I don't. It's a long story."

* * *

16 May

You would think the coincidence, the unremarkable randomness of my father having a cousin Ida in one part of South Florida and my uncle and aunt living off Lake Ida Road in another part of South Florida, would not be a daily conversation starter, especially considering we had this same series of conversations the last time we were here. You, alas, would be wrong.

"Ida? Ida? Who names a lake 'Ida'?"

"I can't believe we're going through this again," I say.

"Heh-heh . . . Ida? Who's Ida? 'Hey, Ida, you want a lake named after you?' . . . Ida must have had money to get a lake. I wonder if Ida, my cousin, knows about this? 'Who's Ida?' I'll be a son of a gun. Ida . . . Nu? Ida gets a lake. Heh-heh."

"Are you about done?"

"You don't think this is odd?"

"Not that odd, no—and less odd still than the last time we were here, when I also didn't think it was that odd."

"You don't get out much, do you?"

We are headed to Panera. Once there, I see him shove two packets of Sweet'N Low into his pocket.

"What are you doing?" I ask.

"The hotel, Ba. I got a coffeepot, but they don't give you

enough of the sweetener, that's all."

Later...

I give you, word for word, part of the actual conversation today on the way to Flakowitz of Boynton restaurant.

[Leo and Marilyn in the back. My father and I in the front. I'm driving.]

Jack: What was the name of the woman who was with Joe?

Leo: Joe?

Jack: I meant Bernie.

Leo: Which Bernie?

Marilyn: Bernie!

Leo: I heard him.

Jack: Bernie! Did it rain, or what?

Leo: Bernie?

Jack: Yeah, the big buxomly thing with Bernie.

Marilyn: Do you know how to work the wipers on this car? We had a car once—

Leo: Ann—

Jack: —with Bernie?

Marilyn: —with wipers. Uh, Ann?

Leo: Ann? Not Ann.

Marilyn: It was Ann.

Leo: It was not Ann!

Marilyn: Then who was it, Leo?

Leo starts humming. "The point is, it lasted three weeks. I think. That was sixty years ago. Who can remember?"

Jack: She was so zaftig, that one. Remember? Wow-wee-wow!

Leo: He got rid of her.

Jack: I think her name was Ann. Where we going again?

Marilyn: Flakowitz.

Jack: Will he be there?

Marilyn: Who?

Jack: Flakowitz.

Marilyn: I don't know.

Jack: What?

Marilyn: I. DON'T. KNOW.

[Leo Friedman begins to hum again.]

[Jack Friedman begins to moan.]

Jack: Where did it all go? Where did it all go?

[Leo continues to hum.]

Jack: You know, I'm going to New York to see Susan. She's got four kids. They all make big bucks—forty, fifty thousand. What do they do again?

Marilyn: You told us already.

Jack: What kind of food they got there?

Marilyn: Deli.

Jack: What?

Marilyn: DELI!

Jack: Kosher?

Marilyn: No.

Jack: Is that legal? Does Flakowitz know?

Marilyn: I don't know.

Jack: What?

Marilyn: I. DON'T. KNOW.

[Leo continues humming.]

Jack: I'm thinking I'm going to get soup.

Marilyn: Good for you. Enjoy yourself.

* * *

17 May

In which Jack Friedman, social geographer (and old Jew), explains why Miami will NOT be a destination today and why the entire place never solved its mass-transportation problems.

"Ach, Miami! What do you got there: the beach, the T-shirts? And then you have to park and walk. Nah!"

Later . . .

We are at Ben's, another kosher deli, but more of a diner. It is open for dinner. Flakowitz is not. For overall quality, Flakowitz, which serves two sides, dessert, and a drink included with the meal, is a tad better. TwoJay's, yet a third diner, has bite-size black-and-whites and great rye bread. Ben's offers pre-meal pretzel rolls and Diet Dr. Brown's Black Cherry.

You really can't go wrong with any of them.

Leo and Marilyn's son, Michael, and his family joined us tonight, and he reminded me that it was our relatives—the extended Friedman family of Palm and Broward counties—that could not follow the intricacies of the butterfly ballot in 2000 and mistakenly punched the chad for Buchanan, thinking they were voting for Gore. Yes, six Jews nationally voted for Buchanan in 2000, along with seventeen of my relatives in South Florida.

I apologize to a hurting nation.

* * *

18 May

In which Jack Friedman has a moment.

After dinner, our last night here, in the car, I noticed my father was oddly quiet.

"What's up, Dad?" I ask.

"I don't know. Seeing Leo and Marilyn and Michael and . . . and . . . and . . . ah, what the hell's her name?"

"Mindy, his wife—"

"Mindy! I know, I know. And what's the other one's name?"

"Carly, their daughter—"

"Carly! I was just going to say that. I'm just sad."

"Why did that make you sad?"

"Because I kept thinking, 'They're all together and I'm sitting here alone. Where is everybody? Where's your mother, Susan, Wayne . . . Where is my family?"

"Susan is in New York and Wayne is in California."

"I got nobody."

"Hello!" I said.

"No, I know *you*—that's not my point—but, you

know . . . ach!"

"You want to go to the casino?"

"Yeah, good idea! Let's go for an hour. What the hell?"

* * *

19 May

When I went to get my father in his room this morning for the trip to the airport, I noticed he had left $5 for the maid and scribbled on a tiny hotel notepad, "Thank you."

* * *

26 May

In which Jack Friedman, after spending the first of two weeks with my sister/his daughter, while I am in the Bahamas, reviews his accommodations.

When I get the gig in the Bahamas, I always schedule a trip to Florida to see Marilyn and Leo. Afterward, I send my dad to New York to see Susan.

"How you doing, Dad?" I ask on the phone.

"Oh, fine, fine. You know, the boys here make big bucks. One of them is pushing forty."

"Dad, that's not really big bucks."

"What are you talking about? One makes thirty. They're all doing well. They all go to work."

"I hear you."

"How's the gig down there?"

"Good. I'm selling books."

"How's the gate?"

"The gate is fine. Susan treating you okay?" I ask, even though she always does.

"Yes, yes, fine, fine. Things are good. There's plenty of food."

* * *

28 May

Let me back up a little. Here was the conversation before I left the gig down here.

"Okay, Dad, you're going to Long Island, I'm going to the Bahamas. Don't call my cell. It will be turned off. Got it?"

"Okay."

"I mean it. I will call you from down there a couple times a week. If you call me, nobody will pick up. okay?"

"Okay. I won't call."

"And Melissa will be with me, so she won't have her phone either."

"Got it."

"You're going to spend time with Susan."

"I know, I know."

"Don't call."

"I won't call. All right, already. Jesus, what a noodge you are."

It's May 28th. My gig is over. I have landed at Fort Lauderdale-Hollywood International Airport and turn on my phone for the first time in two weeks. Among other messages, there are twenty-one calls from my father, twelve messages.

Here they are:

"Hi, Ba, it's Dad. Barry! Hello! All right, you're not there. I'll try the home phone."

"Ba, it's Dad. Do I have a doctor's appointment next week?"

"Did you just try to call me? Okay, call me back."

"Did I call you or did you call me? I have a message here."

"Ba, uh, it's Dad. I just tried calling you. Okay, call me back. I'm at Susan's. I don't know if you know that, so don't call my home phone."

"Are you in the Bahamas, or what? Maybe that's why you're not getting the messages. All right, call me back here."

A message from him that's simply him talking to my sister, nothing to do with me.

"Ba, it's Dad. I was checking my bank balance. What is this check for $148?"

A message where I hear him tell my sister he is leaving a message and that he's cold.

"Hey, Ba, send me my flight information from Astoria. I don't know when the hell I leave."

"Ba, it's Dad. Is Melissa with you? I tried calling her but nobody picked up. All right, I'll try the home phone."

"What is it with this stupid phone? I can't make a call."

JUNE

1 June

In which Jack Friedman, eighty-eight, after hearing that his brother, Leo, ninety-four, got his hearing aids for free from the Veterans Administration, comes up with a breathtaking idea to combat a $1,785 bill that he got for his.

On a phone call with Leo, my father decided he, too, wants free hearing aids and tells his brother, "What if I just re-enlist?"

* * *

2 June

In which Jack Friedman, wounded warrior, unravels the story of the Purple Heart even further.

As it turns out, the VA, in fact, will cover my father's hearing aids, if he has a Purple Heart, which, of course, he does.

I call to tell him.

"Dad, great news. The VA will pay for your hearing aids. We just need to get the certificate that came with the Purple Heart."

"Certificate?"

"Yeah, you got a certificate when you were awarded the Purple Heart. Probably during the ceremony."

"What kind of ceremony?"

"What kind? What kind did they have?"

"There was no ceremony."

"Of course there was."

"Barry, there was no ceremony, I'm telling you. I was in the hospital, and I found the Purple Heart on my bed."

"Found it?"

"Yeah, it was on the bed. I assumed it was mine. What did I know?"

"You *assumed* it was yours?"

"Yeah. It was on the bed."

"Your bed?"

"Who can remember? And, besides, Leo got them to pay for his hearing aids, and he never left stateside. He didn't get a Purple Heart."

"Apparently, neither did you. You may have someone else's Purple Heart."

"All right, look, we'll pay for the hearing aids. No big deal."

* * *

4 June

In which Jack Friedman returns to Tulsa, expresses love and pride for his daughter and grandchildren, and reminds me, again, of his admiration for toil.

"Barry, that Susan, so sweet. She got me a wheelchair at the airport, tipped the woman who wheeled me around, gave me her bed for two weeks. And the kids. All making big bucks. Susan, of course, but Noah, Chris, Emily, Jesse, too . . . and Jesse wants to be a pastor. Yeah, a pastor. I mean, not a Catholic priest, but one of the softer religions."

"Softer religions?"

"Yeah, the maritable ones?"

"Maritable?"

"The ones that let you marry. I mean, I don't know how you become a pastor—he's in computers now—but every night, he made us hold hands, say a prayer before dinner. Nothing bad. It was all right."

"Sounds nice."

"And they *all* work, Ba."
"Amazing! All of them?"
"Every one of them."

* * *

5 June

In which Jack Friedman sees potential gain in loss.

My father lost his money clip at the Hot Rod today. He had, he told me, $215 in the clip, which made this next part of the story hilarious.

"How much money did you have in the clip, sir?" a security guard asked him.

"Uh, two hundred—I mean, three hundred dollars," he said.

* * *

6 June

In which my father, at Owl Head, clarifies the lineage concerns.

"I'm the father, he's the son," he says to a woman at the cash register. "A lot of people get confused."

* * *

8 June

In which Jack Friedman longs for the good old days and bemoans the price we've paid for technological advancement. As a follow-up to Dr. Block's challenge, my father has decided to take the written test to get an Oklahoma license.

Sitting at the motor vehicle bureau, he says, "You know, Ba, if I had a horse and buggy, I wouldn't need a license. See what civilization has done to us?"

During the exam, his eyesight was checked: 20/200 in one eye, 20/40 in the other. The state of Oklahoma, in its infinite wisdom, requires only one good eye—and by good, no worse than 20/45. As for the test itself, he got five out of twenty questions incorrect.

He still got an Oklahoma driver's license.

I still drove home.

* * *

9 June

In which Jack Friedman's political correctness is both hyperbolic and specific.

We're at the Hot Rod Tuesday Night All-You-Can-Eat 2-for-1 Buffet. He has a plate of food and is returning to the table.

"Barry, Barry, I just saw a woman. Enormous. I mean, enormous. And she's eating like there's no tomorrow. Spaghetti and pasta and God knows what. Anyway, her husband—I guess it's her husband—says to her, 'Don't eat that. It's fattening.' I wanted to say, 'It's too late. She's already 65,000 pounds.'"

* * *

10 June

In which the quality of Israeli-made goods is discussed at a register at Walmart.

I was returning some clothes my father bought—because what stylish eighty-eight-year-old doesn't have jean shorts?—when I pulled out my iPhone.

"Hey, hey," said the man behind me at customer service. "What kind of case is that? Damn, that's cool."

"Yeah," I said, explaining its features.

"You get that here?"

"No. Amazon. I think, actually, it's made in Israel."

"Israel? Damn! They make good stuff there. Can't beat stuff made in Israel."

"I guess."

"Israel, yeah, boy! I got to get me one of those cases. My case ain't no good. Israel, huh?"

"Yep."

"That's great, really great. Fun, fun, fun there in Israel."

My father looked at the man and said, "Yeah, well, there's a lot of that going around these days."

The man walked out perplexed—or maybe I was the one who did.

"You know, Ba," my father says, tapping his hearing aids—and, yeah, we paid for them—"these plugs are very resonant."

"Good."

"No, I mean they're resonant."

"Good."

"Very . . . what's the word?"

"Resonant."

"Yeah, yeah, they're resonant. No joke."

"Why would you joke about that?"

"What?"

"Never mind."

"No, I'm just saying the ear plugs are resonant. I sound good. Really. My voice is, how do I say—"

"Resonant."

"Resonant. Yeah."

* * *

16 June

In which my father, as he often does, overwhelms me with his love.

"Ba, I want to go back to Vegas," he says, as we both walk on treadmills at the gym at the Jewish Center. "I have nobody here but you. Don't misunderstand, it's not bad, but I have to call you when I want to go out. I mean, all right, you have time, but it's no good."

* * *

18 June

In which Jack Friedman has many questions about telecommunications in America.

"You're telling me, Ba, I can't get DirecTV because I live in a place that faces north?"

"That's right."

"C'mon. Science, technology, it's the twenty-first century, for crying out loud!"

"Good you noticed."

"I'm a man. Science can't turn me into a woman, so this they should be able to do."

"Wow!"

"What?"

"No. Nothing. Go on."

"Why can't they just turn the thing, the dish [then he actually shifted in his chair]? They can't figure this out? When the guy built the building, he didn't take that into account that you couldn't get TV? What kind of state is this? Oklahoma? Who lives in Oklahoma?"

* * *

21 June

In which Father's Day takes a back seat to life.

My dad's cordless phone is inexplicably in the kitchen cabinet, near his stash of stolen Sweet'N Low packets.

"I give up! I give up!"

"Dad, it's no big deal."

"I need this like a hole in the head."

"It's nothing. I'll hook the phone back up. It's just dead."

"You won't be able to."

"I'm over fifty. I've dedicated my life to this."

"Can you do it?" he asks, as I start to do it.

"I'm doing it."

The job completed, I start heading for the door.

"Here," he says, handing me twenty dollars.
"What are you doing?"
"Can you use the dough?"
"Would you stop! It's Father's Day. I'm not taking twenty dollars. Gimme ten."

* * *

23 June

In which Jack Friedman asks about Genesis and talks about the theological and practical problems with seafood.

"Say, Ba, why is it God, who made all the food in the world—and it's all good, right?—says to the Jews, 'It's not kosher, you can't have any'? Why make food if people can't eat it?"

"I don't know, Dad. God works in mysterious ways, as they say."

"Oh, I don't want an answer."

"All right, because it sounded like you did."

"My question was academic. It's like the apple. You make a Garden of Eden, you put in an apple, but then say, 'Don't touch it.' Then why put it there?"

"Bastard!"

"He shouldn't have done that. And another thing: You'd think with all our technology, they could make shrimp that's easier to eat. What's with the shell? So goddamn tough to get the meat out."

* * *

25 June

In which we learn a little something about the lure of the 2-for-1.

At the Hot Rod casino today, while at the buffet, my father and I heard a loud crash. A man—in his nineties, I'm imagining—has tripped and fallen over his walker and into a wall by the cashier. The walker, meanwhile, has fallen on top of him, pinning him on the ground. Security and others manage to get the walker off him and try valiantly to get him up. I see arms pulling and reaching for the man. He is moaning slightly, obviously scared, in pain, as he eventually sits up straight. More security is called while his friends stand by anxiously.

A few minutes later, though, back at our table, I see the man, back on the walker, making his way, albeit very slowly, through the buffet line.

That's how you play hurt, ladies and gentlemen.

"What do you think, Dad?"

"Guy paid his money. He's going to eat."

* * *

28 June

In which Jack Friedman reminds us, at least rhetorically, why he's Jack Friedman and we're not.

"I'm going back to Vegas. I miss my friends," he says at Owl Head. "I miss my friends."

"You're not going back to Vegas," says Melissa, who has joined us this morning.

"Why can't I go?"

"First of all," I say, "your friends are falling apart and they don't want you."

"They don't want me?"

"They don't want you."

"They want me!"

"Fine, they want you."

"I'm the oldest one in the group. Bill's there, my friend, and his wife. Bad Alzheimer's. Wow-wee-wow! She doesn't recognize him. This Alzheimer's is no joke. He's a cop from Indiana. Nu? Came to Vegas, doesn't gamble—*doesn't gamble*! And Jeannette, the girl I was running with, had a fight with Vicky Mustard—yeah, that's her name, Mustard. Jewish, believe it? And Carole, not the Carole you know, the other Carole, she doesn't go to the Thursday dinners anymore. Anyway, she wanted to marry me."

"Carole?"

"No, what's her name—Jeannette."

"Oh."

"She's a good girl, but I didn't want to get married. She buried two husbands, you know. So, yeah, Vicky Mustard, she's married to Lou. Together they have, like, two million dollars. She moved in with him, but she has a house. I said, 'What are you going to do with two homes?' They said, 'One's our summer home.' I said, 'They're, like, three blocks away.' He's Catholic, sold insurance, goes to church every morning. Gives money to the church. I said, 'What are you doing? The church has plenty of money.' He looks at me. I told him, 'We gave you a God, remember that.' He gets hysterical. And there was this guy, a priest, he left the church because he didn't like the way they were doing things. He married a woman with the . . . the . . . you know, the habit—"

"A nun," Melissa says, trying to help.

"A nun, imagine! He married a nun? A priest marries a nun? C'mon, that's funny. He knows more about Judaism than I do. All right, so tonight, I'm bringing over lemon meringue pie, right?"

"Yes, we're having dinner. You're bringing pie."

"I know, I know."

* * *

29 June

In which Jack Friedman returns from a date. I don't know, but he told me he met someone.

He calls.

"So how was the date?" I ask.

"Nice, nice. I'm home now. We went to Christopher's."

"Christopher's? There's no restaurant called Christopher's."

"Yeah, it's on Lewinsky."

"You mean Lewis?"

"Yeah. No. Wait, not Lewinsky—it's on Peoria, off Morningside."

"You mean Riverside? Charleston's?"

"Yeah, I don't know. Charleston's, I think."

"And?"

"Good. She travels a lot. Her husband died. We'll go out again. I don't know. Maybe four more times. I don't know yet. Maybe we'll all go. You, me, Meliss, and we'll have a foursome."

We take you now to Melissa's reaction.

"I'm not going. Oh, God! Take someone else, I mean it. I can't do this."

"What do you suggest?"

"I don't know. Let's raffle off a chance to go on a double date with your father."

A splendid idea.

Operators are standing by.

JULY

1 July
In which we demand a little respect for the toupee.
The call comes in at seven thirty a.m.

"Ba, I can't go to the gym with you at ten."

"Why?"

"I have a date at ten thirty."

"You got a date at ten thirty? In the morning? With whom?"

"I'll tell you about it later."

Later . . .

At dinner, as Melissa is returning from the restroom, I see my father checking out her ass.

"You look good today, almost like a girl," he says as she sits down.

"So," Melissa asks, "how was your date this morning?"

"She spotted the toupee right away," he says. "She said she didn't like it."

"What a bitch!" I say.

"Cunt," says Melissa.

I mean, we can spot the toupee, mock the toupee—not others.

* * *

2 July

In which the child exhibits bravery in the face of uncertainty.

Oliver Jeffy, eight, son of Cousin Kate and Elon, and Jack Friedman's grand-nephew, asks his mother and me, "Why does Uncle Jack wear a wig?"

"It makes him feel better," says I.

"Can I see him without it?"

"You're too young. It could scar you for life."

Actually, I think the toupee is probably doing that.

* * *

5 July

I'm sure there's a very good reason why my father is watching a rerun of the 2014 Oklahoma State University home opener against Missouri State.

"You know, football," he says, as I enter his apartment at the Mansion, "like basketball. It's a black sport. I don't mean to suggest it's all black."

"I thought that was exactly what you were trying to suggest."

"No. I'm just saying there are a lot of blacks playing the sport, that's all."

* * *

6 July

In which it is only through food preparation that we begin to understand the unique moral compass of the chosen people.

Leaving a surprisingly disappointing buffet-luncheon experience at the River Silk/Stix Casino, my father says, "The chicken was terrible. It was *all* breading. Ba, I don't mean to be ethical, but I think Jews know how to eat better than everyone else."

* * *

8 July

In which Jack Friedman opines on his second son's writing.

"Jack, you should really read Barry's columns," Melissa tells him this morning.

"Yeah, I know, but he only writes about politics. Nothing about economics."

"Economics?" I ask. "Since when do you read about economics?"

"What can I tell you? You don't write about economics."

"How do you know if you don't read me?"

"I don't. I'm just saying. I don't think you do."

Later...

"I won one hundred and two dollars," he says adamantly to the valet attendant, as we wait for the car outside the Hot Rod. "One hundred and two dollars! I got your money, I got your money. You're not getting paid this week. Ha!"

"Congratulations, sir," the driver replies, enjoying this.

"I'm just joking. How goes your life?"

"Very well, sir."

"Don't worry. Wait a while. It'll get worse."

Later...

On the way home, my father asks, "Say, Ba, question: If you go to any restaurant in Mexico, any supermarket, can you get bread or just, you know, the ... the ... tacos?"

"Tacos?"

"Tacos, yeah, you know, the chips."

"I'm familiar with the concept. I'm sure you can get bread, Dad."

"Because I know the Chinese don't eat bread."

* * *

12 July

In which Jack Friedman understands.

"So why don't you and Melissa get married?"

"Oh, we've both been married twice. And it's going well," I tell him. "Why tempt fate?"

"You're right. Women marry—and don't misunderstand me, I think she's devoted and would be a great wife—but they want some security. It'd be one thing if you had a big job and were making the big bucks, but, now, you know, she probably figures, 'Ah, leave it alone.'"

* * *

14 July

In which Jack Friedman takes the notion of sibling rivalry and parks it three rows deep.

"Ba, I have to tell you, all you do for me, I love you."

"Hold on a second, Dad."

I am in the car with Melissa, and I put the call on speaker so she can hear because I'm figuring this could be good.

"Okay, go ahead."

"I say I don't know what I'd do without you. I appreciate it so. I'd be lost without you. I know Susan and Wayne love me, but it's different with them. She works and he's sophisticated."

* * *

18 July

We're at ONEOK Field to watch the Tulsa Drillers on

"Tommy Lasorda Garden Gnome Giveaway Night" with friends Nita and James McPartland. It's 140 degrees, or thereabouts, my father is all in black and just asked Nita and Jim if they were Republicans.

"No," Nita says with a laugh.

"I was attacking a woman in a dark alley," he says, telling, yes, that joke, "and I said, 'Don't scream. It's embarrassing for me too.'"

Nita doesn't laugh, Jim doesn't laugh.

He tells the joke again.

Again, they don't laugh.

"Don't you get it?" he asks.

"They get it, Dad," I say. "They just don't like it."

"You people don't get out much, do you?"

* * *

19 July

The Tao of Jack Friedman, Part 2,694

"So I'm talking to a woman," he says tonight over our hamburgers, "and she asks me the secret to life. So I told her, 'Good health, good food, and a cooperative date.'"

* * *

22 July

In which Jack Friedman reminds us why life is all about choices.

My father has removed the remote control for his hearing aids from his keychain and replaced it with a two-inch piece of useless guitar-shaped plastic that he received at the Hot Rod.

"Don't you need the remote?" I ask.

"I do."

"So why did you take it off?"

"Because it didn't fit."

"Yes, it did."

"Well, they both didn't."

"Why didn't you remove the plastic guitar—you know, the one that does nothing."

"Yeah, I guess I could do that."

* * *

27 July

My father and I sent Leo, his brother, my uncle, a gift card to TooJay's Delicatessen for his birthday.

The phone rings.

"Hello, Barry."

"Leo!"

"What?"

"Leo, how are you?"

"Good. Got your gift."

"Great."

"What?"

"Good that you got the gift card?"

"Good?"

"The gift?"

"Yeah, I got it."

"Good."

"I tried calling your father."

"He probably couldn't hear the phone ring."

"What phone? We're on the phone."

"Never mind. How's Marilyn?"

"She's right here."

"So what are you doing for your birthday?"

"Same as always. Not much new around here. I'm going shooting today, loading tomorrow, shooting the next day, then the podiatrist."

"Perfect birthday week."

"What?"

"I said it was a good birthday week."

"Yes, I guess so. Here, talk to your aunt."

AUGUST

13 August
In which Jack Friedman reminds us it's his world and we understand only a fraction of it.

"Dad, what's the matter? You're cranky today."

"The roads in Oklahoma, the phones, the printers, my ear plugs, nothing's working today. I want to go back to Vegas."

"I don't follow. What does that have to do with Las Vegas? Those things might not work there either."

"They have regular things there."

"Regular things?"

"You know."

* * *

14 August
In which Jack and Barry Friedman, contemporaries, discuss the family.

"Ba, it's just you and me and Bernie."

"Who's Bernie?"

"Your brother."

"No, that's Wayne, your son."

"Right, right, Bernie's dead. I think he died."

"You told me he did."

"I told you?"

"You told me."

"Well, I don't know. I heard that. What did he die of?"

"I don't know."

"But you know he's dead?"

"Yes."

"Who told you?"

"You did."

"Yeah, that's what I heard. Lyla, too. Anyway, tell me something: How did you and I wind up in Oklahoma in our retiring years?"

* * *

18 August
In which Jack Friedman reminds us to never disrespect the buffet.
While waiting in line at the buffet here at the Hot Rod during the Tuesday Night All-You-Can-Eat 2-for-1 Buffet, we see a man through the window actually eating a piece of fried chicken while putting Jell-O mold and mashed potatoes on his plate.
"The man's a savage," my father says as we walk by.

* * *

22 August
In which Jack Friedman makes his demands on life and rediscovers his people.
"So, Ba, tell me about this bowling league."
I had discovered a bowling league announcement on the bulletin board at the Mansion and want to sign up my father.
"It's a bowling league."
"What do you mean? What kind of people?"
"What kind of people? I don't know. Cranky old men like you who bowl."
"I'll rap you right in the mouth. 'Cranky old men . . . ' No, I'm very serious. Are there Jews?"
"Are there Jews?"
"Yes, are there Jews in the bowling league?"
"I think so. I imagine there might be one or two."
"I must have Jews in my bowling league."
"How many do you need?"
"I don't know how many. Seven. Why?"

"I just didn't know if there was a required number."
"A couple."
"You must have Jews in your bowling league? Since when? Were there Jews in your bowling league in Vegas?"
"Yes, many. I didn't know their names, but that's not the point. I feel better. I want Jews."

* * *

23 August

In which we can only imagine how a line must have worked with the ladies during the "silent era."
"How are you, sir?" a waitress asks my father at Village Inn.
"Got a half hour? I'll tell you the whole story."
"Sorry, but I don't," she says.
"That's okay. Wait for the movie. It's in color."
Sometimes there's nothing like the greatest hits.

* * *

24 August

In which Jack Friedman talks about the cycles of life.
At lunch today, we are at the River Silk/Stix buffet. My father is eating fried chicken.
"The chicken's a good animal," he says. "It gives the eggs, and then, when it can't anymore, they kill it and cook it up."

* * *

28 August

In which Jack Friedman gives us sad news about one Dawn.
"Hey, Ba, when's what's-his-name playing at the River Silk?"
"'What's-his-name'?"
"The guy, you know."
"'The guy'?"

"You know, the guy?"
"I don't know."
"C'mon, the guy with the girl. What's his name? He did the song with the ball, I think."
"The ball? Ribbon? Tony Orlando?"
"Yes!"
"Christ, how did I get that right?"
"What?"
"Nothing. Anyway, it's tonight."
"Really? Place is probably jammed."
"For Tony Orlando?"
"No?"
"You know he's not with Dawn anymore?"
"Oh, he dropped them a long time ago. I think one of them died."

* * *

29 August
In which we have evidence of another example of Jack Friedman's magic with the ladies.

Tonight at dinner at Mondo's—as you know, often called Moodo's—my father asks Melissa, "What kind of shirt are you wearing?"
"What kind?"
"I mean the kind."
"I don't know, Jack. It's a shirt."
"Well, it makes you look flat-chested."
"Wow," I say.
"Thanks, Jack."
"Dad, really?"
"What? What did I say?"
"You can't say that to women."
"Why not?"
"Think about it."

"C'mon, she knows I'm joking. Besides, I'm drunk and she's eating salad. C'mon, Meliss, give me a kiss," he says to her, reaching across the booth, grabbing her hand, and kissing it repeatedly.

Of course she lets him.

SEPTEMBER

3 September
In which we are reminded not to try out dusty religious aphorisms on Jack Friedman.

When he lived in Las Vegas, he was diagnosed with atrial fibrillation (Afib), and his cardiologist here wants to find out why he doesn't seem to be suffering from it anymore. Afib, apparently, doesn't just get better in eighty-nine-year-old men.

"Why am I still here?" my father asks a woman sitting in the waiting room.

"Excuse me?"

"I don't mean here at the doctor's office. I mean, you know, here."

"The Lord has you here and alive for a reason. We don't always know what that reason is."

"Yeah, then why did he take my wife so early?"

* * *

7 September
In which Jack Friedman's thoughts on Labor Day turn to that which makes great American cities great, and, of course, shrimp egg foo young.

"I love egg foo young, Ba, you know."

"I do."

"They have the whatchamacallit . . . the pancakes."

"Yes, the—"

"—pancakes."

"Yes, the pancakes."

"Right . . . the pancakes."

"Right."

"I love that so, but with the shrimp. But you know what I hate?"

"What's that?"

"When they make the foo young and then put the shrimp in later. Lay it on top. No good."

"You hate that?"

"Yeah. You have to put the shrimp in the young and cook them together. You got any places like that in Tulsa?"

"Yes, the place you're eating this one from."

"Oh, yeah, yeah. I know."

* * *

11 September

In which Jack Friedman has, yes, another accident.

"Barry, I had an accident," he tells me in a call. "I didn't do anything. This woman sideswiped me. I did nothing. I'm sitting in the middle lane, and I hear the cars scrape together. Her car had two lines, you know, two, what do I call them?"

"Scratches?"

"Scratches, lines, whatever. Mine, one tiny mark. It's fine. But then, listen to this, she calls the cops like she wants to start something. Nu, the cops! What is it with Oklahoma? I swear to God, if the cops had given me a ticket, I would have left the state."

"But they didn't give you a ticket, did they?"

"No, I'm just saying, if they had, I would have left."

"But they didn't."

"That's not the point."

"I think that would be the point. Are you all right?"

"Yeah, I'm just telling you."

"That if the cops had given you a ticket, you would have left Oklahoma. I got it."

"Everything goes wrong in this state."
"Everything?"
"Well, you know what I mean?"
"Sadly, I do."

* * *

14 September

In which, on this Rosh Hashanah morning, Jack Friedman asks the question that has vexed the Jewish people for more than 5,000 years.

"Say, Ba," he whispers, "was Abraham really Jewish?"

* * *

15 September

In which, after a heart catheterization that went extraordinarily well, Jack Friedman does masturbation humor for the cardiology staff.

"Now, Mr. Friedman," says the nurse, "make sure you don't use this hand, this wrist, for twenty-four hours."

"Why?"

"Because that's the wrist we used to find the artery. And it needs to heal."

"But what if I want to play with myself later?"

* * *

19 September

For those who eschew political correctness for brutal honesty, this Jack's for you.

"So, Dad, how was your date last night?"
"What can I tell you? Not so great."
"Why not?"
"Eh, I don't know. She's kind of a dull broad."

* * *

22 September

In which my father and I discuss Yom Kippur, the most important day in all of Judaism, and its defining significance to our people.

"So, Ba, this is the no-eat holiday, right?"

"Yeah."

"So you can't eat?"

"Right."

"You know I can't fast because I get a headache."

"Well, I think you're supposed to get the headache first and then break the fast, not assume the headache and not start fasting."

"So no buffet tonight?"

"We really shouldn't."

"It's two-for-one, you know."

"We are a tempted people."

"What?"

"Nothing."

"So this is the holiday where we tell God how lousy we've been?"

"Yeah."

"Jesus!"

Later...

In which Jack Friedman quantifies the enormity and transcendence of (and his commitment to) the Yom Kippur (Kol Nidre) evening service. And the importance of verbs.

On the way into the synagogue tonight:

"How long will the service last, Ba?"

"Probably two, two and a half hours."

"So long? Is it all going to be in Jewish?"

"You mean Hebrew?"

"Yeah, Hebrew."

"No, there's plenty of English."

"How long again?"

"Look, if you don't want to stay for the whole thing, if you get tired, we can leave early. Not a big deal."

"All right, yeah, good idea. Let's put in an hour."

* * *

26 September
In which Jack Friedman, approaching his eighty-ninth birthday, reminisces as best he can.
"So, Ba, my mother tells me I was born on a very cold day. Very cold. But who can remember?"

* * *

27 September
In which Jack Friedman says goodbye to an old friend as only he can.
"You know, Jim just died. Friend for a lot of years. Devoted Catholic, but a good guy, very generous."
"Jim?"
"Jim."
"Who's Jim?"
"Jim."
"This could go on a while."
"Jim!"

* * *

29 September
In which Jack Friedman, in the midst of a perfectly wonderful and bountiful 2-for-1 buffet here at the Hot Rod, develops a sudden camaraderie with, understanding of, and desire to learn about the Native American experience—and to help them.
"So, Ba, tell me something. The Indians have been getting screwed for years, right?"
"That's right."
"So what's to prevent them from poisoning our food tonight as a way of getting back at the white man?"

"That's a tough one."

"And who runs this place?"

"Members of the Cherokee tribe."

"I'd like to see one. I've never seen one before. What do they look like? And who's their accountant?"

OCTOBER

7 October

In which we remember that Florence Friedman, my mother, Jack Friedman's wife, a woman who didn't suffer fools or bad waitress service gladly, would have been eighty-six today. She died at sixty-nine.

From her greatest hits collection:

On fashion: "Why is it we spend billions and billions of dollars on clothes and everybody still looks like shit?"

On whether she was a virgin before marriage: "Barry, if we only knew I could have. Nobody told us, but you bet your sweet ass I would have."

On people she didn't like: "A fire on them."

On why we never had family photos taken: "Goyim do that. Not Jews."

On people who made the worst of every situation: "Why must you make from everything shit?"

On my first divorce: "Barry, it's okay, really. Nobody died."

On the best moment of her life, part 1 (sitting on a raft in her backyard pool): "I could have more, but I couldn't have better."

On the best moment of her life, part 2 (sitting in a gondola in Sorrento, Italy, with my father): "Jack, we made it here. We finally made it."

On her headstone: "For Family."

"She went too soon, Ba, she went too soon," my father says to me today. He actually says it a lot. "She's probably up there thinking, 'Jack, where the hell are you already? When you getting here'?"

And then this.

"Think she'll remember me?"

***

14 October
This guy is eighty-nine today.

Birthday boy

"What happened, Ba, what happened? I was sixteen two weeks ago."

***

25 October
In which Jack Friedman, over dinner, wonders about Melissa's overall judgment.

"Why did you pick this old guy?" he asks Melissa and then points to me. "You're a good-looking girl. You could find someone in his forties who makes big bucks. A young, strapping guy. What are you doing with him?"

* * *

28 October

In which Jack Friedman reminds us again, as if we need such a reminder, it's never just about the money.

He calls this morning. "So, let me tell you what happened. You got a minute?"

"Does it matter?"

"What?"

"Nothing. What happened?"

"Okay, so I do a little shopping, I go to Panera—I love their soup, did I tell you? You ever have it?—and then I figure, what the hell, I'll go to the casino . . . The whatchamacallit place. And I'm playing, I'm playing, and I win four hundred bucks at blackjack."

"Great!"

"No, wait, wait, that's not the point. So, I'm getting paid and I call over the guy—you know, the guy—you know the guy. Oh, what's the guy's name?"

"The shift manager, pit boss?"

"Yeah, yeah, the guy who runs the floor. Anyway, I tell him I'm hungry, so he says, 'Jack, how are you?' How about that? He knows my name, calls me Jack. And I tell him I'm hungry, and he says, 'Well, you had a good day, you won four hundred dollars, we have a lot of nice restaurants.' And I said, 'Wait a minute. It doesn't matter how much I won. I don't want to pay. I want a comp.' And he says, 'Well, I don't know. We have rules,' blah, blah, blah, so I ask him, 'What do you mean, you don't know? How long have I been playing?' He tells me one hour. I said, 'Bullshit! I've been here for two.' And I say, 'Look, I come here quite often,' you know, to squeeze him a little and let him know how he won't see me again for a long time if I don't get a comp, so he says to me, 'Let me check.' And he comes back with, you ready, a buffet comp. The lousy son of a bitch. A lousy comp to the buffet. Okay, I'm not that hungry, that's not the point, but what's the matter with you people?"

"What do you mean 'you people'? I would have given you a comp."

"You got a cheap state here, Ba. And they charge people for drinks."

"I think that's a state law. I think they have to."

"C'mon, you have a casino, you can't give a lousy drink away?"

"Uncivilized, eh, Dad?"

"But what the hell? I won four hundred bucks. What's new with you, sweetheart?"

* * *

31 October

In which Jack Friedman, after contemplating the Jews in the bowling group, discovers a new dynamic, one with no consistent dynamic.

"You know, Ba, the group in Vegas," he says in a call, "it's falling apart. Sid died, she's the wife. Stanley's the husband. He was the only Jew in the group."

"Did you just find this out?"

"No. I mean, I knew. What?"

"I'm lost."

"Just that Stanley was the only Jew in the group."

"But you're Jewish, Sid is, Solly, Muriel. Actually, there were more Jews in the group than not."

"You're right, you know. And Sol's wife, she's also, but she wanted to get rid of all the furniture from his first marriage when they got married and buy new."

"What does that have to do with anything?"

"I'm just saying. He told her no way. And the other one, you know, the other one, his wife, too—she's also Jewish—wanted to change out the furniture. He said okay."

"Who was that?"

"The other one. You know. What's his name?"

NOVEMBER

2 November
In which Jack Friedman attends a service at a funeral home and sets the eulogist straight.

At the service for Jerry Block, my doctor and my father's doctor, Jerry's son-in-law, an ordained minister, decided it would be a good time to testify about how none of us are getting into heaven unless we accept Jesus as our lord and savior, a presumption my father did not take well or quietly.

"What kind of horseshit is this?" my father asks loud enough for, I'd say, the front six rows to hear.

The sentiment, if not the delivery, I agreed with.

"A man dies and he takes this opportunity to preach?" my father continues. "All right, you're a pastor. How about keeping your mouth shut? The guy opens his Bible. Schmuck. And did he mention Jesus was Jewish? Which he was. No! And I went to synagogue with Jerry. He wore a tallis. He was Jewish."

* * *

7 November
In which Jack Friedman prepares to meet his new doctor.

"So, Ba, what's going to happen on Wednesday?"

"You'll meet Dr. Schumann."

"Jewish guy?"

"Yeah. Although your last doctor was Jewish. Anyway, it's kind of a hello meeting, maybe some tests."

"I'm tired of doctors. Tell me: Does he charge me to say hello?"

"Yeah, he's a doctor. That's how it works. They charge just to say hello."

"Then say hello for me."

* * *

12 November
In which the Legend of the Purple Heart grows.
As we head to the Hot Rod, he sees a billboard for the Army. And we're off.

"So we're in Luzon. Germany had already surrendered, but we're still going to Japan. I'm in the infantry, but engineering came over and said it needed about fifteen guys to help put up a bridge. They said once it was built we could win the war. Whatever. I don't know. Anyway, I was chosen—ach! I was one of the lucky ones. I'm told to go over and pick up this section, which weighs, like, four tons. I said, 'It's too heavy' so they tell me to go pick up another section, which I do. Then we start hearing the shelling and I hear someone yell, 'Drop the bridge and run for cover!' I do, only I drop the section on my big toe. When I look down, I see a gash in my boot and I start to run. Then I hear, '*You're running the wrong way!* Run for cover!' BOOM! Cover? What kind of cover? Then I hear an explosion. BOOM! Next thing I know, I wake up in a hospital. The funny thing with a bomb is it's not that anything hits you, it's the force of the air that knocks you on your ass."

"Okay, so the Purple Heart? When did that happen?" I ask, even though I keep hearing this story, or some approximation of it.

"What? Oh, that. So I'm in the hospital. I get up to go to the bathroom one day and when I come back, there's a Purple Heart lying on my bed. No name, but I assume it's mine. It was on my bed. I think it was my bed. There were a lot of beds. That's how they gave them out, they threw them on the beds. Then they come back, take your information, and engrave your information on the back of the medal."

"But yours isn't engraved."

"What do you want me to tell you?"

"You know, there's no record you ever got a Purple Heart. Susan checked, I checked. There's nothing on your discharge papers, no record in any database. I think, Dad, it might be someone else's medal."

"Ah, let it go. Don't make waves."

"Don't make waves? What kind of waves would I make?"

"You know."

"Okay, so what about the Samurai sword you got? I always imagined you took that off a Japanese soldier in the middle of a fierce *mano a mano* battle."

"Nah, I bought it in Tokyo."

* * *

21 November

In which Jack Friedman inches closer to his faith on a Shabbat morning, and why the Jews are the best.

After a stop at Owl Head, we drive by a church and see its billboard.

"What is it with all the churches in Tulsa? Jesus Christ! Every corner. And what does the sign say? 'Why settle for good when great is inside'?" he reads. "What the hell does that mean? Inside? Inside where? The church? Great's inside? You promise? And each one of these churches needs money to be built, right, so how does it work? They walk into a bank and say 'I need a loan, I'm a church' and then get one. Like this bowling group of mine in Vegas, no Jews. They'd rob a bank if they had to."

"Dad, whoa, what does that even mean? 'They'd rob a bank if they had to'?"

"You know," he says, laughing. "I mean, who knows what they'd do. I give up, Ba, I give up. I'm bored, I'm bored. I need Jews! They're easier to talk to."

* * *

26 November

In which the warmth and solemnity of Thanksgiving are momentarily and deliciously interrupted.

Last night, at around 11:00, my uncle and aunt and I decided that we were, in fact, going to have a traditional Thanksgiving, so my father and I headed to Reasor's, a neighborhood grocery store, to see if there were any turkeys left. Upon arriving in the parking lot, we noticed there was a man in jeans and T-shirt, a store employee, collecting grocery carts, screaming, "Welcome to Reasor's! Welcome to Reasor's!" in a "Redrum, redrum" cadence to everyone getting out of his or her car.

Disturbing.

I digress.

Once inside the store, my father and I did some shopping and then headed to where the turkeys might be, and, lo and behold, who do you think was behind the meat counter? Bingo. Now, were I running the store, I wouldn't have the guy who corrals the carts also be the one who slices the roast pork loin, but who am I to judge?

I approached, gingerly.

"Excuse me," I said, "Do you—"

"—no more turkeys, no more turkeys."

My father, who was with me, asked the only thing you could ask: "What kind of fakakta state is this?"

As my father kept talking about returning to Las Vegas, I thought it would be a good idea for him to go, especially since Chris, Susan's son, the son my father insists makes the big bucks as a systems administrator for a software company (and my father isn't wrong about this), was out there on a gambling mission.

Chris emailed the following to me:

November 28th—That First Night, at the Red Rock

A twenty-three-year-old's to-do list on his first time alone in Las Vegas before picking up his eighty-nine-year-old grandfather from McCarran.

Get Eyebrows Waxed

Walmart
String Cheese
Case of Dasani
Jar of Peanuts
Vienna Fingers

From Uncle Wayne: "The big L.A.-Vegas handoff! Grandpa Jack could use a bottle of water when he lands. Have fun in Vegas!"

To the family: "Just got the handoff text from Wayne, it's game time. Why are all the locals wearing long sleeves?"

Forty minutes in: Did you guys know that I'm supposed to stay with him tonight, at the Red Rock? Also, Tulsa has terrible roads. Jesse and I need to move out of Mom's house, and "Wayne is something else."

"He wants to stop by his first apartment complex and see how much rent is, just in case."

Two hours fifty minutes in: We're on the fourth restroom visit of the trip. This one we left the check-in line for. "Boy, these pills Barry's got me on, I don't get the headaches anymore but now everything I eat, you wouldn't believe these massive loads. But I don't get the headaches."

We check into his room, where I'll be staying with him that first night, at the Red Rock. On the elevator ride up to the eighteenth floor, the man gets quiet, a state of his I've never experienced. We both have aged two years on the walk to the center of the tower. In the gorgeous room in the armchair by the floor-to-ceiling window overlooking the hills he begins to ramble in panic. "I don't like high rooms. I don't want to be up here." He worries about planes striking the building. The front desk sends a bellhop to move us. Our bags and the case of Dasani are on the cart as the bellhop waits with me in the hotel room we don't want as we enter the fifth restroom break of the trip/day/afternoon. It's about now I begin to realize that I didn't take out nearly enough money for the "Sorry about Jack" tips I was going to have to spread around town.

The front desk informs us that the only rooms available on lower floors are handicap-accessible and right next to the elevator. The fourth-floor room is just as grand as the eighteenth, the hills now look taller, and we're both far less out of breath.

A new problem arises "What's this?" Jack asks, holding up a box of chocolate-covered peanuts from a platform on top of the chest of drawers. A plastic sign in front of the platform informs me that the $9 purchase was auto-charged fifteen seconds after the peanuts had been picked off the scale. By a stroke of luck, which would not follow either of us to the tables that week, the front-desk button on the phone puts me right in touch with my new friend at the front desk. She remembered us, and it didn't take much more than "eighty-nine-year-old" and "minbar" for the charges to be canceled and an attendant to come take away the goodies from out in the open. The contents of the fridge, equally booby-trapped, could not be opted out of, thankfully. As far as we know, he didn't stumble across the fridge for the length of the trip.

Safe from airplanes and his own curiosity, we leave for dinner at the cafe at the Suncoast. His oversize baseball cap sat perched crooked on top of the toupee as he ate a salad with a fork and a knife.

November 29th:

It's 8:30 in the morning and Jack wants me to go downstairs to the front desk to check into my own room. He is very concerned that my clothes will wrinkle from staying in the suitcase too long.

After twenty-six hours, a realization: "Now that I've come back and seen it," he says, "I don't think I want to move back."

Ten more minutes of reflection: "Florida! I think I want to go to Florida. I know where the two casinos are."

I suggest we call Jeannette, the woman he used to "run with" before moving to Oklahoma, but he's afraid to and thinks she's mad that he didn't move in with her.

"She's a very nice woman. Christian, you know?" he says. "But she can't cook."

Walking out of In-N-Out Burger following dinner, we're approached by a panhandler. "There are agencies!" Jack bellows. He never breaks stride toward the car. The moment, which I'll remember forever, I have not mentioned again.

November 30th:

We're on the hunt for a special store we need to hit while he is in

Vegas. He needs to buy a special hair dye and ship it to a "lady friend." He doesn't remember the name of the store.

[Personal note, even though Chris didn't say it: My father doesn't remember her name either.] He knows that it's in this shopping center, though. Or perhaps that one down the block. Or the other one, off Rampart.

The store is Sally Beauty. The dye is from L'Oréal. We drove for forty-five minutes.

The visit with his bowling league was shorter than it should have been. The heavy realization that life in the world moves on without you escapes not even Jack Friedman. The reunion is palpably not the joyous and triumphant return he had expected.

We make plans to come back tomorrow to see his friend Bill. He lets me know that he'll be going to Bill's house for a few hours.

Despite the fizzle on the bowling reunion, he seems to be having a good time on the trip. Every single person we've interacted with is asked whether or not they know that Jack used to live here.

On the way to New York New York, I joke about turning into the Orleans. The fear of running into Jeannette nearly brings him to tears.

December 1st:

We do not see Bill. We do not go to Bill's house. It snows.

In Las Vegas.

The valet for the Red Rock is located such that you're always passing the front desk when you come in. Since our second day, every walk past the front desk has been an opportunity for Jack to ask a new person about the hotel shuttle to the airport. His shuttle to the airport has been booked since we arrived. Jack knows this. Jack doesn't know this.

The IHOP waitress is getting the full Jack Friedman this afternoon.

-6 "Miss America"s

-"Does it cost extra to have somebody feed me?"

-"Just last week I was saying to this woman I was attacking in an alley..."

-The one about the parrot.

-"I lived here for nine years, you know?"
-"Decaf coffee, and instead of a spoon, can you stir it with that finger?"
-"Would you believe this is my grandson?"
-"I just want to thank you for last night." "Oh, was that you?"

December 3rd:

It's the day of the mission. We must pick up six black-and-white cookies from Suncoast. As we eat chicken noodle soup ("Make sure you scoop a lot of chicken into the bowl. I don't want too much broth") and bagels at the Bagel Cafe, Jack seems to have gotten the goal confused as he intends to order six cheese pizzas to check into his luggage tomorrow. I've been yelled at for attempting to correct him, and I'm not allowed to say the word "cookie" anymore, for he fears he will get confused by me and he doesn't want to disappoint Barry.

I check my sanity.

"Barry, he won't shut up about the size of these cookies not fitting into his bag. How big are they supposed to be?"

"They'll fit."

"Says they're the size of a large pizza. Now, I wouldn't put it past you, but I doubt they're actually that big."

"They're not that big, not even close."

"Actually he thinks he's supposed to pick up actual pizza. Like with the cheese and the crust. And you like them because they're bigger than the pizza in Tulsa. Did you send us on different missions?"

We staked out the cafe yesterday and he got a cup of coffee there. He's noted that half of the restaurant is now a Subway and he's worried that Subway might not make their pizzas as big as they used to. He's determined to slip the cook $5 to return to the old standards.

In the five minutes that followed "COOKIES! Not pizza. Why did I think it was pizza? Oh. Why did I think it was PIZZA?" Jack Friedman used the word "fuck" twenty-six times.

We got the cookies—five of them—and they were pretty well crushed into crumbs by the time they made it back to Tulsa.

As my mother would say, "A fire on those people."

[Chris told me that after the Friday bowling, he never saw "the Mob" again, and didn't see Jeannette at all.]

DECEMBER

5 December
In which Jack Friedman prepares for a change.

On his return to Tulsa, my father announced at baggage claim where he wants to spend his remaining years.

"Ba, Vegas isn't for me. Everyone's falling apart there. I can't move back there. I want to move to Florida."

"Why Florida?"

"I don't know. I've been thinking about Florida more and more."

"You hate Florida."

"Yeah, I know. Your mother did, too. Called it 'Heaven's Waiting Room.'"

"So why do you want to move there?"

"Why? I don't know. My brother's there. Ida's there. I want to be around family."

"Ida? You'd move to Florida for Ida?"

"You know."

"And what am I, chopped liver?"

"You know what I mean."

"And Ida? She's not even family. She married someone in the family who's now long dead, and then she married another guy who's not in the family and he's long dead. Besides, she doesn't like you. You don't like her, remember?"

"Nah, Ida's all right. You know years ago her son dropped dead walking across Fifth Avenue? Had a heart thing. No, I'm very serious. I've been thinking about Florida more and more. How much are apartments there? And where are those two casinos again?"

6 December

In which Jack Friedman reminds us again why he's Jack Friedman and the rest of us aren't.

Driving by Oral Roberts University and the old City of Faith Hospital:

"I hear Oral locked himself in that tower for years."

"No, he didn't."

"Yes, he did. I read that somewhere."

"You're thinking of Rapunzel."

"No, no, I know about her. Yes, Oral locked himself in the tower until they finally got him out of there and then his son ruined the place."

"Well, you got that part right. But Oral did not lock himself in the tower for years."

"Why not?"

"'Why not?'"

"Yeah, why didn't he?"

"I don't know why he didn't lock himself in the tower for years. What kind of question is that?"

"What do they teach here besides, you know, mythology?"

"Mythology? Oh, that's hilarious. They teach religion, history—"

"So everyone wants to be a pastor?"

"I don't think so. I'm sure many do, though."

"Whose hands are they?" he asks, pointing to the large praying hands in front of the university.

"Whose hands?"

"Yeah, who was the model?"

"The model? How would I know who the model was? But I do know they used to be in front of the hospital and they moved them to this spot."

"Yeah? How much did it cost to move them?"

"I have no idea."

"And what's that building?" he asks, pointing across the street.

"It's a hotel."
"Part of the university."
"No, it's a Sheraton."
"A hotel or a motel?"
"What difference does it make?"
"Well, a hotel is different from a motel. It's fancier."
"Yeah, I know that, but what difference does it make to you now?"
"Plus, there's parking at a motel right outside your door. Called a motor hotel."
"I know this."
"You don't know."

* * *

12 December

In which Jack Friedman issues the most surprising of fatwas and gives a nod toward a new generation of bread products—all while re-emphasizing the theme of the first volume of this trilogy.

"No more bagels. They're too heavy. Okay, the soft roll you can eat, but the bagel, no good."

* * *

21 December

In which Jack Friedman makes lemonade where lesser humans would have trouble even spotting the lemons.

"So, Dad, did you see *Star Wars*?"
"No, every theater was sold out. It's that popular?"
"Apparently so."
"Wow-wee-wow!"
"So what did you wind up seeing?"
"Oh, the film with—you know. Uh, what's her name—with the other one? The two of them, you know."
"*Sisters*? You saw *Sisters*?"

"Yeah, very funny picture. There were only three people in the theater. Good story, though."

22 December

In which Jack Friedman talks health care and mocks my prime earning years.

"So, Ba, what are *you* doing for insurance?"

"Funny you should mention that. Just got a notice that I may be dropped from this particular coverage."

"Why?"

"Apparently, I make too much money for the subsidy."

"*You* make too much? You?"

"Yeah, why are you laughing?"

"You make too much money? Oh, that's funny."

* * *

25 December

In which Jack Friedman soaks in the warmth of Christmas morning.

On *The Danny Kaye Show,* on Get TV, a young Wayne Newton just finished singing "Jingle Bell Rock" and "Somewhere," from *West Side Story,* with the same expressions and movement in both. If Kaye is to be believed, Newton was known as "Mr. Excitement."

Jack Friedman, who's been watching, offers his review:

"Why is this on, anyway? Newton was never that young. He's, like, four times the size now, and, you know, this guy was really nothing. A complete nothing. And how old is Danny Kaye now —one hundred and twelve?"

* * *

27 December

In which we learn that it is not prudent to come to dinner with Jack Friedman without studying French history first, particularly if you're French.

Charles de Gaulle died in 1970. Aurélien Labrosse, my son-in-law, was born in 1987.

Let's begin.

"What the hell was de Gaulle thinking?" my father asks Aurélien. "The Germans just went through the Ardennes Forest. What a dummy!"

"I don't know, Jack," Aurélien says.

"My question's academic."

Anyway, if you bet the under (+/- 7) on Maginot Line references during our post-Christmas lasagna dinner, you lost (and lost badly).

* * *

28 December

In which we learn that Jack Friedman's narrative will not be interrupted by the actual narrative.

"Did you see the Ron Howard movie today?" I ask him, picking him up from the movies. For an eighty-nine-year-old man, he's not afraid to go by himself.

"No, I saw the other one with . . . what's his name?"

"Will Smith."

"Who?"

"Will Smith."

"No. It was the one with the concussion."

"Will Smith—the movie about the NFL."

"What? Yeah, but not the NFL. He was a doctor or something with an accent, whatever his name is."

"Will Smith."

"I don't know what his name is. Anyway, it was a medical story about the heads and damage and—"

"The NFL."

"No, not the NFL. The ones in the league and their brains and these players are dying and nuts and what this fakakta sport does to them. Football, it's such a dumb sport played by—"

"I know: dumb flesh."

"Anyway, how are you, sweetheart? What's the forecast for tomorrow? I want to go to the gym."

* * *

31 December

In which Jack Friedman thanks Aurélien, his granddaughter's husband, and the French people for making life more livable.

At the Hot Rod Tuesday Night All-You-Can-Eat 2-for-1 Buffet, on this New Year's Eve, while peeling his own shrimp, Jack Friedman comments, "You know, Ari [long *ahhh* sound], people got tired of doing this, so in your fancier French restaurants, they hire people who do this for you."

Jack Friedman and his granddaughter, Nina

two
2016

JANUARY

THE YEAR STARTED as the previous year did: with me writing letters to Jim Jakubovitz, CEO of the Charles Schusterman Jewish Community Retirement Center, petitioning to get my father a stipend so he could afford to live there. At the time, rent was about $2,300 per month, out of his price range and mine. Jim had told me years ago that it was going to be a slow process but that at some point we'd get my dad into the place. Every year, every January, I sent a letter.

He didn't get in.

We stay at the Mansion.

2 January

In which Jack Friedman, during pizza before Auri's flight home, talks culinary trends, race relations, American exceptionalism and architecture, and race.

"Ari, what food is indigenous to Oregon? Because in the South, there's fried chicken. In New York, it's pizza. What do you got? What do you eat there besides the grape, the wine? I'm sure in France, well, I'm sure there are French restaurants. Is there such a thing called French pizza? What do they do with the cheese?"

"We have pizza in France," his grandson-in-law says.

"Yeah?"

"Yeah."

"So, do you have a colored problem in France?"

"A colored—no!"

"Good thing you don't live in the South, because wow-wee-wow!"

(Auri looks to me for help. I am powerless.)

"The first time you came to America, was it the first time? I mean, with the skyline?"

"We have cities with skylines. Smaller, you know."

"Yeah, you got?"

P.S. On the way to the airport, my father gave Auri twenty dollars so he could get something to eat during his layover in Denver.

* * *

23 January

In which it's a good thing you have some sense of my father so this will make perfect sense to you.

"I'm cold," my father told Melissa at dinner.

"Put your jacket on," she and I both told him.

"No, I'm not cold, just chilled."

Jack Friedman chilled

29 January

In which Jack Friedman sees others' lives pass before his eyes.

"When I was doing taxes, Ba," my father tells me over dinner, "I was living the high life. Made big money. I was doing a return for a guy in Maine, but he died. Then I was doing one for a woman—you know, what's-her-name in West Virginia?—but then she died. But then bullshit, bullshit. How the hell did we get here?"

* * *

30 January

In which Jack Friedman looks at an Oklahoma icon and finds him lacking.

"Who is this guy Will Rogers?" my father wants to know. "He's supposed to be big in Oklahoma, right? He's nothing. I read this quote: 'Even if you are on the right track, you'll get run over,' or something. What, who . . . that's supposed to be smart? It's the dumbest thing I've ever heard."

FEBRUARY

22 February
In which Jack Friedman talks of the dead, the living, and the in-between.

At dinner tonight:

"You know that picture I have, the one with the whole family?"

"Yeah," says Melissa.

"The whole family's there. They're all dead. You've seen it. I'm the only one that's still kicking. Me and Pitsy. I ran with twenty guys, and now it's just me and Mel and Jerry. You know, Mel's in California. I call him. He gets tired. He can't talk too long. Something with his lung. He takes naps."

"Jack, you were six in that picture," she says. "It was, like, eighty years ago. Of course a lot of those people are dead."

"But they're all gone. Everyone in the picture. What did Jerry Newman die of?"

"Who's Jerry Newman?" I ask.

"Who's Jerry Newman? You don't know Jerry Newman? How can you not know Jerry Newman? He's my mother's sister's son."

"Jerry? Or Bernie?"

"Bernie. Who's Jerry Newman?"

"Jerry Newman? No, Bernie Newman. Where'd you get Jerry?"

"You mentioned it."

"*I* mentioned it?"

"You mentioned. Anyway, how did Bernie die?"

"I don't know."

"You know Lylah died, too, his wife. What'd she die of?"

"How would I know that?"

"Ach, they're all gone, even in Florida. Jerry's got something with his foot. They went back to Nova Scotia. He and Pitsy, who used to run with Mel. He loved her so. They had a terrible falling-out."

"New Rochelle," I tell him.

"What?"

"They moved to New Rochelle, not Nova Scotia."

"Why?"

"I don't know why."

"Anyway, he's still kicking, at least. And what's-her-name's in the home with whatever she's got. And Ida. Ida! Ida's the only one left in Florida."

"What about your brother?" Melissa asks. "He's still alive."

"Yeah, but he wasn't part of the group."

"He still counts, doesn't he?" I ask.

"But, nu. Ida! Ida's still around. She married Jerry, you know? This is another Jerry. We called him Red. He's gone."

* * *

26 February

In which Jack Friedman experiences Oklahoma tax policy.

"Say, Ba," he asks me as I walk into his apartment, "why am I getting forty bucks back on my state taxes?"

"Why?"

"It says I'm getting back forty bucks."

"Good."

"No, not good. I didn't pay in any money. I mean, not a dime in state tax, not a dime in estimates. I mean, nothing, but it says I'm getting back forty bucks. Here, I'll show you."

"I believe you, you don't have to show me. I think that's the tax cut. Everyone gets back something."

"But I didn't pay anything in, I'm telling you!"

"What are you screaming? I don't know why, but, again, I think it's the tax rebate, as I said. It was passed last year. There was a big fight about it. I wrote about it."

"What, you mean in the . . . the . . . paper?"

"Yeah, let's go with that."

"What'd you say?"

"Not important."

"I don't understand. You're a billion-three in debt! What kind of fakakta state gives back money like that?"

"What do you want me to tell you?"

"Forty dollars, nu? Keep the money and fix the goddamn roads. "Oklahoma!" It's not a state, it's a condition."

* * *

29 February

In which Jack Friedman thinks of love with what's-her-name.

"You know, Ba, if I didn't come to Tulsa," he says to me tonight, "Joanne would have taken me in."

"Who's Joanne?"

"You know, Joanne. The girl I was running with."

"You mean Jeannette?"

"What'd I say?"

"Joanne."

"Joanne? No, I meant Jeannette. Joanne? Who's Joanne? Oh, yeah, that's another one."

"You want Jeannette to take you in, you should probably get her name right before you ask."

"I'm eighty-nine, what do you want from my life? I would have gotten it right eventually."

MARCH

3 March

In which Jack Friedman concludes, in a conversation with Melissa, all is right with women's fashion.

"You know, Miss America, I like your head after all. Very fashionable. I know a lot of women are wearing it that short for the summer. It's cooler."

* * *

18 March

In which we take another trip to the MotherLand. This is a short one, just a weekend. My father will fly up to New York, while I go on to the Bahamas.

We're with Gail Cohen in Palm Beach, Florida.

"How do you know her, Ba?"

"Facebook."

"What's that?"

"Oh, boy!"

With Gail Cohen in West Palm Beach

APRIL

2 April

My father likes his gin-and-tonics the way he likes his hair: tall.

* * *

22 April

In which Jack Friedman reminds us it really is his world and he can claim it anytime he wants it.

Back from the Motherland (Delray Beach). As we walk into Village Inn, my father picks up a copy of the latest issue of *The Tulsa Voice,* the alternative-news biweekly for which I actually write.

"Are you in this week, Ba?"

"Yeah, in all the time."

"What do you write about, politics?"

"Yeah."

"Oh, here you are," he says, finding me. 'The War on

Women,'" he reads. "What's it about?"

"The war on women."

"Yeah?"

"Yeah."

"There's a war on women?"

"Yeah."

He calls the waitress over.

"Say, miss? Miss? You want to meet a celebrity?"

"Sure," she says.

"He's in this paper."

"Really?" she says.

"Yeah, I'm Jack Friedman, I'm the father."

* * *

26 April

In which, just when you think you know the act, Jack Friedman trots out the new material and then finishes with a crowd-pleaser.

As we head into the Hot Rod for the Tuesday Night All-You-Can-Eat 2-for-1 Buffet, my father puts on his Members Only windbreaker and approaches the valet, an attractive woman with the whitest of teeth and the blondest of hair.

"How goes your life, Miss America?"

"I'm okay. And you?"

"Got a half hour, I'll tell you the whole story."

"I don't have that much time, sir."

"Better yet, wait for the movie. It's in color. Hey, is it cold in there?"

"A little, yes. Good thing you have your jacket."

"Oh, this. I don't need this. I'm a skier. Have been for years. My whole life."

"You were?"

"Sure. Okay, love, thanks for your time."

"'You're a skier'?" I ask.

*\ *\ *

28 April
In which Jack Friedman sets priorities.
This from my brother, Wayne.
"So Dad called and said, 'I was going to call you earlier for your birthday, but I was at the casino, hot at the tables, and I was drinking.'"

*\ *\ *

29 April
In which Jack Friedman, embodying an important and ignored demographic, masters Netflix.
"What the hell is the name of that show with the kids?"
"The kids?"
"The kids, the college kids. There's a bunch of them."
"A bunch of kids?"
"Yeah, they sit around and talk, you know. This one and then the other one and . . . it's good."
"I'm trying here, Dad, I really am."
"Oh, you know, the girl is in it, the pretty one, she was married to what's-his-name?"
"You're not talking about *Friends,* are you?"
"Yes, yes, *Friends.* I've seen, like, forty of them. They run them in a row, one after another. Good writing, very funny."
Later . . .
"So this show tomorrow, is it a farm show?" He's asking about *Fiddler on the Roof.*
"Well, it's a local production, if that's what you mean. I hear it's good."
"Any Jews in it?"
"I don't know. Probably not."
"Do they know Jewish?"
"That's actually hilarious. I don't know."

"How much is it?"
"Forty bucks a ticket."
"Forget it."

* * *

30 April

Perhaps you're thinking, "No, your father did *not* pull out his bottom denture at Owl Head to show you where it hurt at the exact moment you first bit into your bagel."

Well, you would be wrong.

MAY

8 May
My mother, Jack's wife, at sixteen.

My mother, at sixteen

20 May

In which Jack Friedman looks for a person to thank.

"So, Dad, Sunday at the synagogue, we have a dinner. It's not free, but someone paid for your ticket but wants to remain anonymous."

"What?"

"Someone wanted to buy you dinner."

"Who?"

"She's anonymous."

"So who do I thank?"

"You don't. She's anonymous."

"Do you know her?"

"No."

"Then who is she?"

"She's anonymous."

"What'd she say?"

"She didn't say anything. In fact, I'm not entirely sure she's a she. But for argument's sake, let's say she is. She just wants to buy you a ticket at this dinner."

"Why?"

"She likes you on Facebook."

"Likes me on where?"

"It's a really long story."

"You making me a celebrity?"

"Yeah."

"You getting rich off my fame?"

"Yeah, that's what I'm doing."

"So who is she?"

"I don't know. She's anonymous."

"So I can't thank anyone?"

"No."

"I have to thank her. Do you know her?"

"No, she's anonymous. I don't know. She called the office, if she's a she, and said, 'I want to buy Jack Friedman a ticket to the dinner, but keep my name anonymous.'"

"What if she comes up to me at dinner?"
"Then thank her."
"How will I know it's her?"
"How many people do you think wanted to buy you dinner?"
"But I have to thank someone. You can't give me a name?"
"I don't know the name. She's anonymous."
"Ach! All right—anonymous. Should I wear a suit?"
"A sport coat, no tie."
"And you don't know her?"

* * *

21 May

In which Jack Friedman, amid windshield wipers and free hot dogs, contemplates the end.

The day begins at the Napa Auto Parts grand reopening sale.

"So what are you getting again?"
"Windshield wipers, Dad."
"Why?"
"I need them."
"How do you know?"
"They streak—the wipers are frayed."
"On the car."
"Yes, on the car."
"Do you need to get special electric ones?"
"No. They're normal blades."
"But your car's electric."
"Yeah, but blades are blades."
"You mean blades for the wipers?"
"Yeah."
"Do I need them?"
"No."
"How do you know?"
"I know. I just changed them."

"Maybe we should get some anyway. It's good to have a spare set around."

(After purchase is made, I notice, as part of the grand reopening, the store is giving away hot dogs and soda.)

"Here, Dad, I got you a hot dog."

"What kind of hot dog?"

"A hot dog hot dog. What do you mean what kind?"

"You forgot the mustard."

(I go back to the grill area. There's no mustard.)

"There's no mustard," I tell him. "Ketchup they have."

"Ketchup? Who eats it with ketchup? Oklahoma! And what do you mean no mustard? You serve hot dogs, you don't have mustard?"

"You want the hotdog or not?"

"Give me the hot dog, yes. Is it kosher?"

"I doubt it."

"How can you eat this without mustard? . . . Say, Ba, let me ask you," he says, let's call it thirty seconds later. "What does the Jewish religion think about suicide?"

"I don't know. Why?"

"I mean, like the Catholics, you kill yourself, you don't get in right away."

"In?"

"Heaven, you know. They don't let you in. You have to take a written test first."

"That's funny."

"Well, I mean, they don't make you sit down and actually take a test, but they make you do some things before they let you in."

(We interrupt the proceedings for a moment for a call I make to Melissa.)

"Free hot dogs, baby, and four dollar wiper blades!"

"You're the man. Wait, you're eating hot dogs from a Napa Auto Parts store at ten thirty in the morning?" she asks.

"Yeah, I had to. They were free."

"But no mustard!" my father screams from the passenger side.

"Let me go," I say to Melissa. "I'll be home soon."

"So, anyway, Ba, I was wondering," he says after I hang up, "what Jews think about suicide, that's all."

"Why?"

"No reason. Where we going now?"

"You wanted coffee, you said, remember?"

"Yeah, let's go to Old World, the bagel place."

"If you're going to get it wrong, get it right. It's Owl Head."

"What?"

"Nothing."

"But who can eat? I love their coffee. But get me a scrambled egg on a soft roll. Their bagels are too heavy, too . . . What do I call it? Voluptuous."

* * *

22 May

In which we are reminded why Congregation B'nai Emunah should have a two-drink maximum.

When did Jack Friedman get drunk? If I had to guess, it was after the third time he motioned to the server as if he were pumping the trigger on a gun, as he usually does when he wants a refill of any kind, to fill up his wine glass, but before he fell asleep on Didi Ralph's shoulder during a video salute to past synagogue presidents.

"What happened?" he asked, stumbling out of the lobby.

"You're drunk," said Melissa.

"It's wine. I'm not drunk. You can't get drunk on wine."

"You just did."

It took two of us to get him upstairs, one on each arm. In the hallway to his apartment was the first time we heard, "I'm dying, I'm dying."

"No, you're not," Melissa said. "You're just drunk."

"No, I'm dying."

To the bed we got him. He fell backward, protecting, of course, his hair.

"I'm dying, I'm dying. Florence, I'm coming."

"You're not going to die," Melissa said, lying down next to him. "You're eighty-nine and you're drunk on wine. It's the first time. You usually drink gin. I'll put it in your baby book."

"What's your name, lady?" he asked, feeling her arm around him.

"Melissa. I'm cuddling with you. You got a woman in bed. How about that?"

"I can't have sex with you tonight. I'm too exhausted."

"Jack, try to sleep."

"Oh, oh, oh, what happened?" he repeated. "I'm going to die. It's all right. Florence," he said again, repeating my mother's name, "I'm coming."

"You're not going to die, Dad, don't worry."

"Thank you, thank you for being here. Take five thousand out of my account. I don't care. You deserve it."

"Is that five thousand each," I asked, "for Melissa and me, or five thousand total? I'm just curious."

"Oh, what happened, what happened? What is this thing on my head?"

"It's a cold wash rag," said Melissa. "I put it there."

He turned the TV on, for some reason. He was watching, for some reason, *Grey's Anatomy*. It's all he's been watching for weeks.

"I'm dying," he moaned again.

"You're not dying."

"I'm dying."

Just then, George, the doctor who's in love with Elaine, came on the screen.

"Oh, this guy's an idiot," my father said, dead cold sober.

"Go home, both of you, go home. I'm fine, I'm fine," he said, straightening out his toupee once he removed the offending cloth.

He was watching the show, the toupee was fine, my father safely in bed. We knew all was well and we left.

* * *

23 May

Jack Friedman, a surprisingly not-hungover Jack Friedman, on the way to the dentist this afternoon, remarks about the firemen at various intersections around town, boots out, collecting donations.

"What are they selling, boots?"

"Dad, they're collecting for charity."

"Oh, okay, because I figured 'boots?' Who the hell's buying boots now? It's spring."

* * *

24 May

In which Jack Friedman sees Melissa moving on.

As my father and I return from our morning stop at Old World (formerly known as Owl Head, actually called Old School), there is a car in the driveway he doesn't recognize.

"Whose car is that, Ba?" he asks as we drive up.

"Don't know."

"It's probably the new man. Melissa is probably moving him in."

* * *

28 May

In which, it being Memorial Day Weekend, the conversation, once again, turns to Jack Friedman's time with First Cavalry in the Philippines during World War II. And we hear the story again. Sort of.

"Tell me again, Dad, what happened in the war?"

"Well, we started bombing this bridge and then the Japanese started shelling, so the sergeant said, 'Run.' I then dropped something on my toe—"

"—whoa, whoa, whoa, you dropped something on your toe? I thought you said you were hit with a piece of flying bridge."

"No, no, I dropped something on my foot."

"What'd you drop?"

"Who can remember? It was so long ago."

"You really don't remember what you were holding?"

"It was something. I was holding it and dropped it. I then heard the sergeant scream, 'You're running the *wrong* way!' And the BOOM! And, later, I took off my boot and saw my toe and passed out. I then woke up in the hospital. Well, it was a tent, really."

"And then?"

"I got up to go to the bathroom, and when I came back, there was a Purple Heart on my cot. I mean, I think it was my cot."

* * *

31 May

In which Jack Friedman brings the praise, sort of.

I am at the Mansion.

"Ba, I gotta tell you, these pills you have me on—blood pressure pills, the whatnot, the other stuff, the way you laid them out in the . . . the, you know."

"Pillbox?"

"Yeah, perfect. I haven't felt this good in years. Not a headache, a bellyache, nothing. Of course, it's all going to fall apart tomorrow. But, no joke, you deserve some credit for this, you really do. And, of course, the doctor."

Later . . .

Good friends Laura Belmonte and Susan Arrington are kind

enough to bring my father a fanny pack, embroidered with the word "SMILE" on the pouch. You would have thought someone had bought him a condo in Boca Raton, he was so excited. Unfortunately, a small piece of plastic piping was left in one of the pockets, piping that affected neither the look nor the operation of the aforementioned fanny pack. You would think finding a small piece of plastic piping in a used fanny pack would not fill a full thirty minutes of commentary.

You, of course, don't know Jack.

"What the hell is this?" he asks.

"Looks like a piece of plastic," I say.

"What kind of plastic?"

"Plastic."

"Plastic?"

"Yeah, plastic."

"What does it do?"

"What does plastic ever do?"

"Maybe it has to do with the shape."

"Probably."

"It's not like I'm going to wear it all the time, anyway. I mean, when I wear dungarees I won't, because they have back pockets, but when I wear these summer pants"—he motions to his Nike Sweats, with the thick white line down each leg—I will."

"Yeah, good idea."

"But the plastic's bothering me. I mean, I don't know. It came right out. Should I throw it out?"

"I would."

"I'll put it back in."

JUNE

8 June

In which Jack Friedman reminds us that Tulsa is a tale of two cities, even or maybe especially for the two Friedmans, and then makes a bold prediction.

"Ba, I'm bored. Tulsa . . . Tulsa? Who comes to Tulsa? I gotta get out of here. That stinking dollar they take at the casino. On each bet, mind you! I'm going back to Vegas. But you need to stay."

The vig that the Native American tribes take at area casinos—and it's only fifty cents—never ceases to annoy him.

"Why do I need to stay?" I ask.

"C'mon, it's your town, you know people, you write, the thing for the newspaper. You'll make your fortune here."

Wait. What?

* * *

11 June

In which Jack Friedman prepares for the move to his new apartment, a smaller one-bedroom, at the Mansion, across the hall from his present residence.

"Ba, you going to take my typewriters?" he says while packing.

"No."

"Why not?"

"They're broken, for one thing, and nobody uses typewriters, for another."

"They're not broken. The ball just doesn't work on the IBM, and the other one, I don't know, there's something going on with the wheel. It doesn't move."

"That means they're broken. And why do you have two, anyway?"

"In case I need a spare."

"A spare? But they're both broken."

"They're not broken. They just don't work."

"Just throw them out. Tell you what: I'll throw them out."

"Ah, broken—they're not broken."

"They're broken."

"Why can't you just put them in the car?"

"Because they're heavy *and* broken and, not to put too fine a point on this, you're moving across the hall."

"Oh, right. I already brought other stuff down to the car."

"Why would you—? Of course you did."

"Can't you sell them? They're good typewriters."

"They're forty years old, and, again, they're broken, and, again-again, nobody uses typewriters. Nobody's going to buy them."

"C'mon, you couldn't get a hundred bucks for them? They're good for labels."

"You have a computer that does that. Everyone has a computer that does that. And very few people use labels. And even those who do don't make their labels on typewriters anymore."

"Yeah, but, you know, I don't know, they're good to have around. You're going to get me a new typewriter, right?"

"If you insist."

"You'll call your guy?"

"Dad, he's not really my guy. It's someone on eBay who sells IBM Selectric typewriters."

"You know, I got a whole thing of balls for those, and sheets for labels with the, uh, you know—"

"They peel off?"

"Yeah. What am I going to do, let them go to waste?"

"Of course not."

* * *

18 June

In which Jack Friedman has a plan to deal with boredom and then touches on the dynamic between fathers and sons.

"I think I'm going to get a job," my father says to me on the way to Owl Head.

"Where?"

"I don't know. A job. Why can't I get a job?"

"Nobody's going to hire you."
"Why not?"
"You're almost ninety."
"I'll lie about my age."
"They'll want to see your license."
"I'll make up a fake one. I'll change the dates."
"What could go wrong there?"
"I'll tell 'em I'm sixty-five."
"Sixty-five? And you'll just change the dates on your license?"
"Yes."
"Since when did you become a master counterfeiter?"
"I can pass for sixty-five! What do you know? You're just jealous you don't look like me."

* * *

19 June

You may be cool, but you're not Jack Friedman-in-a-plastic-and-felt-fedora-at-Dollar Tree cool.

Happy Father's Day to a man who wrings more out of life than any man I've ever known.

* * *

20 June

In which we can only imagine Jack Friedman in his prime with the ladies. They didn't stand a chance.

Last night at dinner, across the table from Melissa and Gregory (her son), he says to Melissa, "You know, your hair looks very good now that it's growing back. Beautiful. Very good-looking girl. No joke. If I were sitting next to you, and if not for him"—he points to me—"swear to God, I'd make a play for you."

* * *

23 June

In which Jack Friedman just wants to remind each and every one of you that you're going to have to up your game if you want to make an impression.

Upon leaving his biannual checkup with Dr. John Schumann, a good friend, a fabulous doctor, *and* president of OU-Tulsa, my father says, "What a nice man. Good doctor, very good. And you know him?"

"Yeah, he's a friend. Plus, we know him from the synagogue."

"Jewish?"

"Yeah."

"Does the synagogue know he's Jewish?"

"I'm sure it's come up."

"Is he your doctor, too?"

"Yeah, he usually examines us both on the same day, remember?"

"I've seen him before today?"

"Yes, about four times."

"No, it hasn't been four times. Maybe three."

"Okay, three."

"That's right, that's right, yes, yes. Wait. I've seen him?"

"Yeah."

"I knew the building looked familiar. So what kind of doctor is he?"

"What kind? Internal medicine."

"So he's not a specialist, just a GP and, what, president of the university?"

"Yeah."

"Wow-wee-wow! What does he do as president?"

* * *

28 June

In which Jack Friedman and the buffet waitress, I'm confident in saying, have one of the great conversations of all time, and remind us all, if such reminders were necessary, that coffee is the universal language.

"You know, in Las Vegas, everyone is overweight," my father tells the waitress at the Hot Rod, who, how to put this delicately, is overweight. "Before the casinos, they were underweight."

"Well, my dad was from Vegas," the woman responds. "I lived there as a girl. He married an Italian hooker."

"Well, I lived there for nine years until my son dragged me to Tulsa. Tulsa! Who comes to Tulsa?"

"She was a whore," the waitress continues. "We had to move after she lost his money gambling."

"Well, my wife died sixteen years ago. She worked as a costume designer, so I ran to Vegas. I'm pushing ninety."

"I'm sixty-seven."

"I'm older than you."

"We lived in seventeen states. You want any more coffee?"

"Is the pope Catholic?"

* * *

30 June

In which, after a brief discussion about gambling in a Native American casino, Jack Friedman comes face to face with nature and blinks.

"Funny thing about gambling, Ba," he tells me as I meet him while he's playing crap. "Sometimes you win, sometimes you lose. You're up, you're down, you never know. Who ever thought I'd be doing this in my retiring years? But this still burns me—the buck they take every hand."

"I thought it was fifty cents."

"It's a lousy buck at crap. That's all right, though, I'm winning. But it still bothers me. Why do they do that?"

"Because they can. Don't play if it bothers you."

"No, it's not that."

"It sounds like it's that."

"Why do they have gambling in this city if they don't want gambling? And it's not even in the city. It's in Cahootsville."

"Catoosa."

"What did I say?"

"It's actually funnier your way. But it's Catoosa."

"Whatever. They name a tribe Catoosa. What kind of fakakta name is that? And crap they don't play with dice but with cards and the wheel thing, the . . ."

"Roulette?"

"Yeah, roulette, they don't spin the thing. They do the other thing. Ach, I give up!"

We then leave the Hot Rod, first stopping to get beverages from the soda machines the casino provides for free.

"This is nice they do this," he says. "They'd never do it in Vegas."

"Yeah, but they don't charge the lousy buck."

"You're right. You know, you're right."

"It happens."

We exit the Hot Rod.

"What is this, water?" he says, seeing a puddle as we step outside.

"You wait here. I'll get the car."

"Here?"

"Here. By the bench."

"Look at this rain."

"Dad, it rained."

"What kind of rain?"

"What *kind* of rain? Rain."

"Wow-wee-wow, look at this. It rained. Was it supposed to?"

"I don't know."

"I mean, was it in the forecast?"

"I don't know."

"How long did it rain?"

"I don't know."

"Look at this. It's wet. I wonder if the bench is wet. [He checks.] Yeah, it's wet."

"That's because it rained."

"Was it a heavy rain?"

"I don't know. I was inside with you."

"Did you hear it?"

"The rain? No."

"Well, I'll be."

"Dad, it's rain. You're going to be ninety soon. You've experienced rain before. Why is this so fascinating?"

"Yes, but I was in Vegas for nine years. It didn't rain."

"But you're familiar with the concept."

"Hey, I'm not knocking it. It cooled things down. And it gave the car a wash. Is it still raining?"

"Clearly no."

"You know, this casino's all right, except for that lousy buck they take. It burns me so."

"Bastards!"

JULY

1 July

In which we are reminded to never doubt Jack Friedman's prescience.

While eating our usual Friday-night pizza at Uncle Vinny's in Broken Arrow with my Uncle Ed (my father's brother-in-law), and Anita, Ed's wife, we made the decision to go to Dairy Queen after the meal, a place we had gone to previously.

"This time, Ba," my father says, about an hour before we'll be there, "I don't want vanilla. I had vanilla last time. I want chocolate. Do they have chocolate or just vanilla?"

"You're kidding, right? No, just vanilla. Of course they have chocolate. Who opens an ice cream store and serves just vanilla?"

"They're not going to have chocolate."

"Of course they are."

"This always happens."

"What always happens?"

"They never have chocolate."

"Of course they do. How many times have you not gotten chocolate when you wanted it?"

"I'm just saying I don't want vanilla, I want chocolate. And a small one. My capacity to eat is not what it used to be. I think because I played a lot of tennis in Vegas—every day, four-game sets, I don't know. I have no appetite. I don't know what the hell is wrong with me." The slice of pizza and half a meatball hero are about gone from his plate.

We arrive at Dairy Queen.

"Don't forget: chocolate," he reminds me. "I want chocolate. Not vanilla."

"I got it!"

"Sure, why not."

I approach the guy behind the counter. I'm a little concerned because I don't see a chocolate-dispensing machine, but maybe it's not out front for some reason. What do I know?

"I'll have a small chocolate cone."

"Sir, the chocolate machine is broken. We just have vanilla."

"Seriously?"

"Yeah, sorry."

"You've got to be kidding."

"No, really, the chocolate machine broke. We just have vanilla."

"You seriously don't have chocolate?"

"We don't."

"Do you have any idea what this is going to cost me?"

"Excuse me?"

"Never mind. I mean, there actually is a chocolate machine most nights, though, right?"

"Yeah, and it's been broken for a couple of hours."

"Mother of God!"

"Sir?"

"I can't go back there without chocolate ice cream. You don't understand."

"Sorry. Can I get you something else?"

"Can it be fixed? I mean, I'll wait."

"Not tonight."

"What do you suggest? Because my father wants a chocolate cone."

"You could get him a chocolate shell on a vanilla cone?"

"I guess that could work."

I bring it back to the table.

He takes a bite.

"Hey, this is vanilla under the chocolate."

"Dad, I know. You're not going to believe this, but they're out of chocolate."

"What do you mean they're out of chocolate?"

"The machine broke."

"What do you mean the machine broke?"

"I don't know what that means, except it's broken and there's no chocolate."

"I told you they wouldn't have chocolate."

"No, they have it. It's just the machine is broken. They don't have it tonight."

"So what's this chocolate shell? The chocolate-shell machine is not broken?"

"Apparently not. Maybe there are two machines. I really don't know."

"So, what, you can't get chocolate in Oklahoma?"

"I'm sure some places have it—just not here, just not tonight."

"I gotta get out of this state. Nu, you can't get chocolate."

He's got a point. We're going to have to move.

* * *

3 July

My father and I are at Cracker Barrel and he has ordered Fruit Loops.

"Hey, miss. Miss," he says. "Does it cost extra to have someone feed me?"

* * *

6 July

In which Jack Friedman means no rhetorical harm.

At dinner tonight, the waiter, African American, brought my dad his coffee just the way he likes it.

"Attaboy," my father says.

* * *

8 July

In which Jack Friedman once again wonders what might have been with what's-her-name.

"I should have gotten married, Ba, after your mom died."

"Who would you have married? Who would have married you?"

"Oh, c'mon, you know, what's-her-name in Vegas. The one in the trailer who buried the two husbands—oh, what was her name? She would have married me."

* * *

10 July

In which Jack Friedman, presently in New York with his daughter (my sister), Susan, who weighs more than 300 pounds, shows off some of his irrepressible charm with the ladies.

Let Susan pick up the story by way of a text I just received:

"Have you ever seen the Kate Hudson commercials where she's selling her workout outfits?"

"No, I haven't. Why?" I replied.

"Well, Dad said her body is gorgeous—and why don't I look like her?"

"Well, why don't you?"

"Fuck you."

My sister, ladies and gentlemen.

* * *

18 July

In which Susan, at a cemetery with her father, files another report.

"Went to the cemetery yesterday, and I have to tell you it was something," she tells me. "I sat on the bench and watched this man walk to each and every stone. He stopped and read them, looked around for me, told me something about that person, and then moved on. It was a bit surreal. Here is this ninety-year-old man looking at his family. But of course, being our father, he then reminded us—the boys were there, too—about the cost of cemetery plots and how, as he continues to pay the family center association dues for all his children, he can get us all one. Barry, he kept offering me a spot."

"Did you take him up on his offer?" I asked.

* * *

23 July

Susan reports: "Today, at lunch, he grabbed a woman by the arm, a waitress, who was heavily tattooed.

"'Hold it, dear,' he said. 'I want to read your arm.'"

* * *

30 July
In which Jack Friedman prepares to return to Tulsa from Mastic Beach, New York, and Susan shares some thoughts and, in the process, explores the family dynamic.

"I spent four weeks with him. Nothing. No compliments, only complaints. And you make *one* phone call and tell him he's got money in the mail, and he tells me, 'Barry made my day.' Fuck you, Barry."

AUGUST

2 August
In which Jack Friedman returns to Tulsa from New York a changed man. And of course when I say "changed," I mean not at all.

The scene: He is on the other side of airport security, behind two bulletproof-glass doors and windows. He sees me, extends three fingers in the air. I see his mouth moving. I have no idea what he's saying because, as mentioned, he is behind two bulletproof-glass doors and windows.

" . . . planes. Three planes! Not one, not two, but three planes!" he's screaming, still with three fingers raised, as he comes toward me. "Did you hear me? Three. Hello, sweetheart, how are you?"

"Fine."

"Nu? Three planes. Three! Did you ever?"

(Nephew Jesse, his grandson, who accompanied him on the trip, looks like he's ready to shoot heroin between his toes.)

"There was something wrong with that last plane," my father says to Jesse.

"Yes," Jesse agrees, exhausted.

"But three planes! Three! Did you know it was going to be three?"

Later at the Hot Rod valet—yes, he wanted to go to the casino right from the airport to eat at the buffet. It was around dinnertime, c'mon!

"Why do they make it so goddamn cold in here?"

"So, Dad, did you have a good time?"

"They all work. All of them. They get up, they go to work. They all work! Susan, Emily . . . all of them, even this one next to me. And they wouldn't let me drive. But they all work. How about that? All of them!"

Dinner almost over, Jesse suggests they play craps.

"You know what burns me: that lousy buck they take on every roll."

"Again."

"What? First time I brought it up. And it's not a roll—they play with cards. Did you ever? Cards! Oklahoma . . . Oklahoma! But that buck, it burns me."

"It burns me too," says Jesse, because he's a good grandson. "You want to play, Jack?"

"Oh, come on, you had me on three planes and now you want to play? All right, we'll play for an hour or so."

* * *

3 August

In which Jack Friedman discusses Hitler and falls in love with a country singer.

After a trip to Walmart for fitted sheets and milk, on the way to the Hot Rod, my father discusses science improbabilities with his grandson.

"There have been many cases where people without brains give birth to people with brains," my father says.

"Many cases?" asks Jesse.

"Well, you know what I mean. And maybe this is a bad example, but if you wiped out Hitler's brain and all he could do was breathe, would he still be a miserable son of a bitch?"

We drive the rest of the trip to the Hot Rod in silence. Later on, at the Flip Side, the surprisingly good burger place inside the casino, the conversation continues.

"I think I'm ready to die," my father says to nobody in particular.

"Why is that?" I ask.

"No reason, nothing bad."

"Nothing bad?"

"Hey, who's that?" he asks, staring at a photo of Martina McBride, who will soon be appearing at the Joint.

"Martina McBride."

"I think I'm in love. I want to marry her. How can I get her to marry me?"

* * *

6 August

In which Jack Friedman vies to be the crankiest man in America.

I arrive at his apartment.

"Barry, I'm sick of this fucking place."

"Morning."

"Morning. Okay, first off, I can't sleep."

"Why can't you sleep?"

"The toilet seat for one."

"You can't sleep because of the toilet seat?"

"It's not setting right, so I pushed it down and it's fine. But who the hell knows?"

I check. It was a plastic seat that needed to be locked. I locked it.

"It needed to be locked. I locked it. What else?"

"What do you mean it's locked?"

"It needed to be locked."

"You sure it's locked?"

"It's locked. What else is bothering you?"
"The kitchen cabinet doors. They're still not on."
"They've been ordered."
"They've been ordered for two years now."
(He moved in six weeks ago.)
"They're coming, I promise."
"When?"
"I don't know. So what's bothering you?"
"I don't know."
"Why is everything annoying you?"
"Everything is not annoying me."
"Fine, but you seem annoyed."
"I'm not annoyed, but . . . I'm, you know, how do I phrase it?"
"Annoyed."
"Nah, it's a miserable day. Is it raining or wet or drizzling or what?"
"Raining."
"Was this in the forecast?"
"I don't know."
"Is it supposed to rain all day?"
"I don't know."
"I mean, is it forecast to rain all day?"
"I know what you meant. I don't know."
We leave for Owl Head.
"What a miserable day. Is it supposed to rain all day?"
"Still don't know. Why don't you take yourself to the movies?"
"Ach, the movies. Till you find out what's playing. There's, like, twenty movies and to know what they're all about. Movies? No, I don't want to go to the movies. All right, maybe I'll go to the movies. It's such a miserable day with this rain. What's playing?"
"I'm driving."
"I mean, what's showing?"

We're now at Owl Head.

"Why is this so goddamn hot?" he asks, after ordering and picking up his egg sandwich.

"Because they needed to cook it."

"But to make it so hot. Who can eat it like this? I can't even pick it up. All right, what's playing at the movies?"

I check my phone and I start reading to him titles of about nine of the twenty pictures playing.

"All right, I'll go see . . . what's it called again?"

"*The Infiltrator*."

"What time?"

"Four thirty."

"Why four thirty?"

"Why four thirty? Why not four thirty?"

"You know, I'm going to go, see one, and then slide over to that one."

"You're going to slide over from one movie to another? This is not a Vegas buffet, you know."

"No, you know what they got there. You walk in and it's this huge place and there's, like, twenty-five movies. You can go to any one you want. They design it like that. I go to all of them, I don't care."

"Okay. But you should go to the movies, even if you only go to one."

"Yeah, might as well. It's such a miserable day. Is it supposed to rain all day or what?"

"I still don't know."

* * *

7 August

In which Jack Friedman opines on the history of Nevada, Part 1:

"You know why Nevada has gambling?" he asks in a call.

"Why?"

"Because they can't grow anything in that state. It's all sand."

"Go on."

"The whole place is a desert. It's un-arable."

"Un-arable?"

"There's no agricultural, ah, what do you call it? Nothing will grow. It's the worst climate anywhere, so they allowed casinos 'cause it's the only industry that'll make it."

* * *

9 August

In which Jack Friedman confronts aging ... with questions.

"So why do they give you this aging *and* give you the rest of the shit?"

"You've already lost me. What rest of what shit?"

"No, they say, 'Here's old age, but here's disease, here's this, here's that.' Why do they do that?"

"They?"

"Yeah. They give you a long life and everything hurts. What good is it? Ach."

"I don't know."

"Look, I'm not really asking. My question's academic."

"Thank God."

* * *

11 August

In which Jack Friedman reviews the bill for his flat tire and has some questions for Tulsa officials.

My father had a flat tire earlier this morning. I meet him at Robertson Tire.

"How much?"

"One hundred sixty-five dollars."

"Why so much?"

"Well, they had to tow the car to the tire place."

"Why couldn't they just fix it where it was?"

"Because you had it in a Mazzio's parking lot."

"Oh, c'mon, it was right down the block."

"But that's not where their tires are."

"Ach. I give up. I'm going back to Vegas."

"Right. Because nobody in Vegas gets a flat."

"It's these goddamn roads in Tulsa. What are they putting on them?"

* * *

12 August

In which, I kid you not, it happened again at Dairy Queen. Again at fucking Dairy Queen this happened!

"I'd like a small chocolate ice cream cone," I say.

"We're out of chocolate," says the teen behind the counter. "Machine needs to be cleaned."

"How is that possible?"

"The machine's dirty."

"I understand that. But it's Friday at eight. This happened before. The machine was broken. I can't believe this, the coincidence."

"Well, sir, the machine's not broken, it just needs to be cleaned. And we do it every night."

"I appreciate the distinction, but it's Friday, shouldn't this be done before—never mind. I'll have vanilla."

A few minutes later. "Dad, they're out of chocolate."

"What do you mean?"

"They don't have chocolate."

"No chocolate?"

"No chocolate."

"How can they not have chocolate?"

"I know, right?"

"What did the guy say?"

"That they're out of chocolate."

"Didn't this happen—"

"—Yes, it did."

"Oklahoma. I gotta get out of here."

"I don't blame you."

"So what's this?"

I hand him a vanilla cone with a chocolate shell topping. Thought I'd try it again.

"It's vanilla ice cream with a chocolate shell. You remember? It's the best I could do."

"Is that legal?"

"Yeah."

"What if they find out?"

"I won't tell them."

"Ach! Must be a Republican!"

* * *

18 August

In which we are reminded, if such reminders were necessary, that Jack Friedman is one tough sumbitch to please.

We are at Owl Head.

"Why do they make this roll so goddamn hot?"

"And we're off! Because you said you wanted it toasted."

"All right, toasted, but I can barely touch it. I'll have to wait for it to cool down."

"Good plan."

"What is this?"

"The blueberry cream cheese you ordered."

"Why so much?"

"Because that's how much they give you."

"It's too much."

"You want less?"

"No, but why do they give you so much? I can only eat half."

"They don't know that."

"You'll have to take half."

"I don't want a croissant and blueberry cream cheese."

"C'mon, I can't finish it."

"I don't want it."

"All right, it's just that I can't finish. I don't know what's going on with my appetite. Maybe it's the gym."

"Look, when we leave here, I have to run some errands. You want to come with me?"

"What do you have to do?"

"Go to T-Mobile and then buy some Half-and-Half."

"That's all?"

"What, you're disappointed? You don't like my errands?"

"No, but yesterday I went shopping."

"Okay, you win."

"No, I'll go with you, but where do you have to go, again?"

"T-Mobile and then to buy some Half-and-Half."

"All right, what the hell, I'll go. Then what?"

"I'm taking you home."

"Good, because I want to watch TV."

* * *

23 August

In which Jack Friedman brings his A-game to the Hot Rod Valet.

The first stop, obviously, on our Tuesday Night All-You-Can-Eat 2-for-1 Buffet soiree is the valet, where we almost always meet the same attendant, a woman around forty-five, bleach-blonde, tattooed, sweet, big smile, who always helps my dad out of the car.

"Hello, Miss America, how goes your life?" my father asks.

"Just fine."

"That bad, huh? Don't worry, it'll get worse."

"How are you, Jack?"

"Wait for the movie. It's in color. It's a porno flick. Did I tell you about the woman who walks into a bar with a parrot on her shoulder?"

And of course he has, and of course she lets him tell it again.

Finishing the joke, he says, "All right, love, behave yourself, and if you can't, take my number. Nobody calls. *Nobody calls.*"

"Have fun tonight, Jack. Win some money."

"Here," he says, suddenly reaching into his Nike sweatsuit jacket pocket and pulling out a bite-size Snickers, which I'm guessing is between two and three weeks old. Smashed, but still wrapped.

"Thank you," she says, looking at me.

"I have no idea," I mouth.

As we walk into the casino, I ask, "Really, Dad, a Snickers bar?"

"Yeah, I forgot I even had it. I figured I'd give it to her—what the hell?"

"Smooth."

* * *

26 August

A plea: For the love of God, would you people in the service industry leave room in the coffee cup for my father to add his five containers of Half & Half, three ice cubes, and four packs of Sweet'N Low? Man worked hard his whole life, he's turning ninety, his son dragged him to "Oklahoma," and this is how the world thanks him? He's *verklempt* over this.

"What's the matter with these people?" he asks. "They don't drink coffee?"

* * *

27 August

In which Jack Friedman's fame grows.

My father and I go to Mondo's tonight, and what's the first thing Chris Aloisio, one of the owners, says?

"Hey, Barry, tell your father not to worry. I've got chocolate ice cream for him."

Is that sweet or what?

"What a nice dinner!" my father says. "They give you too much goddamn food, though. Who the hell can eat it all? I don't know what happened to my appetite. Hey, how'd they know about the chocolate ice cream? Did you tell them? Was good, too. But they give you too much."

* * *

28 August

In which Jack Friedman deconstructs corporate America, and it's brilliant.

"Dad, this week we'll go to Mondo's again."

"Yes, yes! We'll split the chicken parm because I can't finish a whole one. My appetite—"

"—and we'll get some chocolate ice cream again. They like when we come in."

"Imagine? You can't get chocolate at the other place."

"I'm sure they have it."

"Nah, it's bullshit. They never did. Maybe one day because the owner wanted it. They don't have."

"I'm sure they've had it."

"Nah. Besides, the name—what is it?"

"Dairy Queen."

"You know, it means the cow, the white milk. Vanilla."

"'Cow' means 'white milk'? Since when?"

"You think not? Then why can we never get any?"

"You win."

* * *

30 August

In which one would think Jack Friedman would be happy after discovering hard-boiled eggs at Jason's Deli. One would be wrong.

"Huh, huh, who found hard-boiled eggs for you?" says I, as I come up to him at the salad bar.

"Ach, I got hard-boiled eggs at home. I need theirs? But all right, I'll have one. But how come this guy's got them and the other Jason doesn't?"

"I don't know, Dad, but I don't know that Jason is actually there—or even exists."

"My question is academic. You know, if I walked in with my own plate, I could walk right up to the salad bar. They'd never know."

SEPTEMBER

1 September
In which the normal encounters with Jack Friedman seem eerie.
He called at 7:55 this morning just to say he was going to the gym and wanted me to know that if I called, his phone would be in the locker and that's why he wasn't picking up and to just leave the message.

"Okay, sweetheart?"

"Okay."

"Because I'll be in the gym."

"Okay."

"Okay?"

"Okay."

* * *

2 September
In which Jack Friedman reminds us to never take the first rejection.
We're eating hamburgers at a place called Ron's.

"Why are my hands so goddamn sticky, Ba?"

"Clearly the food's fault."

"And why don't I have a napkin?"

"Because you threw it on the plate when you were done with the burger and the waitress took it away."

"Say, miss," he says, spotting another waitress, "can I get another napkin, love?"

"Absolutely," she says, giving him one. "Anything else?"

"I'd like you to give me a bath."

"I can't do that, sir," she replies good-naturedly.

"Why not? I'll behave."

* * *

6 September

In which you'll want to stay off the roads.

"Say, Ba, I think I need to get my left eye checked. The right one's good, but the left, I see double sometimes, not always, but it's very blurry. Don't misunderstand me. It's not bad."

"That's not good."

"No. So when I drive, I close it and just use the right and I can see fine," he says, putting his palm over the offending eye to show me how he does it.

"You close it, cover it, and drive with just one? Oh, my God!"

"What?"

"You're a eighty-nine-year-old man driving around with his hand over one eye. Why would I think this might be a problem?"

"It's these goddamn roads. They don't allow parallel parking."

* * *

10 September

In which, heading to the crap table at the new River Silk Casino, Jack Friedman gives gambling tips and then offers some much-needed insights into Native American history.

"You know with crap, you win," he says. "You lose, you're up, you're down. And in blackjack, you win, you lose, but it's a softer game. Crap, you can lose very fast, but here they play with cards, not dice. I wonder why."

"I can't explain this again."

"Cards, nu? And how come the Apaches don't have a casino? I mean, they were fierce. And the Sioux. Those were the two biggies. Which one killed Custer? Are the Apaches in Oklahoma? Do they have casinos?"

"I don't think so."

"I wonder why not."

"Shame we can't ask them."

"What's with the Creek and the Whatchamacallit?"

"The Cherokee? What do you mean?"

"Did they fight?"

"I don't know."

"You know, we gave them the casinos because we felt bad about taking their land. And now they're getting us back. Oh, boy!"

Later...

It won't mean much to those not in Tulsa (and may not even matter to those who are here), but when the city closes the highway exit on Denver, as well as 15th Street, because of the farmers market, combined with the construction on 21st, it's very tough getting to my father's apartment. That seems like a first-world problem, and it is, but a ninety-year-old man who wants an egg on a soft roll (not a bagel—it's "too voluptuous") should not be denied or delayed.

He's not driving this week on account of that eye, so I took him to the movies this morning and dropped him off. I told him when and where I'd meet him.

"I'll be fine."

I did the same thing with my children—and back then they said the same thing.

* * *

11 September

In which we are reminded why Jack Friedman, his protestations about how the first one had no alcohol notwithstanding, never gets the second gin-and-tonic.

He woke from his nap at a booth at Mondo's Ristorante Italiano and asked the question that has been flummoxing the country's greatest minds for decades.

"So how come Oklahoma City doesn't have camels anymore? What the hell happened to their camels?"

* * *

13 September

In which my father and I run some errands, so of course the conversation turns to Tahitian dietary habits and sticking it to the Man.

"What the hell do they eat in Tahiti?" he asks this morning when I come to pick him up. "Probably fish," he says, answering his own question. "I mean, what's the difference between Tahitian food and Chinese food? It's mostly rice and sauce, right?"

"Absolutely," I say.

"Tahitian food? I never had any. Probably a lot of fish. Is it spicy?"

"I'm sure some of it is. Okay, look, I have to run into UPS. You want to stay in the car?"

"Yeah, I'll have a cookie."

* * *

14 September

In which Jack Friedman reminds passersby who's the star of the show and who's the other guy.

A girl, the Hot Rod valet, approaches us.

"Are you Jack Friedman?" she asks.

"Who, me?" my father asks, surprised. "How do you know me?"

"You kidding? I follow you on Facebook all the time."

"Oh, yeah, yeah. Yeah?"

"Do you read them?"

"Well, no, I mean, yeah, I don't read all of them, but some."

"Oh, you're really famous. They're hysterical."

"Well, there's a lot of that going around."

"Is this Barry Friedman?" she asks. "Omigod! I love him. Your son's amazing."

"Well," my father says, "I was in Vegas for twelve years."

"I read your son all the time. He's my hero."

"I went there from Atlantic City after my wife died. Gorgeous woman."

* * *

15 September

In which Jack Friedman blames the crowd.

To review the best of my father's act:

1) Telling every woman he meets, "May you never know the horrors of stretch marks."

2) The joke about the woman who walks into a bar with a parrot on her shoulder and is told that animals are not allowed. "Animal?!" she screams. "This is not an animal, it's an award-winning parrot." "I was talking to the parrot," says the bartender.

3) The joke about the man who comes home and discovers his wife is in bed with another man. The husband shoots the man, and his wife says, "You know, you keep doing stupid things like that, you'll lose all your friends."

So today, my father had cataract surgery, complete with anesthesia, which made him, as it would anyone, a little loopy. Just imagine, if you will, the comedy festival that went on pre- and post-op. He was telling those jokes multiple times to the same nurses, sometimes with different punchlines; for instance, on Joke No. 3, the punchline was changed to the very unfunny "What are you doing here?"

Sitting in the waiting area, I heard all this. Then, after coming out of surgery, he told the same nurse about never knowing the horrors of stretch marks three times in—yes, I timed it—two minutes. And she gave him zero reaction. I mean, nothing. All three times. After the last attempt, my father said, "No stretch marks. It's a blessing! Get it? C'mon, who gives you a blessing like that?"

On the way out of the clinic, we passed this nurse in the hallway, and she said, "Mr. Friedman, it's been a pleasure. Take care of yourself," to which he responded, "You, too, dear, and thank you for your time. Behave yourself. And if you can't, take my number."

* * *

16 September

In which Shonda Rhimes has no idea.

Four times I have gone to my father's apartment since his cataract surgery and four times he has been binge-watching *Grey's Anatomy*.

"Dad, why are you watching this?"

"I don't know."

"Do you like the show?"

"Eh. I turn on the TV, the Netflix, and it's there. I leave it."

* * *

17 September

In which Jack Friedman sums up a life well lived.

"Remember Melinda?"

"Yeah, I do. She worked with you."

"She worked in Don's office. She died. Cancer. Never told anyone. She was Filipino."

* * *

18 September

In which I give you Jack Friedman, political pundit who gives wise advice.

I walk into the Mansion to find him in his desk chair, two feet away from the TV, watching, of course, *Grey's Anatomy*, screaming on the phone. I find out he is talking to his old friend Bill in Las Vegas. For those unfamiliar with the cast of characters in these parts, Bill was his partner in crime at Vegas buffets, the man who co-founded the Slide, the devilishly smart plan of arriving at the breakfast buffet late, hanging around and then sliding into the lunch feast undetected as soon as it opens.

"You cannot vote for Trump, you hockey puck, and put that man in the White House!" I hear my father scream. "No, no, no! You're a savage, you know that. Now, how's your wife? You still bowling?"

* * *

19 September

In which Jack Friedman gets mail.

My father's toupees, much discussed in these parts, came to him today: one box labeled "Dawn," one labeled "Star," from an online women's wig emporium. He also received his copy of *Essence* magazine.

* * *

23 September

In which Jack Friedman wins the day.

"So I ran into this Nazi today, said 'Good morning,' and then I shot him."

* * *

24 September

Sometimes conversationally with my father, you just have to hold on and hope you don't get hurt.

"Hey, Ba, I need to stop and get a gallon of milk and a gallon of orange juice," he says as we're headed to dinner. "The big ones, the double gallons."

"I don't understand."

"You know, the big ones, the gallons, the double ones, you know, because I eat a lot of cereal and I have juice every morning, so let's go to your guy at, what is it, when we're done eating, at, you know—"

"The bagel place? Trader Joe's?"

"Yeah, yeah, I want the, uh, soft roll and the blue cheese."

"Blueberry cream cheese?"

"Yeah, they have great coffee there. What brand do they use? And who knew your guy there is from Austria?"

"Aaron?"

"Yeah, his parents are from Austria. Who knew? Did you know he was from Austria? Anyway, I love his coffee."

"I know."

"Great coffee. How does he make it?"

"Actually, I make it. I combine two or three brands, add the Half-and-Half, the Sweet 'N Low, and—"

"I know. I love their coffee. But don't forget. I need a gallon of milk and a gallon of orange juice—"

"Can I make a suggestion?"

"—because I eat a lot of cereal."

"Yeah, I know."

"I mix it with the Rice Krispies, it's very good."

"Why don't you get a half gallon of each?"

"What do you mean?"

"You're not going to go through a gallon of each. They could go bad. And even if you do run out, it's not like you have a lot to do. We can get more."

"Well, when I run out, I just use Half-and-Half and water it down."

"That sounds awful."

"I've only done it once, when I ran out. I put it on the corn flakes."

"But again, you really just need a half gallon."

"That's what I said."

"Okay, so you don't want a gallon?"

"No, no."

"Because earlier you said you wanted a gallon of each."

"No. C'mon, you know what I meant when I said a gallon."

"That you really meant a half gallon?"

"Yeah, because I use it on my cereal, that's all. I have it in the morning."

* * *

26 September

We're at my father's apartment at the Mansion and he has slept through the presidential-candidate debate. He wakes just as they're signing off.

"What happened?" he asks.

"You slept through it."

"Oh, yeah, the debate, right. So what was the outcome?"

* * *

29 September

In which Jack Friedman, almost ninety, defines man.

"Ba," he says, calling me. "I'm not sleeping. I need to get laid."

* * *

30 September

We are at the River Stix and my father, dressed in a FUBU short and a particularly bad toupee, has wandered off.

Later...

Jack Friedman has been found.

"Dad!"

"Where the hell you been?"

"Waiting for you."

"What time is it?"

"Ten thirty."

"I thought you said ten."

"I did. It's ten thirty."

"Oh, right. So we were supposed to meet at ten."

"Right."

"What time is it now?"

"Ten thirty."

"I thought it was late."

"You okay?"

"Yeah, won thirty-six dollars, but they take that lousy buck."

"I know."

"Did you try calling?"

"Yeah, about five times."

"I thought I heard the phone ring."

"Why didn't you pick up?"

"I figured, who would be trying to call me?"

"Many people would answer the phone to find out."

"Yeah, I guess so. Did you leave a message?"

"No."

"Why not?"

"Because you don't know how to get the messages even if I do."

"Yeah, this stupid phone. All right, let's get out of here. I'm tired. What kind of life is this for me? Who knew I'd find gambling in my retiring years?"

OCTOBER

1 October

In which Jack Friedman takes us on a magical rhetorical ride before going to Owl Head.

Scene: He comes downstairs from his apartment wearing glasses prescribed to him pre-cataract surgery. They are the plastic wraparound kind that are preposterous anywhere but in such a clinic.

"Dad, you shouldn't wear those anymore. Not good for your eyes since the surgery."

"I know, I know."

"But you're wearing them."

"Yeah."

"But you really shouldn't."

"I don't, I don't. I just put them on, that's all. I have the sunglasses, which I use for the sunny days, and the reading glasses I use just for work. These"—he takes off the ones he's wearing—"I just wear for everyday." He puts them back on.

"But they're not good for your eyes."

"I know, I know. I don't wear them. I don't wear any glasses during the day."

You have to know when you've lost.

"Okay, what else is going on?"

"I'm tired, achy. You know, I used to play tennis every day, so I got up and started doing taxes. I'm not active, so I can't sleep."

"So you're tired, huh?"

"Nah, I'm not tired."

"But you just said you were tired."

"Tired, you know, eh, tired. I'm not . . . I'm, you know, blah. I think I'll take a nap when I get back. I feel fatigued, logy. So, tonight, what's the story?"

"You're coming over at seven to stay with Gregory."
"Seven?"
"Seven."
"You want me to be there at seven?"
"Yes, seven."
"OK, so I'll come over at six, six thirty."
"Perfect."

* * *

3 October

In which, on this holiest of holy Jewish holidays, my father reminds us to personalize religion.

There was a point in the service where the Torah was taken from the Ark and, while music played and prayers were being chanted, was paraded around the sanctuary by the rabbi, cantor, and other dignitaries, so those congregants who so wished could touch it with their hands or lay their tallis (prayer shawl) or prayer book upon it. It was also at this point the congregation turned its backs from the bima (stage) to follow the processional. As my father and I were sitting in the front row of the back section—and directly in the path of the Torah—we were actually facing the congregation, as it turned its collective gaze to follow.

"Hey, Ba," my father didn't quite whisper, "why's everyone looking at me?"

Years ago, when my father lived in Las Vegas, I took him to Rosh Hashanah services in Summerlin, west of the city. During the morning session, the rabbi, a Russian in sneakers, along with a co-rabbi, his wife, also in sneakers, also Russian, began the prayer called Al Cheyt, which is a litany of confessions Jews say on Rosh Hashanah, all beginning with the preface "For the sin of . . ." that deal with things like selfishness, cruelty, arrogance, greed, etc. We are asking God to forgive us for those sins against family, friends, ourselves, and God himself.

My father and I were not members of this synagogue (we were guests: My rabbi in Tulsa made a few calls, as they say in Vegas, and got us into the service), but we were nevertheless surrounded by congregants who welcomed us, when, apparently, my father decided the list was too long and too severe.

"Jesus Christ!" he said after one too many "For the sin of . . .," "how fucking bad are we?"

Yeah, we left pretty quickly.

Later . . .

"Hey, Ba, where's Melissa?"

"She's got a migraine."

"Well, listen, the world is filled with millions of people, all with the same noses, all with the same heads."

* * *

14 October

This man's having a birthday.

"Ninety? Ninety! I was sixteen two weeks ago. I turned around and what happened?"

From the, count 'em, two Filipinos with whom he's bowled on his championship team, to the Slide, to the possible thieving of the Purple Heart, to Jeannette . . . Janine . . . Carol, whatever the hell her name is, to "Where's your mother, Ba, where's your mother?" . . . to uncovering the secrets behind Dairy Queen's unconscionable business model, I give you my father, Jack Friedman, on the first day of his tenth decade.

"What does the world want from my life?"

And may you and yours never know the horror of stretch marks.

* * *

18 October

In which Jack Friedman's magic with the ladies is not only beyond understanding, but also it's beyond comprehension.

At the Hot Rod Tuesday Night All-You-Can-Eat 2-for-1 Buffet, a waitress approaches with my father's root beer.

"Hello, love. How goes your life? You behaving yourself?"

"Never."

"No? Why not?"

"Why not?" she responds. "That's no fun."

"Yeah. I was standing on the corner the other day with a cigarette hanging out of my mouth and said to this girl, 'How are you?' and she said, 'Fine.'"

Silence.

I look at the waitress. She looks at me. We both look at him.

The silence continues.

She looks back at me and points to my father.

"I just love him."

Later . . .

On the way back to the Mansion: "Say, Ba, so what do you

think I should do? Take the six-month extension or the year they're offering me?"

"I don't know. You like the place?"

"Yeah, it's fine. Besides, I don't feel like moving again. What do they charge if you break the lease?"

"I think they charge two months, but don't worry about it."

'Ah, what the hell, I'll do a year. It's the same price. Don't misunderstand me, everything's fine, but how much longer am I going to live, anyway?"

* * *

23 October

In which Jack Friedman reminds us all what we have to look forward to.

"What the hell are these?" he asks while we drive to the River Silk. "Stores?"

"Yeah."

"What kind of stores?"

"Stores, you know. Stores."

"They put stores here?"

"It's a busy intersection. Why wouldn't they put stores here?"

"What, they sell different kinds of things or is it one store?"

"It's a strip mall."

"A what?"

"Strip mall! More than one store."

"Nu? Stores. They're short. They need more stores. Ach, I give up!"

"You give up?"

"Where do I belong, Barry, where do I belong?"

"Where do you think you belong?"

"Oklahoma. I'm bored to death here. Fix these goddamn roads already."

"Why are you in such a lousy mood tonight?"

"'Cause I'm ninety. That's what happens. You become a miserable bastard. Everything annoys me. I'm entitled."

"You're entitled?"

"That's old age, baby. What can I tell you?"

Later...

Jack Friedman worries about those in the construction community. Melissa and her anxiety will be going on a cruise this week. Her mother will be coming to Tulsa for a few days to help me with Gregory.

"Who's going to cook for your husband," my father asks Cindy, Melissa's mom, "while she's away?"

"He cooks for himself, Jack."

"Really?"

"You want me to meet him at the door with a drink and his slippers, too?"

"Well, it's just that he's in construction," my father says.

* * *

24 October

Another 355 to go.

My father, who had a birthday ten days ago—he turned ninety—announced to everyone at Owl Head that he was "pushing ninety-one."

Later...

Who says you can't measure love? This morning at breakfast: "Barry, I appreciate everything you do for me. I don't know what I'd do without you. The pills you lay out, driving me around."

"You're welcome, Dad, I love you."

"Really, I can't thank you enough. That's why I give you some money for the accounting work you do for me."

* * *

25 October

In which Jack Friedman gives us another reason to hate The Wall Street Journal.

"These crosswords, I can't finish it. I don't know what the hell they want. It's not that it's complicated or difficult. It's their phraseology [pronounced "phrase-ee-ology"]. For instance, oh, I don't know, but you know, like, it'll say 'cold,' so you think 'frost,' but no, they want 'a frost.' They cheat, the miserable bastards. I'm filing a protest."

* * *

26 October

Something is bothering Jack Friedman

"You know, in the old days you could slide across the seat from the passenger side to the driver's," he says. "Now, with these bucket seats and the hole between them, you have to get out of the car and come around."

"What else you gotta do today?"

"It's not that. But if it's raining, you get wet."

"You get wet? You're blaming that on the automobile industry?"

"Who told them to change seats? I liked the seats the way they were. Now you have to unbuckle, get out, get back in."

"I don't know that anyone told them, Dad. I think things just develop and change. And, really, *this* is what you're going to bitch about today?"

"Yes! I don't like your modern world."

* * *

29 October

In which we join Jack Friedman as he returns from the movies and reminds us what's important about Tom Cruise.

"Hey, Dad, what'd you see?"

"Oh, you know, that picture with the . . . oh, what's the name of it? You know!"

"*Girl on a Train?*"

"Who?"

"*Girl on a Train.*"

"No! Girl on a what? No. I saw the other one. Oh, what's the name of it . . . with the idiot?"

"The idiot? Uh, Tom Cruise?"

"No! Who?"

"Tom Cruise."

"Maybe."

"*Jack Reacher?*"

"Yeah."

"Tom Cruise."

"Yeah, yeah, yeah. John Reasor or something. He was very good. Good story. You know he's very short."

* * *

30 October

In which we are reminded, if such reminders were necessary, Jack Friedman takes the conversation wherever he wants.

We're driving.

"So, Melissa, she's on a cruise in the Gulf, right?"

"Yep."

"So she's, what, in the Gulf?"

"Yeah. In the Gulf."

"They go to Mexico or just ride around?"

"They stop a few places."

"Can she bring me back a T-shirt?"

"I'll ask."

"What kind of water are they known for?"

"Kind of . . .? I don't know."

"No, I mean, do they get many storms?"

"Yeah."

"They're not that bad, though, right?"

"No, some are bad."

"Yeah, but they're not like the ocean. So what's the name of the boat?"

"I don't know."

"What do you mean you don't know? You don't get out much, do you?"

"Why don't I know the name of the cruise she's on? I just don't know."

"What do they charge those ships to go through the Panama Canal?"

"I have no idea. But it's not going through the Panama Canal."

"I wonder how much it is to take a speedboat through the canal."

"I don't know that, either. Do you want to take a speedboat through the canal?"

"It's gotta be less, but still, eight, nine hundred. It's too much. You ever been?"

"No."

"Oh, I thought you were on a cruise."

"I have, a couple of times, but never through the Panama Canal. I was on one off the coast of California."

"Did you have a gig?"

"Yeah."

"How'd it pay?"

"Good."

(At this point, my father looks out the window on Highway 51, west of Tulsa.)

"Who owns those cattle? The state?"

NOVEMBER

8 November

In which Jack Friedman casts his first ballot in Oklahoma and has questions.

"Is my name on this ballot?"

"No."

"Then how do they know it's me?"

"You registered, that's why they gave you a ballot.'

"But can't someone make, like, a hundred thousand copies of the form and fill them out themselves?"

"Yeah, but without the machine to insert the form, what good will it do them?"

"Yeah, I guess you're right. But how do they know I voted?"

"You came and signed in."

"Yeah, but can't someone change the marks who I voted for? What about the guy I gave the pen to?"

"I don't think he'd change your ballot."

"Why not?"

"He's the pen guy. Besides, you didn't give him your ballot. You put it into the machine yourself."

"Yeah, you're right. But there's nothing on the ballot that tells them it's me?"

"Nothing."

"That's odd. Couldn't I mark it?"

"Secret ballot. Do you want to mark it?"

"Yeah, I guess you're right. So, all those state questions. What do Republicans want, since this is a solid Republican state?"

"A fabulous question, that."

Later...

While cutting into a piece of prime rib at the Hot Rod Tuesday Night All-You-Can-Eat 2-for-1 Buffet here in Tulsa, he puts the election into perspective.

"I wonder, if we were at a buffet in a Jerusalem casino right now, if this meat would be kosher."

* * *

9 November
In which you-know-who has an opinion.

Jack Friedman, ninety, enters the car on the way to Owl Head and bellows, "We have to leave the country! What the hell happened? Run the numbers again. They made a mistake. And both Houses the Republicans got! And Trump? What the hell is everybody so angry about?"

* * *

11 November

Jack Friedman en route to the Philippines

This is my father on his way to the Philippines during World War II. If you're new to these parts, he was supposed to go to Italy, but his mother, my grandmother Riva, didn't want him to go to (and here's the pronunciation) "Youpe." So she feigned an illness, which got him a two-day pass home. When he returned, the Army told him he was going to the Pacific. And the rest is history (or complete fiction) about the Purple Heart story.

Later...

Driving past Saint Francis Hospital in Tulsa, my father asks, "Saint Francis? Did they name it that because he relocated here?"

"He lived in Italy in the twelfth and thirteenth century."

"Oh. So when's Hanukkah in Oklahoma?"
"Sometime in December."
"You get much snow here, or what?"

* * *

16 November
In which Jack Friedman remembers and wonders why I don't.
Last night, at the Hot Rod Tuesday Night All-You-Can-Eat 2-for-1 Buffet:
"I spoke to Mel last night," he says.
"Your friend growing up?"
"Yeah, his mother lived to one hundred. He lives in Fullerton."
"How's he doing?"
"Not well. He's in bed most of the time. He takes a lot of naps, he told me."
"He told you that?"
"Well, you know, he was in bed when I called. He's not going to make it."
"Make it?"
"To one hundred."
"Wow. That's a lofty goal."
"They're all gone. Milty, Benny, Red. Then there was George Poporoff. Handsome guy. But a conceited son of a bitch. He's gone. I wonder what ever happened to Bucky."
"Bucky?"
"You remember Bucky."
"Why would I remember Bucky?"
"You know. He was very short. His sister was short. He had two short parents."
"That's hilarious, but he was your friend growing up . . . in the 1930s. Believe me, I don't know him."
"Oh, yeah, that's right. I thought you knew him. Buffet's good tonight."

* * *

18 November

In which Jack Friedman goes to the dermatologist, part 1.

"You know, I lived in Vegas for twelve years and never wore a shirt," my father says upon greeting the doctor.

Part 2:

"You'll never guess what the skin guy whispered in my ear, Ba," my father says after the exam.

"I was sitting there. He didn't whisper anything. I was looking at the two of you the whole time. He was only in the room for about forty-five seconds."

"I'm telling you! He didn't want you to hear."

"Okay, what didn't he want me to hear?"

"He said, 'Jack, I want to look like you when I get to be ninety.'"

"You sure? Why would he whisper that to you?"

"I swear that's what he said."

"He didn't say that."

"What do you know?"

"I know he didn't say that."

"Ach!"

"Ach!"

* * *

23 November

Jack Friedman's Magic with the Ladies, Part the Infinity.

Today we meet Rhonda, a friend of Joe Trizza's, one of the owners of Owl Head. He ushers her to our table because Joe is an evil, evil man who likes torturing his friends.

And we're off.

Introductions are made.

"Please sit," my father says.

"This is Jack Friedman. I'm Barry," I say.

"I'm the father."

(He tells the parrot joke, the one about the man who shoots his friend in bed with his wife, and then mentions, apropos of nothing, how he does a lot of heavy breathing.)

"I'm Rhonda."

"You know, I'm ninety. Had a birthday in October. Nine-oh."

"You look good for ninety," says Rhonda.

"Well, it's a rented body. Your name again, dear?"

"Rhonda."

"You from here?"

"I live in Houston."

"So what brings you to exciting Tulsa?"

"Visiting."

"Republicans?" my father asks. "So, you know, there's a Rhonda Shimes on TV. She's one of the actresses on this doctor show."

"You mean Shonda Rhimes, who created *Grey's Anatomy*," says I.

"What'd I say?"

"Close enough."

"So, Rhonda, where you from?" he asks again.

"Houston."

"In the city or a ranch? You know, your state is known for ranches."

"In the city," she says.

"Well, I've lived in a lot of different places," he says. "New York and the Philippines . . . well, that was during the war."

He tells Rhonda the Purple Heart story.

"You got a Purple Heart from running the wrong way?" asks Rhonda.

"Yeah, I went to the bathroom, I came back, and it was on my bed. Anyway, I'm from Las Vegas, until he [pointing to me] dragged me out of there. Said I couldn't live alone, so he brings me to Tulsa, where they haven't fixed their roads since 1912. How old was I when you brought me here, ninety-two?"

"You're not ninety-two yet."

"I played a lot of tennis and golf there."

"You've never played golf in Las Vegas."

"I played four-game sets instead of eight sets, and we played four-hole golf."

"Four-hole golf? What the hell is that? You don't even play golf!"

"What do you know? You don't know. I played a lot of ball. We were all over ninety-five, so we only played four holes."

"How old is your dad?" Rhonda whispers to me. "He's aged, like, five years since I've been here."

"So have I," I say.

* * *

26 November

In which Jack Friedman, calling from California on a trip to Wayne's, opines on Fidel Castro.

"So I heard on the news today that Mr. Castro died. Did you know one time he came to Brooklyn—I think in 1957—he stopped on 57th Street, near my friend Morris' house? He never forgot that."

"Castro or Morris?"

I actually got a laugh out of him.

"Yeah, so he died," he continues. "Took him a long time."

* * *

29 November

His trip to California over, my dad calls from Phoenix on his way back to Tulsa to talk family and lodging.

"So, Dad, how was your trip?"

"Very nice. Did you know that the Best Western has a full breakfast?"

"I did not know that. But how was Wayne, Hope, Francesca?"

"Great. He came and got me every day. Every day!"

"What a guy. So how are they?"

"Fine, fine. But what a breakfast! They had everything, you name it. Where'd you find this place?"

"Wayne found it."

"What a great place. I mean, a full breakfast."

"Great, but what did you do for Thanksgiving?"

"Oh, went to his friend's or his cousin's. Was very nice. They had turkey... But the Best Western, gorgeous place. And they don't charge you anything. I gave the girl a tip at the end of the week—five bucks. She was worth more. I mean, a full breakfast! And I got a hundred dollars back because I stayed a week. And Wayne wants me to come back next year."

"You should go."

"You gotta get me at the Best Western again."

Later...

I meet my father right outside baggage claim.

"Barry, I met a woman. Very nice. She's in a wheelchair. You'll meet her. She's coming out now. Someone's pushing her. I'm taking her to dinner. She doesn't know I'm Jewish."

DECEMBER

5 December

In which you can't stop Jack Friedman, you can only hope to contain him.

Wayne calls with some added detail about our father's trip to California for Thanksgiving. At this Thanksgiving dinner—it's a dinner Wayne has taken him to before—the parrot joke was not working well, Wayne tells me. Neither, unfortunately, was my father's opening salvo, in which he says to a woman, any woman, "I want to thank you again for last night," and then quickly adds, "You were supposed to say, 'Oh, was that you?'"

Jack Friedman, yes, scripts your part as well.

My father, Wayne says, then moved to another part of the room, where he tried the act yet again with yet another woman. This time, though, absolutely nothing. Brutal. The parrot joke delivered, the woman looked at him as if to say, "I'm not even hearing you," so, because the man is indefatigable, he said, "I want to thank you again for last night," which was met with a blank stare.

"You're supposed to say, 'Oh, was that you?'" he said. His entire act had fallen on deaf ears.

Literally.

The woman was deaf. Completely. Totally. And my father didn't notice. Oh, sure, Wayne thought of saving the woman from this onslaught, but this was comedy gold in the making.

* * *

7 December

We interrupt the end of the republic for some Aristotelian logic by Jack Friedman.

I notice this morning that his hairpiece looks like the one Al Pacino wore when he played Phil Spector.

"Dad, what happened?" I ask as he enters the car.

"What? I washed it. It looks better, don't you think?"

"Dad, not going to lie to you. It's too big. Besides, in washing it, you apparently tore the hair from the mesh because there's a piece of white gauze sticking out above your ear."

"I'll just wear a hat and flatten it down, that's all."

"Trust me on this one. You've got to throw this one out."

"What do you know? You don't wear a toupee. You don't know what looks good."

* * *

9 December

In which Jack Friedman wrestles with the concept of Uber.
"All right, so just give me the card."
"The card?"
"The card for the car with the number. Now, what do I do? I call this . . . what is it? Who?"
"Uber."
"Uber? What kind of name is that?"
"It's a name, what can I tell you? And there's no calling. It's an app on your phone."
"What's on my phone?"
"Never mind."
"All right, so Uber . . . the guy is going to know where I am. Question: Who the hell knows the address to these places? I'll just tell them I want to go to Walmart and he'll know which one or do I have to tell him? How many you got in this town, anyway —Uber?"

* * *

10 December
We try Uber. We get in the car at the Mansion.
"How much to take me to Vegas?" my father asks the driver.

* * *

15 December
Jack Friedman this morning on *The Wall Street Journal*: "Cancel that goddamn paper! The crossword puzzle— impossible."
"Well, it's a smart guy who puts it together."
"He's not smart, he's sneaky. Sometimes he's classy, sometimes he's, what do you call it, historical. So cancel it. Get me the Tulsa paper. At least with the, what is it, the *World* [*Tulsa World*], you can get movie times. *The Wall Street Journal,* I can't find a goddamn movie listing."

"It's a national paper, Dad. They can't give you Tulsa movie times."

"That's probably why. But I don't care. Cancel it anyway."

* * *

18 December

In which Jack Friedman and Melissa discuss God's mysterious ways.

"So why, if God is so good," my father asks at dinner, "did he allow Hitler to shoot himself and not give him cancer?"

"What?" she asks.

"Hitler," he says. "Adolf."

"No, I got that part. But thanks for clearing up which Hitler you're talking about."

* * *

20 December

Jack Friedman, on the way to the dermatologist yet again, talks about women and aging.

"Where did it all go? Where did it all go? I was sixteen two weeks ago. I turned around and, *whammo*, ninety! Ninety? I look at a woman now and I wonder not how she's going to be in bed, but what kind of housekeeper she'll be. Ach!"

Later...

Jack Friedman, after being told about his basal-cell-carcinoma diagnosis at the skin clinic, doesn't like the diagnosis.

As he's putting his shirt back on: "Shoulder blade? What kind of shoulder blade? It's not on the back?"

"Shoulder blade is your upper back."

"I didn't know. I thought it was the back."

"It is your back, Dad."

"I give up. I thought it was on my back."

"Oh, my God! Dad, it is on your back."

"Ach!"

"It's nothing, Dad. It's going to be taken care of."

"I know, but I thought it was on the back."

"Does it matter where it is?"

"Doctor told you it was on the shoulder blade. He saw it?"

"Of course he saw it. That's why we're here. It's visible. I can see it."

"Why can't I see it?"

"Because it's behind you."

"Why didn't I see it?"

"Have you looked?"

"No. I can't see it. I need a rearview mirror."

"Okay. I'll get you one of those."

"And he gets fifty bucks for this?"

"What are you talking about?"

"I have to pay him fifty bucks to scrape this off. I'm going back to Vegas. It didn't cost me anything in Vegas. Never paid a dime. I had a lot of these done. You weren't around. Fifty bucks?"

"Where are you getting fifty dollars from? That's your office-visit charge. It's going to be in the thousands. You're covered, don't worry."

"To take off a thing like this. C'mon. I'm done with doctors. Done. Hey, is this doctor Jewish?"

"I don't know. Ask him."

"I'm not going to ask him. His name's Pittman, right?"

"Yes."

"I think he's Jewish."

"Why?"

"Because all the names that end in 'man' are Jewish. Friedman, Pittman. Yeah, he's Jewish."

"Wow!"

"But the shoulder blade. Who knew? I thought it was the back."

* * *

22 December

In which Jack Friedman has the chills but carries on with his appointed rounds.

He calls in a panic, he's shivering, doesn't know what to do. I get over there. *Grey's Anatomy,* as usual, is on. I get a blanket, make him some coffee, he settles down.

"Ah, Barry, I'm dying, I'm dying."

Moments later: "Okay, so much better, so much better. You make a good cup of coffee." Then, seeing Christina, the Sandra Oh character: "Oh, this is the Asian girl. She's a Jew. Nu?"

* * *

24 December

Love is priceless, sort of.

My father is still sick, so I decide to spend last night at his apartment. He's not hungry, and there isn't much to eat, so I make myself an egg-matzo-and-Muenster-cheese sandwich with a refreshing glass of pineapple soda, followed by a miniature chocolate doughnut and some spumoni ice cream. I then join him in the living room for an evening of *Grey's Anatomy* binge-watching. (He's right, by the way, Izzy can give you a headache.) Let me back up a minute to say my father is not his usual ebullient self. The toupee is actually off, he's wearing a bathrobe, he looks a little like Whitey Bulger. He is slumped down in his chair, moaning rhythmically when George appears onscreen. My father sits up, like he's throwing off twenty years, and starts pointing and screaming at the screen, "This guy I never liked! What a schmuck! He loves this one, he loves that one. Ach, please!"

Later, before my father decides to go to bed, he begins to tell me how appreciative he is of my being there.

"Ba, if you weren't here, if you weren't here, what would I do? Go in the bedroom, under the handkerchiefs, there's an envelope. There's five, six hundred dollars in there. Take a hundred."

"Don't be ridiculous," I tell him. "It's insulting. You're not paying me a hundred dollars to come take care of you. I love you. Just give me fifty."

Later . . .

A remarkable recovery. He wants to go to the Hot Rod. He's hungry, too. We go. We head first to the snack bar because the chicken sandwich is really good.

"Two pieces they give you, Ba, two pieces! And lettuce and tomato."

He then sees the upcoming acts on a message board.

"Priscilla Presley," he says. "She really needs the money? What does she do, anyway? And you mean what's-his-name didn't leave her a couple of bucks?"

"You mean Elvis?" I ask.

"Yeah, whatever. I'm sure he left her a million."

"It was more than that, Dad."

"No, he didn't have that much. Maybe two million."

"How do you know that?"

"I don't know. But I assume."

My father then notices Wayne Newton will also be appearing.

"Wayne Newton? Who's that?"

"You remember. 'Danke Schoen'?"

"Oh, yeah. He's, like, a thousand years old. Ba, people actually pay money to see these people?"

* * *

31 December

In which Jack Friedman, on this New Year's Eve, reminds us it's all about longevity.

At Mondo's Ristorante Italiano on Brookside, where old silent movies, including *Our Gang* clips, are played on two screens, I say, "You know, every one of these actors is dead."

"Jackie Cooper is not dead," he says.

"Yes, he is."

"He was in the last *Superman* movie with what's-his-name. You don't know what you're talking about."

"Christopher Reeve. Also dead."

"Jackie Cooper is dead?"

"Yeah."

"I'll be a son of a gun. He was just in the movie. Ach! How old?"

"I'll check." [I do.] "He was eighty-nine."

"Eighty-nine? Ah-ha! I'm ninety. I beat him."

Later ...

You may be cool, but you're not "a ninety-year-old man in a plastic Happy New Year hat, drunk off your ass, having just taken the River Stix Casino for $130" cool.

three
2017

THE YEAR STARTED with yet another letter to Jim Jakubovitz about getting my father into the retirement center. Still no available apartment, but more important, still no approval of the stipend for him to get in. We're not any closer, but not any further away. It looks like he'll be at the Mansion, albeit in a one-bedroom apartment, for another year. Donald Trump being elected, I can see in retrospect, put a pall on the year's early activities. I notice I began many of these posts, perhaps too many, with "In which we interrupt the end of the republic . . ."

I make no apologies.

JANUARY

4 January
In which we interrupt the end of the republic to address an old reason for a new ailment.

At Dr. John Schumann's office, my father's new doctor (his previous one threw himself off his twentieth-floor balcony—sometimes I do, in fact, wish for a less bumpy narrative), my father said to the nurse after she determined his blood pressure was high: "Yeah, ever since getting the Purple Heart, I've had high blood pressure."

* * *

8 January

In which Jack Friedman, tired of Grey's Anatomy, *orders* The Blair Witch Project *on pay-per-view and lies about the women who were in his life.*

"Ba, I'm telling you, I'm bored. If not for this TV, I'd go back to Vegas."

"What did you do in Vegas? You went to casinos, you watched TV, you went out to dinner, you went to movies. What's the difference? You do all that now."

"I bowled and had three girlfriends."

"You did not have three girlfriends."

"You don't know."

"I know you didn't have three girlfriends."

"You don't know from nothing. I had three."

"Who?"

"There was Jennifer—"

"You mean Jeannette?"

"What did I say?"

"Jennifer."

"Oh. You know she's got a bad leg."

"Jeannette has a bad leg?"

"Yeah, she's walking with the what-do-you-call-it?"

"The walker."

"No, it's the thing you hold on to with both hands and walk."

"It's called a walker."

"Really?"

"Yeah."

"Ninety! Ninety! Where did it all go?"

"I don't know, Dad. I really don't."

"Now, what did I order again? What kind of movie?"

"Doesn't matter."

"You know you can order porno," he tells me. "I think it's in the 800 channels."

"Who were the other three girlfriends you had, by the way?"
"What? I had three girlfriends?"

* * *

9 January
In which Jack Friedman speaks on celestial matters and toppings.
This morning at Owl Head, Jack Friedman encounters a Latina worker, which may or may not have factored into his retort when she said "Hi" in the sweetest, shyest voice.
"Behave yourself," he says, "the pope's watching."
"Pope?" she asks, not understanding.
"Pope!" he says again, and actually mimes the miter.
She smiles. "Ah, pope!"
"Say, love," he asks, reminding us all what's really important, "where's my cream cheese?"

* * *

11 January
It's probably how Samson felt.
My father, on his way to pre-op, inexplicably left the house without his toupee, which, all things considered, he took quite well.
"Where's your hair?" I asked.
"I wear it, I don't wear it."
"Glad we cleared that up."
"What?"
"Nothing."
At the pre-op, we were told he had to have another EKG before they could perform the surgery to remove his skin lesion, a prospect that, all things considered, he didn't take so well.
"Doctors don't know what the fuck they're doing," he said to me when we were left alone in the examination room. "Doctors! Nu. Anyway, I don't want to go with him."

"Okay, we'll go home."

"I want to put my hair on, my lucky hair."

"Fine. Wait—you have lucky hair?"

"Yes! It makes things better."

* * *

14 January

In which we take another break before the end of the republic.

The irrepressible Florence Friedman once said of her husband/my father, Jack, "When it comes to compliments, Barry, your father gives ice in the wintertime."

To wit . . .

Earlier today, my father and I were talking about our annual trip to Boca Raton to see his brother, Leo, now ninety-five, and his sister-in-law, Marilyn, now ninety-three. This is our fifth or sixth trip down there.

"They're excited we're coming, Ba. We'll eat, we'll go to the casino. They like when we come down. And for some reason, they like you. They enjoy your company."

"For some reason?"

"You know what I mean. Marilyn doesn't like talking to anyone in the family, but you she likes talking to. What do you talk to her about?"

"I don't know. I talk to her."

"About what?"

"Politics, family, you. She likes the Heat."

"The Heat?"

"Basketball."

"Yeah?"

"Yeah."

"Anyway, she likes you. I don't know why."

* * *

21 January

In which Jack Friedman, if he were so inclined, would write to someone at Mondelez International Cadbury, the current holding company for Halls cough drops, about the product line.

"Oh, Ba, these drops you bought for the throat. The yellow ones! Oh, God, the yellow ones are fantastic. They lubricate the throat, they moisten it. Fantastic. But the cherry ones do nothing. I mean, nothing. But the yellow. What are they, yellow, honey, or what? We have to buy more yellow. Where do we get the yellow? Remember, don't buy the red. The throat feels very good. Very soothing. But you have to get the yellow. Do not buy the red, the cherry!"

FEBRUARY

3 February

A little break from the end of the republic to remind you that Jack Friedman, ninety, is not really a detail-oriented guy anymore. And my sister gets a new name.

"So why are you going to Poland?"

"We're not going to Poland, we're going to Iceland."

"Well, you know what I mean. Why do they call it Iceland? Is it covered in ice?"

"They have ice, yeah."

"A lot?"

"Yeah, I guess."

"How much?"

"How much? I don't know, probably enough to warrant the name."

"Bring me back a T-shirt."

"Okay."

"So, Poland. That's interesting. You know, my mother's from Austria."

"Iceland!"

"I know, I know. That's interesting. Why Poland?"

"Jesus! Iceland!"

"And you're going after Nova Scotia?"

"Nova Scotia? I'm doing comedy in the Bahamas, if that's what you mean."

"Yeah, yeah. And then I'm going to see Cynthia."

"Susan."

"What'd I say?"

"Cynthia."

"She's dead, you know."

"I know."

"And Normie went blind, but he's dead, too. They don't have a stone up yet."

"I didn't know."

"I wonder how he died."

"I don't know."

* * *

5 February

In which we take a break from the end of the republic to share with you Jack Friedman's thoughts on the Super Bowl.

"Why do they run up the middle? Dummies! This is a dumb sport played with dumb flesh."

One of the announcers mentions New England's Julian Edelman. "Jewish?" my father asks, adding, "How much do these lineman make? A million or two, right? To stand there and block! C'mon!"

He slept through Lady Gaga's halftime show.

Later...

My father has just stolen, as best I can tell, fifty-five packs of Sweet'N Low from Panera. He did so in front of the cashier and then asked for a small bag into which he can put the aforementioned stolen Sweet'N Low, as the theft exceeded his pocket space.

"Dad, really?" I ask as we leave the place.

"What did you want me to do? I had no place to put them."
Later...
As we drive west on the Cimarron Turnpike, he spots cattle.
"So where the hell are they going? Do they even know? And what do they eat?"
"Grass."
"But it's all gray."
"Gray?"
"Yeah, you know, but they probably eat the dry grass and that's how we get salt-free milk."

* * *

9 February
In which we interrupt the end of the republic so Jack Friedman can review recent and not-so-recent deaths, and which professions should ensure immortality.

[Pay close attention to Bernie Newman. Though mentioned previously, he will figure prominently in our ongoing tale.]
"So what the hell did Bernie Newman die of?"
"I don't know Bernie."
"He was my cousin! You know him."
"I don't know him."
"We were very close."
"You hadn't talked to him in forty years."
"C'mon, he's family. Someone should make a phone call."
"Well, they did. That's how you know he died."
"True. But how did he die? He was younger than me."
"I don't know."
"And Lylah, his wife, died. How'd she go? She was something."
"I don't know her either."
"Ugh. Very cold woman."
"Okay."
"Ach, I give up. You know Leo went in his sleep."

"Leo? I don't know."

"Leo! Not Meltzer—well, he died, too—but the other one."

"Didn't know either one of them."

"Yeah, Ida couldn't wake him. She woke up, he didn't. So, what, you try to take a breath and can't? I guess you try to get up, huh?"

"Yeah, I guess. Dad, look, they were in their nineties. They lived long lives. Maybe that's the best way to go."

"Yeah, you're right, but Bernie died, and, imagine, he was a colonel in the Army, too."

* * *

13 February

In which Jack Friedman schools us on European agricultural challenges throughout history.

Last night, after I served him my semi-famous homemade pizza, he begins.

"You know, in Italy, this is all they eat because they don't grow much."

"What?"

"Yeah, they don't have the climate or the land, so that's why they eat so much pizza and pasta."

"Where do you think pasta comes from?" asks Melissa. "Wheat."

"Yes, but someone was telling me they don't have the land, nothing grows, so there's not enough food, and that's why they have to import so much."

"Who told you that?" ask I.

"When we were in Italy—you were there, remember?—the guy told us."

"What guy?"

"Anyway, they don't have the land. It's arid."

"It borders the Mediterranean."

(Melissa, at this point, does a little research.)

"Jack," she reads, "'Italy grows rice, wheat, corn, tomatoes, olives, grapes, cherries, apricots, nectarines, sugar beets, and soybeans.'"

(I do some research.)

"Dad, Italy is, like, sixth in the world in food sustainability."

"That's why," he says, "they have to import so much from the other five."

"No, Jack, it's why they *don't*," says Melissa.

"I don't mean now," he says. "I meant during the Roman Empire."

* * *

16 February

In which we interrupt the end of the republic for some truly disturbing coiffing news.

My father enters the car this morning wearing a new toupee. Bigger, lighter, puffier, bouncier.

"Ah, you got a new piece, I see."

"No, no," he says, "I've had this one for years. I'm giving the other one a rest."

* * *

19 February

In which we interrupt the end of the republic to bring you another Beckett-ian Jack Friedman moment.

"So, Jack," Melissa asks, "your brother Leo is ninety-five?"

"No, no," my father replies, emphatically, "he's going to be ninety-six in July."

* * *

23 February

In which we interrupt the end of the republic so a slightly annoyed

Jack Friedman can explain his revolutionary marketing reset for the emergency services/first-responders industry.

Driving back to his apartment, we notice an ambulance up ahead, lights flashing, blocking traffic. Paramedics are tending to the person on the gurney. Police are directing traffic. It is rush hour.

"Nu," my father says, *"here* he picks up a customer."

* * *

24 February

In which Jack Friedman tries to process this eighty-degree February day in Oklahoma.

"How the hell do you dress for this weather? It's hot, it's cold, it's hot, it's cold. Oklahoma!"

"Well, I'm not sure you can blame Oklahoma for this?"

"Do I wear a sweater, do I not wear a sweater?"

"Well, you could just watch the forecast before you go out, or open a patio door and walk outside, and then you'd know whether to put on the sweater or not."

"So you're telling me if I were asleep for a hundred years and woke up and expected it to be cold, because it was February, I wouldn't know what to wear?"

* * *

25 February

Forgot to take a picture of the pancake and eggs that Joe Trizza at Owl Head made for my father this morning.

"Who the hell can eat all this? I wish you had told me. I can eat one, maybe. I have no appetite. You know, I used to play a lot of tennis, but now, I don't know, I don't eat much. I think I'm a vegetarian. It's too much. Hey, if pancakes aren't on the menu, where does he get the batter? You'll have to help me. Here"—he hands me the bacon—"eat this."

MARCH

1 March
In which we interrupt the end of the republic so Jack Friedman can speak on the very fine line between life and death.

Biting into his "croy-sant" at Owl Head, my father laments the recent poor decisions of immediate family members: "If my brother were alive today, he'd be spinning in his grave."

* * *

4 March
In which we interrupt the end of the republic so Jack Friedman can discuss the Gregorian calendar over a vegetable pizza (and somewhere, Carroll O'Connor smiles).

"So Jesus was the first Jew, right?" my father asks.

"What are you talking about? No, he wasn't," I say.

"Yeah. We gave them a god, and then, when he converted, they got the new calendar."

"What are you talking about? That didn't happen."

"What do you know?" he asks. "When I told my friends in Vegas—you know, there were only two Jews in the group—me and, uh, what's-his-name. Oh, yeah, Sid, and he converted, nu? His wife was Jewish. She had Alzheimer's. Bad scene. Anyway, we gave them a god, they got shook up."

"Imagine that."

* * *

6 March
In which we interrupt the end of the republic so Jack Friedman can hear the call of a prospective client.

"Say, Ba, what if Aaron at whatchamacallit, Owl Head, asks you to be his accountant?"

"Why would he ask me? I'm not an accountant."

"But you help me."

"I'm still not an accountant."

"What if he asks me?"

"He's not going to ask you."

"Why not?"

"Because a) you're ninety, b) it's not a good idea to mix business and pleasure, c) you know nothing about Oklahoma tax law, and, d) most important, he already has an accountant."

"He could die," my father says.

* * *

11 March

In which we interrupt the end of the republic so we can play "Name That Celebrity" with Jack Friedman.

Pulling into the River Styx Casino (River Spirit, if you're just joining us), we notice a long line at the valet.

"What? It's crowded tonight," my father says. "What day is it?"

"Saturday."

"Why should it be busy on Saturday?"

"Seems like a perfect day to be busy."

"But why is it so busy?"

"We just covered that."

"Oh, I know why it's busy."

"Okay. Why's that?"

"That singer is here."

"What singer?"

"Oh, you know."

"No, I don't."

"Yeah, you do. He's the guy with the . . . uh, you know. Oh, what's his name? The guy with the . . . ach!"

"Dad, I can't help you."

"You know the guy. He was at the other place. The singer. The idiot."

* * *

12 March

In which we interrupt the end of the republic for another episode of "End-of-Life Musings with Jack Friedman."

On today's show: forgiveness . . . or maybe not.

"So, Ba, let me ask, if you die in your sleep, what happens? Do you wake up and then die or just, you know, that's it—you're dead?"

"I don't know. Maybe both happen."

"I mean, like Red Meltzer, he died in his sleep. What did he die of?"

"I don't know. I didn't know Red Meltzer."

"He was a buddy from school. You didn't know him?"

"Wasn't alive."

"Oh, yeah, that's right. You're too young. You know he married Pitsy?"

"No."

"But what did he die of?"

"I don't know."

"Boy oh boy, in his sleep. Did he just drift off or did he wake up in pain and then die?"

"You said Pitsy found him dead in the morning, so, apparently, whatever it was, it wasn't enough to wake her."

"Very true. It's not like he woke up suddenly and screamed at her, 'I hate you!' before he died. He just did."

* * *

13 March

In which we interrupt the end of the republic so that Jack Friedman can discuss the type of journalism that speaks to him in these troubling times.

Recently, I canceled my father's *Wall Street Journal* and got him a subscription to the *Tulsa World,* mostly because he was unhappy with the crossword puzzle in the *Journal*. ("They cheat, Ba, with those words they want. They try to trick you. Ach!") For the past few days, inexplicably, he has received both papers. The verdict is in.

"The local paper, Ba, what's it called?"

"The *Tulsa World*."

"The what?"

"The *Tulsa World*."

"Much better, much better paper."

"Why do you say that?"

"Because, you know, with *The Wall Street Journal*, it's all politics and then you have the stock market and it's all about Mr. Trump and you can't even find out when a goddamn movie's playing."

"And the *World*?"

"It's a pleasure. You know, it's . . . uh, what can I say? It's easier, there's more nonsense in it."

"Nonsense?"

"You know what I mean. The writers—I don't know who they are, but they, you know, they write. Fine. The editors have these notes, and they have two crossword puzzles. Two!"

* * *

21 March

In which Jack Friedman just asked the new girl at Owl Head to feed him and to rub his belly.

But then added, "I'm just joking, love. How goes your life?"

* * *

26 March

In which there's something about Mary.

Mary at Golden Gate, the best Chinese restaurant in all of Tulsa (I will brook no discussion on this), will make shrimp egg foo young only with a four-hour lead time. Today, I called at 4:20 p.m. for a 7:30 p.m. pickup. Close enough, I assumed. I gave the order to Brandon, who owns the place along with Mary (or at least I assume that's the relationship; there's not a lot of kibitzing among us when I'm there), and he said, "You killing me. I can't now."

"I need at seven thirty. Can you?"

"Yeah, yeah, seven thirty, that's okay, but we are slammed."

"Okay, great," I say. "I'll get back to you in a few minutes with the rest of the order."

I do. This time, I get Mary on the phone.

"Mary, hi, it's Barry—"

"I know it's you. Barry, what wrong with you?"

"What did I do?"

"I no cook for you no more!"

"How come?"

"You give me only three hours for foo young."

"No good?"

"No!"

"Sorry."

"Ach! Okay, I cook for you. You want egg?"

"Shrimp."

"Ach! Okay, fine. What else?"

"Pot stickers, shrimp lo mein, Mongolian beef."

"What Mongolian beef? I make Peking beef."

"Is that close?"

"I know no Mongolian beef. Mongolian beef, no! I make Peking beef. You like."

"Fine."

"Fried rice or steamed rice?"

"Steamed."

"You want steamed, why?"

"Okay, fried."

"Dumplings steamed or fried?"

"Whatever you think."

"You come at seven thirty. Not before. Buh-bye." She hangs up.

Later...

Something About Mary, the Conclusion (the Golden Gate Affair):

"Your guy makes a great—what the hell is this again?" my father asks when we go to pick it up.

"Shrimp egg foo young, Dad."

"Very good. The shrimp is inside, not placed on top like so many guys do."

"That's why it takes so long to make. Four hours."

"Why so long?"

"Why? That seems to be the wonder tonight."

"Yeah, it's just shrimp and egg, what's the big deal?"

"'What's the big deal?' Mary's not going to be happy."

"Mary?"

"Mary."

"Who's Mary?"

"Who's Mary? How can you ask such a question?"

"Mary?"

"She cooks this especially for you."

"For me?"

"For you."

"Why?"

"She likes you."

"Me?"

"Yes, you."

"Me?"

"Christ, are we going to do this all night?"

"Do what?"

* * *

27 March

In which we interrupt the end of the republic so Jack Friedman can give us more of his special way with the ladies.

To Melissa at dinner: "I'm surprised you don't put on weight, as much as you eat."

* * *

28 March

In which we interrupt the end of the republic so Jack Friedman can make the necessary corrections.

At the Hot Rod Tuesday Night All-You-Can-Eat 2-for-1 Buffet, we see Jacqueline, a Native American hostess, we see every week.

"Hello, Miss America. How goes your life?" my father asks, the irony somewhat lost. "So I was attacking this girl in an alley," he says without transition, "and I said, 'Stand still.'"

Jacqueline, who has heard the joke exactly 1,453 times, smiles but looks troubled, for this doesn't appear to be the punchline.

She, of course, is right. My father has forgotten a punchline to a terrible joke and somehow has made the joke worse by an even more terrible punchline. The heretofore horrendous punchline is "Don't scream. It's embarrassing for me, too," as you may remember. I then go to get dumplings. Jacqueline leaves. When I return to the table, Jacqueline is already there, and I hear my father say, "So I was attacking this girl in an alley and I said—"

"Dad," I interrupt, "you just told her this joke two minutes ago."

"Quiet! What do you know about women? Anyway"—he turns his attention back to Jacqueline—"I said, 'Don't scream. It's embarrassing for me too,'" now getting the punchline correct.

"I just love your dad," Jacqueline says.

* * *

31 March

In which we interrupt the end of the republic to review Jack Friedman's morning exercise class (and its participants) at the Tulsa Jewish Community Retirement Center.

"Ba," he says, calling me after what he does whatever he is doing at the community center's workout room (we are members of the place, even though he is still not a resident), "I'm sitting at the, uh, whatchamacallit, workout, uh . . . well, it's not really exercise . . . it's a limbering class. You get limber and move. Anyway, everyone's in chairs, you know, and a guy, must be in his hundreds, falls off. Goes down, boom! He can't get up. I mean, straight down. All right, so then he gets up—they help him—and sits back down, but he can't do any of the moves. He just sits. He broke his legs days earlier or something, I don't know. Anyway, these two women, I guess they're Jewish, and I start talking, and when I told them I was in my nineties, they got hysterical. One said, 'Ninety! I thought you were in your fifties.'"

"Would you knock it off? She did not say you were in your fifties."

"Fifties to sixties, I swear."

"She did not."

"You weren't there, you don't know."

"Dad, c'mon! You look great, but you don't look fifty-five, you don't look sixty. That much I know."

"You think you look good?"

"Not sure where that came from. Look, be honest, she did not say you looked sixty."

"What? I don't know what she said. Maybe she said sixty, seventy, eighty, who knows? I like the class, though."

APRIL

1 April

In which we interrupt the end of the republic to review the concepts of sons and fathers and patience.

The phone rings.

"Ba, it's Dad." [Ed. note: You gotta love he still announces who he is.] "What's the weather like?"

"I don't know. I haven't been outside."

"Is it hot or cold or what?"

"I don't know. I haven't been out."

"I'll bring a sweater, a jacket, something, what do you think? This fakakta weather in Oklahoma!"

"Why don't you open your door and check?"

"Well, that's not going to help me. It opens to the hallway."

"Your *patio* door."

"Oh, oh, oh, yeah. Good idea. I'll do that. I never thought of that."

"You never thought of that? Really? Anyway, I'll see you at noon, okay?"

"Noon."

"Noon."

"Goodbye."

(Eleven seconds later, the phone rings.)

"Ba, it's Dad. What time did you say again—noon or one?"

Later...

Walking into Owl Head, Jack Friedman says to his second son, "And what the hell happened to you?"

"Me? What happened to me?"

"You got smarter as you got older."

* * *

2 April

In which my father is in a rare terrible mood—so bad, in fact, that Melissa told him at breakfast, "I've seen slugs covered in salt happier than you."

* * *

5 April
In which Aunt Marilyn wants to make sure there's no confusion.

Next week, my father and I will head to Florida for our annual trip to see Leo and Marilyn. They have been married seventy-two years.

I emailed Marilyn to confirm we were coming and asked how she was doing.

Her response came this morning.

"YOUR UNCLE WANTS TO KNOW WHAT TIME?????? NOW YOU KNOW HOW WE ARE."

* * *

6 April
In which we interrupt the end of the republic so Jack Friedman can once again go over final plans.

As many of you know, one of the benefits of being a Friedman is, upon birth, you are automatically given a free burial plot in the Yankov-Leibish Family Circle grave, on Long Island. The caveat to all this is that you have to be Jewish; hence, my sister, who converted years back, is out. Not quite sure who in the family checks such things—my guess it's the feared Ida Meltzer, though there is some discussion that she turned this awesome responsibility over to her daughter—but my father is pretty adamant about this perk and the rules.

"You know what a plot costs these days?" he asks.

"I know."

"You don't know."

"Okay, I don't know."

"Thousands."

"Okay, I got it."

"Forget it. I'm not paying your dues anymore."

"All right, I'm sorry. I understand."

Anyway, the point of him bringing this up today was twofold.

"You get me back to your mother when I die. I don't care what it costs."

"I told you before. I'll get you back to Mom."

"No, you won't. I don't trust you."

"I promise. I'll get you back."

"No, you won't."

"We can go now if you want."

The second point was to discuss my relationship with Melissa.

"You can get in," he said, "but she can't because you're not married, and because she's not Jewish. So here's what you do. If she gets sick, God forbid, marry her right away and then she'll be eligible."

"What if she doesn't want to be buried up there?"

"Does she know what a plot costs?"

"I'll tell her."

"Look, if she doesn't, she doesn't. That's her business. But these things are not cheap, no joke."

On the south shore of Long Island

* * *

11 April

In which Jack Friedman just asked the lovely woman next to him in bulkhead seating what the flight attendant was saying, before he seamlessly transitioned into his Purple Heart story.

"Thank you, sir, for your service," she says.

"Yeah, well, there's a lot of that going around," he replies.

Later...

On the flight from Dallas to Fort Lauderdale, my father is sitting next to an actual veteran, a veteran who has lost both legs, a veteran fitted with two prosthetics. My father has not yet noticed, in part because he's screaming to the pilot to turn up the heat on the plane, in part because he's musing why nobody checks bags anymore, in part because he's busy doing the parrot joke for everyone who walks down the aisle. Anyway, while I wait for the "Brothers in Arms" moment, my father tells the vet about the bridge falling on his toe in Manila—in response to the vet's recounting of some real horror story of war.

"Hey, sir," the vet says to my father after hearing about the Purple Heart my father was awarded, "you've got quite a head of hair on you. Damn! Let's see what's under your hat."

This could be my most favorite flight ever.

Later...

I'm going to be sixty soon, I've been traveling pretty regularly for thirty years, and I'm now using my first baggage cart. What a pleasure. Now to find Juanita, the airport rep who pushed my father through security, and who has taken him somewhere in a wheelchair. Perhaps to Alamo to get the rental, perhaps back to her home in Trinidad. They were getting along quite well, actually.

Later...

Upon checking in at Alamo, we get a five-car upgrade, subcompact to minivan, because, as Thai, the man behind the counter, asks, "How old are your uncle and father and aunt?"

"In their nineties."

"Let's make them comfortable, then."

Nevertheless, Jack Friedman responds, "Who the hell needs such a big car? Think of the gas."

Later . . .

Upon checking in at Embassy Suites, the second room is given at half-price on a rate that's already good ($109/night, which includes free breakfast, a mini-suite, parking, and internet).

Jack Friedman responds, "Ach, you paid too much! Who needs a suite? Two rooms, two TVs, who needs? How much time do you think you're going to be in your room, anyway? And the buffet, you know, I don't eat that much."

The call to Aunt Marilyn to plan tonight's festivities goes about how you'd expect.

"Marilyn, Barry. We're here."

"Super. Listen, your uncle doesn't want to do anything. He's cranky about Passover, he's cranky about everything. Here, you talk to him."

"Leo, how are you?"

"Terrible. I told your father for months I can't move."

"So don't move. What if we bring Chinese food in?"

"All right. What time you coming?"

"Six."

"Make it five."

"Okay, five. What do you want?"

"Talk to Marilyn."

She gets on the phone.

"Marilyn, you want Chinese food?"

"Super! I want dumplings and egg foo young. Don't bring ice cream. I have."

"What does Leo want?"

She screams: "*Leo, what do you want?*"

He answers from another room. "*Nothing!*"

P.S. The China Gardens in Delray Beach is closed for Passover. Why do they hate the Jews so much?

Later...

Other Chinese food has been procured.

Leo Friedman, ninety-five, lifelong liberal Democrat and card-carrying member of the National Rifle Association, has left the organization. Says Leo, "What am I wasting my money supporting these people, these politicians? All they want is money. Every week they call. I mean, if you shoot, you should be a member. I stopped shooting, so I don't need it."

[Ed. note: Probably good that a ninety-five-year-old man with macular degeneration stops shooting.]

"They make a hundred grand a year and retire with four-million-dollar pensions. What the hell's going on? I said, 'Enough.'"

* * *

12 April

In which Aunt Marilyn and Uncle Leo always remember to buy me gumdrops.

"So, Ba, what does 'Boca Raton' mean, anyway?" my father asks.

"'Rich Jews.'"

"You're joking, right?"

"Just barely."

"And what's this Yamato Road? I bet some Japanese guy came here, thinking they were going to win the war, to get a foothold in the place."

"That's exactly right."

We're now at Panera. ("I love Panera so, Ba. I got one where I live.")

For those who asked about my uncle's shooting habits: "Hey, Leo, what kind of guns did you shoot?" I ask him.

"Smith & Wesson, .357 Magnum, .45 ACP Colt, and .45 Long."

"Anything else? Any other guns?"

"Barry," Leo says sternly, "that's enough information."

Later...

Oh, there may be more fun than repeatedly reading Chinese fortunes to three essentially blind, deaf ninety-year-old Jews who, upon further reflection, don't really care much about age-old Asian-fortune-cookie wisdom, or, as it turns out, what you're reading to them, but at the moment, I can't think of what that may be.

Later...

I am at the valet at Seminole Casino Coconut Creek and see my father approach, smiling.

"Ba, I won a hundred and twenty dollars in, like, fifteen minutes, but they only had $15 tables. Fifteen dollars! Can you believe it? Fifteen dollars. Okay, ten dollars, but fifteen dollars. The nerve. Fifteen-dollar tables. How do they have the nerve... Fifteen dollars?"

"But you won."

"Yeah, but you know what you're talking about here? Fifteen-dollar tables. You lose very fast. You win very fast, too. That's not five dollars per play, that's fifteen dollars."

"But you won!"

"Yeah, but, c'mon, fifteen-dollar tables. Do you remember them being fifteen dollars last year? I don't know. I looked around. I couldn't find anything but fifteen-dollar tables, so I sat down at a table. Fifteen dollars!"

"That's great, though. And you gotta stop saying 'Fifteen dollars.'"

"Yeah, but I don't play fifteen dollars. It's not even a weekend. How do they get away with fifteen-dollar tables? They have players who play fifteen dollars?"

"Apparently so."

"C'mon, fifteen dollars, no way, baby. They're not playing. I checked. They don't get that lousy buck the way they do in Oklahoma, but fifteen dollars? Fifteen! I don't play fifteen dollars. All right, but I ran after I won. I'm not playing fifteen-dollar tables. But the tables were packed."

"You said they're not getting the players."

"You know what I mean."

"Absolutely. Anyway, good. You won."

"Yeah, but fifteen-dollar tables. Ach, please. Did you ever? Fifteen dollars . . . that's per hand!"

* * *

13 April

At the buffet this morning, my father had two eggs, a pancake, French toast, a bowl of fruit, a banana, a glass of orange juice, and two cups of coffee.

"Who the hell can eat like this?" he asks.

"Apparently you."

"You know what I mean."

"Absolutely."

"You can't eat like this every day—you'd be as big as a house. But it's nice the hotel does this. Why do they do this?"

"I don't know."

"Did I tell you about my win last night?"

"You might have mentioned it."

"Fifteen-dollar tables. Wow-wee-wow! Did I tell you?"

Later . . .

A trip, once again, to Palm Beach today to visit good friend Gail Cohen, realtor, to look at multimillion-dollar homes. ("She doesn't think we're looking to buy, does she, Ba?" asked my father), and to scope out Mar-a-Lago. Gail took us to the world-famous Breakers Palm Beach Resort, where we had soft drinks and watched tiny fish swim inside the bar countertop. Disconcerting, really, when they, the really unimpressive tiny fish, come out from underneath mock reefs, also built inside the counter.

These guppies, plankton—I really don't know fish—are as attractive as roaches are when you turn on the light in the middle of the night, not to be judgmental. Why, you ask, did we pick that place at all? Well, to use the Breakers valet—it's thirty bucks, but if you buy something at the hotel, anything, like a Diet Coke or a club soda for, say, twenty-two dollars, the valet is free. This was about winning, and you have to wake up pretty early in the morning, even in Palm Beach, to outsmart three Jews in a minivan.

Later...

About eighteen months ago, I started shaving with a blade. I didn't think it was going to be a good idea, and today it wasn't. This morning I cut my chin. It started bleeding. Twelve hours later, it's still bleeding. Is this normal?

* * *

14 April

Interior: Embassy Suites breakfast buffet

"What a dream I had last night! What a dream!" my father says.

"Tell me."

"You remember, oh, what's-her-name? Anyway, she was in my dream. What the hell was she doing in my dream?"

"Who?"

"You remember!"

"I have no idea."

"I saw her after Mom. Remember, she was the, oh, you know—"

"You mean Marlene?"

"Yes! She lived in New York. She was what's-her-name's daughter and they lived in, oh, where the hell did they live?"

"Rockaway?"

"No, not Rockaway! What kind of Rockaway?"

"Hey, I took a shot here."

"Anyway, I was running with her after mom died."

"And?"

"Well, then she died."

"Great story."

Later...

On the way to Leo and Marilyn's:

"I can't get over this," says my father. "Lake Ida Road. What, did she move here and get a road named after her?"

"Who?"

"Ida."

It. Never. Stops.

Later...

We stop at Walgreens. A man in front of me has a family-size box of Good & Plenty and a large package of peanuts.

"Sir," the clerk says, "those are four for four dollars but not two for two dollars."

The man is not happy.

"What do you mean?"

"Those are not two for two dollars," the clerk repeats. "You gotta buy four or it's full price."

"Why would they do that?"

"I don't know, sir."

"That's crazy. So, I can get four for the same price as I'm getting two?"

This momentarily stumps the clerk, who says, "I don't know. This comes to three dollars and nineteen cents."

"Oh, that's fine," says the man. "This, too," he adds, sliding over, hand to God, two Fleet enema boxes.

In the middle of all this, my father has called me four times. The first three times, the phone has stymied him, so I don't hear anything, but by the fourth call, I hear him screaming to nobody in particular, "A gallon of no-fat milk! Leo and Marilyn need a gallon of no-fat milk. Remember, no-fat milk, gallon of no-fat milk. Okay, goodbye."

Later...

"Marilyn, just want to make sure, how long you and Leo been married?"

"Seventy-two years," she tells me.

"Jesus!"

"Yeah, the first seventy were wonderful."

Later...

The trip to Key West is out, Ida is in. Dinner is scheduled for four p.m. tomorrow. The restaurant hasn't been chosen, but I'm sure the word "portions" will be a determining factor in the ultimate selection.

Later...

In which having a conversation is very much like not having one, especially if you have already had it.

"So, Dad, listen if we go to Key West tomorrow, we won't get back in time to have dinner with Ida. We talked about this yesterday. Which do you want to do? I'm fine either way."

"Well, Ida . . . Ida, you're right . . . Ida. [Inaudible.] Key West. [Inaudible.]"

"But would you rather have dinner with her or go to Key West?"

"Dinner? What do you mean, dinner? With her?"

"Yeah. Dinner with her."

"What do you want to eat?"

"I don't know. It's still Friday."

"Yeah, I mean . . . dinner. Who knows what she's doing? I guess I could give her a call, give her a ring. She's family, you know. She's a cousin. Well, she's not really a cousin. She married a cousin. What did she say to you?"

"I didn't talk to her."

"You didn't talk to her?"

"No. She's your cousin. Why would I talk to her?"

"She's always running with a new fella, you know. Her husband died in his sleep."

"I know, but . . . tomorrow. What do you want to do? Which would you prefer doing?"

"What do you think? I'll see if she wants to go to Key West."

"No, no, no! She's not coming to Key West with us. It's about dinner with her. Tomorrow!"

"All right! Let me call her. [Inaudible.] Ida. Do you know her number? That's right, I have it. How long has she lived here?"

* * *

15 April

Interior: Embassy Suites breakfast buffet

"You know, Ba, this is a great deal, this breakfast. If you lived around here, you could walk in right off the street every day and eat for free. The guy at the front there doesn't always check if you're staying at the hotel."

"Reason enough to move to Boca."

"Hey, no joke. Anyway, so I know he's ninety-five and constipated, but what's the matter with Leo? He doesn't seem happy."

We were so close, so close. We saw the sign, we passed the sign, and nothing. Another sign. Again, nothing. We did it. I'm free.

Nope.

"Lake Ida Road? How can you forget Ida?" he asks. "I wonder if she knows. You know we're seeing her later?"

"I think you mentioned something about it."

And then, for reasons that defy understanding, Jack Friedman has Miami on his mind.

"So, Miami . . . let me get this straight. The settlers came there in the seventeen and eighteen hundreds, threw the Indians out, so they could build hotels."

"That's not even remotely close to what happened."

"Well, you know what I mean."

Later . . .

Ida calls. Marilyn puts her on speaker.

"Ida, how are you?"

"Marilyn, what can I tell you?" says Ida. "I have a lot of ailments."

Later...

"There's character in that face," Leo says, seeing a picture of Melissa.

To dinner we go.

Before we get out of the car, Ida meets us in the driveway.

"You're late. Okay, you have to meet my friend Murray. He's very nice."

Later...

A perfectly good table at Flakowitz is thwarted, as Ida demands a booth. Says the hostess to Murray, "Okay, fine, you want to wait for a booth, wait. Now sit down, so I can do my job."

Later...

Ida: "I'm eating expensive. Lamb chops. I don't care."

Later...

A party of four, who have arrived milliseconds after us, is now ordering before us. Ida has noticed, is not happy, and has made her displeasure known.

Later...

Ida, eighty-six, to Murray, ninety-one, about her desirability and attention she receives from other men. "You better be careful, better treat me nice. They're still coming after me."

Later...

The meal arrives.

Murray, surveying his plate: "Now this is a beautiful piece of liver."

Later...

Ida: "Why'd she take the bread so fast? I wanted to take some home. Ach!"

Later...

Ida on her latest cruise experience: "I need a wheelchair, but they cost on the ship. They're very expensive, but we saw one on the second floor, so we took it."

Ida, Manny, a menu, Jack Friedman

* * *

16 April

A rather quiet morning here at the buffet, though, in casing the joint all week (and here I thought he was just eating), my father has determined that the later you get here, the better chance you have of not being asked to show your room key, a concept, as it turns out, he doesn't expect me to fully understand.

"After nine, there's nobody there, Ba. You can walk right in."

"But we have room keys. What difference does it make? And why do you keep bringing this up?"

"Ach, what do you know? You're from Oklahoma."

Later...

In which we set the record for the shortest time at the beach ever.

We go without Leo and Marilyn, who don't like the beach—as opposed to Jack Friedman who, well . . .

"So, Dad, we're here. You want to get out of the car?"

"Nah, the sand. I don't like walking on the sand. Never have. You know, the sand. Till you get it out of your shoes. The water. I don't like the water."

"Then why are we here?"
"I thought it'd be nice to see."
"Well, there it is."
"Where?"
I point to the water. "There."
"Oh, yeah. Okay, wanna get a cup of coffee?"
"Sure."
"I wonder if there's a Panera around."
Later...

For, I can only estimate, the seventeenth time since he found out we're planning to take a trip there, my father wants to know why Hitler never invaded Iceland.

* * *

17 April

In which we spend all day at Marilyn and Leo's, where my uncle is still constipated and my aunt keeps talking about the possibility of administering the Fleet.

Here's just the dinner experience:

We sit down after takeout arrives. Leo is mumbling, unhappy with Trump and hackers in the Department of Commerce, my father is talking about tennis and how I ripped him out of Vegas, and Marilyn has just about had it with both of them. My cousin Michael, Leo and Marilyn's son, and I have brought food from Ruven's Restaurant, yet another deli.

"Did we have to buy this food or could we just rent it?" my father asks.

"We bought it, Jack," says Marilyn, already annoyed.

"All right, don't get shook up, I just want to know if we bought it or rented it. We could rent it, you know. Haven't you ever rented food?"

"Jack!"

"Leo," my father asks, "you want some chicken?"

Nothing.

"Leo, you want some chicken?"

"What?"

"Chicken?"

"He's got steak," Marilyn says.

"What?"

"He's got steak."

"No, I don't need steak," my father says. "I got chicken. I can't eat red meat."

"What?" I say. "Yes, you can."

"Not you. Leo!" Marilyn screams. "Jack wants to know if you want chicken!"

"The kitchen?"

"What?" my father and Marilyn ask in unison

"Yes, I told you what I'm eating," Leo says, "but you don't listen. You're in your own world. I don't want this. I don't know why you get all this food."

"We could have rented the food," my father says again. "We didn't have to buy it. And how do you cut this? It's a big piece."

"Dad, eat what you want," Michael says to his father.

Michael then shows my father how to cut the chicken.

"Did the chicken give its life willingly or was it forced into the oven?" my father asks. "Leo, you sure you don't want any chicken? It's good, it's soft."

"Jack!" Marilyn screams.

"What? Okay, I'm just asking. Does he want corn or potatoes? I can't eat all this. I have no appetite anymore. I'm not as active. It's too much food. Why do they give so much?"

"Dad, Leo's not feeling well," I say.

"That's why I told him," he says, "to drink warm coffee before, because it loosens everything up."

"Jack!"

"What? It loosens the hard food. It makes it move through the body."

"What are you two talking about?" Leo asks.

"Dad, what do you want to eat?" Michael asks Leo.

"He can't hear you," Marilyn says.
"I can hear him," says Leo.
"Then what ... do ... you ... want ... to .... eat?"
"Tuna."
"Here, Barry," my father says, "take some chicken."
"I don't want chicken."
"Why not? What are you eating?"
"Pizza."
"You got pizza at the deli?"
"Leftovers."
"Did you warm it up?"
"Yes."
"Is that legal?"
"Yes, Jack," says Marilyn, "it's legal."
"Did this chicken give its life willingly or was it forced into the oven?"
"You asked us that already," says Marilyn.
"Well?"

On the way home, I stopped at CVS and bought an electric razor.

* * *

17 April

At Fort Lauderdale Hollywood International Airport:

Nephew Chris Ruch has my father and is ushering him up to Long Island, where he will spend the next month with Susan Ruch, the best sister in all the land, along with her four kids, including Chris ("They all work, you know, her kids. They all make big bucks and there's, like, seven cars in the driveway," my father likes to remind Melissa and me fourteen times a day. "We get it, Dad, we get it!" we always say), while I head to the Bahamas. Anyway, yesterday, at dinner, where Chris joined us, Leo said he and my father should leave for the airport at three p.m. You won't be surprised when I tell you it's a nine p.m. flight and around a twenty-five-minute ride to the airport.

Just got a text from Chris, who said they arrived at the airport at five, a full four hours before the flight, which gave them plenty of time for dinner and to go over the flight details and sleeping arrangements at Susan's six thousand times.

Jack Friedman and his grandson, Chris

* * *

24 April

In which a random guy in the Bahamas channels Jack Friedman.

Tonight, around seven thirty, with the sun going down, a man walks by my villa and says, "You have a great room, you know that?"

"Yes, I do."

"I walk by every day and you're always sitting out on your patio. You read a little bit, you type, you look up at the ocean and the sky, and then you look down again, then up at the beach, then down again. You type. You stop typing."

"Yeah, I've been busy this week."

"That's funny. You really don't do much during the day, do you?"

"Nope."

"All right, good talking to you."

"You, too."

MAY

2 May

In which Jack Friedman opines on civic responsibility.

From the Mastic Beach Regional Office:

Susan's son Chris was recently called for jury duty, to which my father, who is still visiting in New York, replied, "Oh, I've been called many times, but I never served."

"Why not, Grandpa?" Chris asked.

"Because I'm an accountant and do tax work. They don't like that."

* * *

24 May

In which Jack Friedman takes stock, literally, and is unhappy with what he finds.

He calls.

"Say, Ba, what happened to my liquid?"

"Liquid?"

"My blue liquid."

"Blue . . . what, you mean your mouthwash?"

"Yeah. What happened?"

"What happened? I don't know. Maybe you used it all."

"Someone took it."

"I doubt someone took it. And who would take it?"

"No, I had a full bottle before I left and now there's, like, an inch left. Did you use any?"

"Did I come over to your house and gargle? No."

"It's okay if you did."

"Dad, thank you, but I didn't use your mouthwash."

"Did Melissa?"

"Without calling her, I can assure you she didn't come over and use your mouthwash from the Dollar Store."

"Then who the hell took it?"

"Maybe you're forgetting how much you had when you left."

"No, no, no, no! I had a full bottle. I remember."

"Dad, you can't remember your daughter's name half the time."

"Cynthia?"

"Susan. Anyway, I'm just saying it's possible you're forgetting how much was in the bottle."

"I remember exactly how much was in the bottle. It was full. I know what it was! They had a lot of workers in and out of the apartment. I bet they used it."

"You think the workers from the apartment used your mouthwash?"

"What else could it be? I mean, it's okay, I'll buy more. I use it, you know, for the mouth, but where the hell would it go? Ach, I give up."

Later . . .

"Did you hear from Madigan?" my father asks, referring to a tax client from the old days.

"No, nothing."

"I wonder what the hell happened to him. I can't get him on the phone."

"Don't know what to tell you, Dad."

"Who knows? He probably died."

* * *

27 May

In which Jack Friedman expounds on God, fowl, and bread products.

Nine a.m., outside the Mansion. He enters the car.

"I'm so pissed off!"

"Why? It's early. Nothing happened yet."

"Why did he take her?"

"'Take her'? You mean Mom, God?"

"Yeah. What, he had to take her? Nothing else to do. It's bullshit. And here I am pushing ninety-one. Ach!"

"Maybe it wasn't God who took her."

"He took her, he took her. And what the hell's going on here?" he asks, pointing to a flock of ducks walking toward the car. "They having a meeting? All right, where we going?"

"Bagel place."

"Can you get me an egg on a soft roll? Not a bagel. The bagels are too tough to chew, too voluptuous."

* * *

28 May

In which Jack Friedman sees the conspiracy and hears the call of the desert.

For reasons that defy understanding, his refrigerator door came off in his hand.

"I lived in twenty-five different apartments and I've never had this happen. Never! Oklahoma! Some state! I give up! Nothing's working out. Nothing. The accident last year and now this."

"Two things in eighteen months isn't so bad," says I, "and you're blaming Oklahoma for this?"

"I give up. I'm going back to Vegas."

* * *

29 May

In which Jack Friedman reminds us why growing old sucks, while simultaneously and relentlessly body-slamming the English language until it cries for mercy.

"Ah, Ba, I'm bored. Well, when I say I'm bored, I don't mean bored. It's just I got nothing to do."

"That sounds like boredom to me."

"Nah, it's not that. It's just, what can I say, I'm not endeavoring. You? You're young, well, younger, you got your, uh, what is it, the, the . . . writing?"

"Yes, that's exactly what it is."

"See, that's what I mean. You're endeavoring. I'm not endeavoring."

* * *

30 May

In which nobody does non sequiturs like Jack Friedman does non sequiturs.

Coming home from the Tuesday Night All-You-Can-Eat 2-for-1 Buffet at the Hot Rod:

"Say, Ba, what does a head weigh?" my father asks.

"A what?"

"A head."

"A human head?" Melissa clarifies.

"Yeah, you know, generally speaking."

"Generally speaking?" I ask.

"Why would you want to know that?" Melissa asks.

"I mean, I guess it would depend, huh?" my father answers. "Anyway, my question is academic."

JUNE

1 June

In which Jack Friedman reminds us yet again how easy it is to get through life unscathed and without disappointment.

On the way back to his apartment, I ask if he needs anything at the store.

"No, I got everything I need: Frosted Flakes, the mouthwash.

I'm good."

* * *

4 June

In which Jack Friedman finds a way to fight the thieves of oral hygiene. The mouthwash looms large.

At Costco today, my father bought, count 'em, three 50.5-ounce bottles of Kirkland Mouthwash.

"Dad, why did you buy three huge bottles? You've already got two unopened ones at home."

"Those are not these, and I like their blue. These are blue. They got a nice blue."

* * *

5 June

In which Jack Friedman wants service.

"I need a servant," he says, getting into the car this morning on the way to his stretching class at the Hebrew Home.

"Why do you say that?"

"I have to get up, open the blinds, make the coffee, take my pills, and then get the orange juice. It's too much to do. I should have someone do that for me. You know, a servant, a wife."

"Well, I'm sure when you put it like that, you'll have no problem finding one."

"What's the matter? I'm ninety. Don't I deserve one?"

"Another good line."

"What do you know? You're from Oklahoma!"

* * *

8 June

It's the "of course" that makes it art.

This morning at Owl Head:

"Ba, you think Mom's waiting for me?"
"If there's a place where one waits, sure."
"Or do you think she met someone?"
"Mom's dead, Dad, how would she meet someone?"
"Well, I mean a dead guy, of course."

* * *

10 June

In which Jack Friedman wants you cellphone impresarios and electronics big shots throughout the land to know that he's on to you.

"I've noticed, Ba, when I turn the cell off, I mean off entirely, with this button"—he shows me the button—"the battery doesn't run down like it does when it's on."

"What a bunch of sneaky bastards they are, huh?"

"I mean, I always charge it anyway, that's not my point."

"Of course not."

* * *

11 June

In which Jack Friedman recognizes the problem and sees the solution.

"I'm bored, Ba. I think I need a hooker."

* * *

12 June

In which Jack Friedman and I will spend the rest of our lives living rent-free inside David Mamet's head.

We're at Owl Head.

"Get me that turkey on a soft roll. I love it so."

"It's nine in the morning, Dad."

"I don't have much of an appetite anymore because I'm not active."

"So you don't want the turkey?"

"I can't consume as much because I'm not active, I don't know what it is. Turkey, I don't know. You're right. Get me the white cheese."

[Editor's note: cream cheese]

"Where's Owen?" he asks as we enter.

"Aaron."

"The owner, the short guy. He's from Austria, you know. I am, too. So are you."

"I know."

"Does he have any kids?"

"No."

"Why not?"

"I don't know why not."

"He makes a good sandwich."

"Speaking of, the sandwich I gave you yesterday, how was it?"

"Oh, was great. Delicious."

"Wasn't sure you'd like it."

"Wait. No, I didn't eat it."

"I thought you said you did."

"I thought you meant the other one."

"What other one?"

"I had chicken last week."

"So you didn't have the sandwich?"

"Why?"

"Why?"

"No, I have it in the refrigerator. It's good with coffee."

* * *

13 June

In which we interrupt the end of the republic (and this is not funny anymore) so Jack Friedman can remind us of things jurisprudence has yet to get to.

At the Hot Rod Tuesday Night All-You-Can-Eat 2-for-1

Buffet, he spots a woman, large, in a floral-patterned dress, tattooed, with a big plate of food, heading to her table.

"Look at this," he says. "I think I'm in love."

"Dad, be nice."

"What, what'd I say?"

"You know what you said."

"Jack!" says Melissa.

"You'll be there soon enough," he says, just as she puts another bite of lemon meringue pie in her mouth. "There really should be a law," he adds, still staring at the woman, "about the size of bosoms."

* * *

14 June

In which Jack Friedman comes face-to-face with the social condition.

We drive by Tulsa's Little Light House, where a sign reads, "Helping Children with Special Needs."

"Little Light House," my father asks, "helping children with social needs. So, what, they help kids who can't get dates?"

"That's exactly right, Dad, exactly what they do."

"Yeah?"

"No! It's 'special.'"

"What?"

"Special, not social."

"What is? Them?"

"Yes, they deal with special-needs kids."

"Why did I think it said 'social'?"

"Why did you think . . .? I stopped asking myself questions like that years ago."

* * *

15 June

In which Jack Friedman reminds us, yet again, why it's Jack Friedman's world and the rest of us are relegated to ordering off the menu.

At Owl Head today, Joe Trizza made my father a special breakfast: pancakes, eggs, bacon. He does it just for my father. That's how great this place and he and Aaron Quinton are. Anyway, a man who knows me and my writing comes over.

I introduce him to my father.

"I love this guy's writing," the man says to my father, pointing at me.

"Who, him?" my father asks. "I'm the father. I knew him when he was this tall," he adds, placing his hands about eighteen inches apart. "I have pictures, I swear."

"Well, I really do," says the man, shaking my father's hand. "It's a pleasure to meet you both."

"I'd get up," says my father, "but I'm in the middle of a pancake."

* * *

17 June

In which Jack Friedman, ninety, sets his terms, and they're as brutal as they are specific.

On the way to Owl Head:

"Ba, I think I want to get married again."

"Here we go."

"What?"

"You want to get married again."

"Yeah, what's the matter?"

"Who are you going to marry?"

"I don't know. I want a fifty-year-old woman."

"Fifty?"

"Yeah, divorced. Something like that."

"Why's that?"

"Well, at fifty, they're still running around. By sixty, they lose half their activities, and by seventy, they're finished."

Later...

We enter the Flip Side, the snack bar at the Hot Rod.

"So, Dad, you want a burger, right?"

"A burger? What do you mean?"

"A burger, you know."

"You mean like a hamburger?"

"Yeah. You're familiar with the concept. You said you wanted one earlier. Or I could get you the chicken like you usually get."

"Well, you know, the chicken. It's a different kind of eating."

"That it is. So which one do you want?"

"I don't know. All right, get me the hamburger."

"You want cheese?"

"Cheese?"

"Yes, cheese."

"Nah. Cheese. Cheese? No! I had two pieces of Muenster, earlier, on the, you know, bread, and it got stuck here." He taps his chest.

"You want a raw onion, though, right?"

"What do you mean?"

"On your burger. You like that."

"I don't know if I like it, but it has a good taste. Okay, yeah. No. I don't know. What do you think?"

"I can get you a raw onion."

"If you can, but if you can't, no sweat."

"Fine. Okay, you find us a seat."

[Ed. note: He does, and I go to order. I hear him scream across the seating area: "Ba, no bun, medium rare! Don't forget the French!" I wave. Then I return to the table.]

"Did you tell them no bun?"

"I did, but, Dad, you can take the bun off if they forget."

"Yeah, I guess that's true. Take some of the fries when they get here. I can't finish them all. What did you get?"

"Chicken."

* * *

19 June
In which a middle-aged Vietnamese woman is about to give my father a pedicure. We wait.

"Hello, Miss America," he says. Pointing down to his feet, he adds, "This is the World War II foot."

Later . . .

The women working at 61 Nails don't understand English, and he isn't wearing his hearing aids. He keeps screaming, "You're running the wrong way! Boom!" in describing the bridge that fell on his toe in the Philippines. They keep smiling and filing.

It's an astonishing dynamic.

Later . . .

The bridge that fell on his toe is now a bomb. (This is a developing story.)

Later . . .

"Where you from, dear?"

"Vietnam."

"Oh, I was in the Philippines. You ever been there?"

Later . . .

"I got a Purple Heart. I was in the hospital for six months. No joke. This was the Philippines, not Japan. This was forty years ago. That toe there." He points.

Later . . .

A woman enters, takes the seat next to my father, and overhears the talk of the bomb, the toe, and the bridge (yes, there is now a bomb and a bridge in the story).

"Were you in the service?" she asks.

"Excuse me, dear?"

"Were you in the service?"

"Is the pope Catholic?"

"Well, thank you for your service."

"There's a lot of that going around."

"I'm sorry, what?"

"I'm the father," he says, pointing to me.

"Well, thank you again for your service."

"I'm pushing ninety-one."

"Wow."

"How did I get that old? I was sixteen two weeks ago. Where did it all go? Where did it all go? I was just saying to this girl I was attacking—"

"Dad, no!"

"What? That's my son," he says to the woman.

Amy, the pedicurist, has put away her tools, for she is finished. My father stands up and decides this would be a good time to hug her.

"Very nice job, very nice," he says. "Ba, did you pay her?"

"I paid her."

"What'd you pay her?"

"I paid her, don't worry."

"I'm not worried. But did you pay her?"

"I paid her."

"Did you give her a tip?"

"Yes."

"You gave her?"

"I gave her."

My father to Amy: "Did he pay you?"

"Yes," she says.

"Ba, did you give her a tip?"

"I gave her a tip."

"What'd you give her?"

"For the love of the Vietcong, I gave her a tip."

"All right, all right, let's go. I was just asking."

On the way out, Amy, clearly fatigued and recently hugged yet again, walks us to the door.

"So," I ask, because she has told me to return every month or so for my own pedicure, "I should bring my father back next month, yes?"

"No, no, no," Amy says quickly, her hands almost clasped in prayer. "Two! He come back two months, not one. Two!"

In the car, my father—swear to all the gods out there—asks, "Did you pay her?"

Later...

Like a lot of fathers, my father falls asleep in front of the television. Even with his toupee doing whatever it wants and his glasses half on, half off, it's oddly beautiful and reassuring.

"If the belly's moving up and down," my mother once told me years ago about the same visual, "I know he's okay."

* * *

20 June

In which Jack Friedman works the Tuesday Night All-You-Can-Eat 2-for-1 Buffet at the Hot Rod like Sinatra in the Main Room at the Sands.

It's crowded, I'm at the register, and my father, as he sometimes does, goes ahead to the check-in line, trying to time my arrival with the actual handing of the receipt to the hostess who's seating people (told you these Tuesday nights were not for the unprepared). Anyway, I see him hug one of the buffet waitresses who's walking by, and I can tell by his body language that he is telling her the parrot joke. Moments later, another buffet waitress walks by, another hug, and then, for reasons not clear, they escort him to the front of the line and then to a table.

I arrive moments later.

"Nice move, Dad. Very impressive."

"Yeah, they came over. I don't know. I think the big one wants me. What should I do?"

* * *

23 June

In which your sleights of hand are no match for Jack Friedman's superior intellect and deconstruction.

Point the First: Outside Owl Head, there are huge planters.

Today, they were watered, resulting in runoff, meaning the parking lot is wet.

"What the hell's going on?" my father asks, seeing the water. "Why is the ground wet? They watering the ground?"

"Well, they're actually watering the flowers over there."

"They need this much water? Who does that?"

"Water it?"

"Yeah, I mean, who comes and waters it?"

"I don't know. People. I'm sure they have a service."

"Did it rain or what?"

"They watered the plants."

"I know, I know. I'm just asking."

Later...

We leave Owl Head and see, across Peoria Avenue, Tropical Smoothie Cafe, and a sign: "Grand Opening: Now Open."

"So they're just now open?" he asks.

"Apparently so."

"Just today?"

"I don't know about today, but I'm sure just recently."

"'Now Open.' Nu? What do they sell?"

"Smoothies."

"Smoothies? Like . . . what? Smoothies? Like shakes."

"Yeah, more or less."

"You think it affects Owen at the bagel place?"

"Aaron."

"Aaron. What'd I say?"

"Owen."

"Who's Owen?"

"Aaron."

"What?"

"Never mind."

"You think his business is affected?"

"No."

"Why not?"

"He doesn't sell smoothies."

"Oh, yeah, that's right."

Later...

We drive by a house that's clearly in the process of being built.

"What are they doing, building it or tearing it down?" my father asks.

"They're building it. You can see the drywall, the windows going in, all the workers, the cement guys."

"Yeah, but what's with all the wood stacked up?"

Later...

We pull into the parking lot to pick up the hearing aids he swears he doesn't need and see a sign: "Tuesday Morning."

"Tuesday Morning?" Who names a store Tuesday Morning?" he asks.

"I don't know."

"What kind of name is that? Tuesday Morning? Tuesday Morning . . . can you shop there on Wednesday?"

"I'm sure you can."

"My question's academic."

* * *

24 June

If it's Saturday, it must be time for "Jack Friedman's Fashion, Health, and Beauty Tips."

Dental Care

"Why can I hear your teeth?" I ask, watching him and his teeth fight a croissant. "You didn't put them in today, did you?"

"No, I wait until after I eat, because otherwise it gets caught in the glue."

"But doesn't the food now get caught under your teeth?"

"Yeah, but I rinse it out later."

"Later?"

"When I get home."

"But you know, it's not a good idea now to swish your teeth

around in decaf coffee that has four Sweet'N Lows and God knows how much Half-and-Half."

"What do you want from my life?"

Shaving

"Dad, how much cologne or aftershave are you wearing?"

"I'm not wearing anything."

"C'mon!"

"I swear."

"Dad."

"Nothing. I mean I have some pre-shave on, that's all."

"Why do you have pre-shave on? You haven't shaved."

"Yeah, I forgot. I was waiting for it to dry and then something came up."

"What came up? And how long do you wait?"

"I wait. I don't know. That's okay, I'll shave when I get home. No sweat."

Wardrobe

"So, tonight, Ba, if we go to the casino, should I change outfits?" he asks. He is presently wearing sweatpants with a white stripe down each leg, blue slip-on canvas shoes, ankle socks, and a black pullover with a zipper up half the shirt.

"Maybe so."

"I've got a gray shirt with a collar. It's a good-looking shirt."

"Perfect."

Hair

"What's going on with your hair today?"

"I washed it."

"How do you do that?"

"I take it off and wash it in the sink. I scrub it with a brush."

"What could possibly go wrong?"

"What?"

"Nothing."

* * *

25 June

In which there's nothing like being caught inside a Jack Friedman compliment on a Sunday night.

Tonight, at Mondo's (or "Modo's," "Mottel's," "Dondo's," "Coso's," or "You know, that place with the dish we like"), my father looks at Melissa—after telling her to move the table away from her stomach in case she eats too much and "gets stuffed"—and says, "You know, you're the prettiest almost-wife he's ever had," and then, pointing in my direction, tells her, "Really, no joke. If we weren't related, I'd make a play for you."

* * *

28 June

In which I can only assume the train had jumped the tracks long before I got there.

Here's what I know. I walked into the lobby outside the Tulsa Jewish Community Center workout facility and saw my father and an elderly Japanese couple—he was sitting, they were standing—and heard him say, "No, no, the Philippines—this was, like, forty years ago. World War II. I was in the First Cavalry Division. I wasn't on a horse. Anyway, it's where I got the Purple Heart. So, where are you two from?"

* * *

30 June

Jack Friedman on reincarnation and naps (spoiler alert: He doesn't like one of them):

"When you die, Ba, you are immediately reborn as a baby somewhere and you don't know from nothing until one day you're walking, you see someone and think, 'Where do I know them from?' It's from your previous life. Why does God do it like that? Ach, I give up!"

Later . . .

Jack Friedman is watching UFC.

"What kind of cockamamie . . . what the hell? You can kick somebody in the balls? No wonder they don't let you wear shoes. You imagine Joe Louis in this sport? The dumbest thing I've ever seen."

Later . . .

"So I spoke to Mel. You remember Mel?"

"Why would I remember Mel?"

"He was my best friend growing up."

"Same question."

"Oh, right, you weren't born yet. Anyway, his wife tells me he takes naps. Naps? Nu?"

"You take naps."

"I don't take naps."

"You fall asleep on the sofa in the middle of the day."

"That's not a nap."

"It's not?"

"No, Mel's wife says he goes into bed. I don't go into bed."

"So you think falling asleep on the sofa in the middle of the day isn't a nap?"

"I doze."

"You doze?"

"Yes."

"That's a nap."

"What do you know? You're from Oklahoma."

Dozing on the Long Island Railroad

JULY

2 July
In which Jack Friedman gives a health update on Jack Friedman.
"I haven't had a cold, a headache, nothing since I came to Oklahoma. I mean, an occasional rash, but that's cleared up."

* * *

3 July
In which I don't know how you ladies productively go about your daily lives in the presence of such a smooth operator.
Today at Costco, walking out with his shopping cart, my father said to the girl staffing the entrance/exit, "Why don't you hop in, and I'll wheel you to my place?"

* * *

6 July

In which Jack Friedman takes a slight fall but stays focused.

A neighbor emails me: "I live at the Mansion House. Sometime within the last hour I heard a terrific noise from above. I got myself dressed and went up to see what was going on. Your dad answered the door. Don't freak. He had fallen. He was/is dizzy but nothing appears to have been broken. He couldn't find his glasses, and I found them for him near the kitchen on the floor. They'd been catapulted that far. He fell near the desk. He made me promise not to call you. But, of course, I'm contacting you. He appears to be okay, but the dizziness is worrisome, he sways when he stands up."

And then a follow-up text.

"If it makes you feel better, he did mention his Purple Heart."

So I go over there. My father's fine, sitting, wants half a turkey sandwich—"just a half"—and then asks me about the person who came to help him.

"She reads you," he says, "in the, uh, you know . . ."

"Yeah, I know."

"Very nice woman. But she reads you. She have a husband?"

"I don't know."

"Oh, yeah, we talked. Very nice woman. What's her name?"

"Pamela. Pamela Caldwell."

"Caldwell?" he asks. "Not Jewish."

P.S. Thank you, Pamela.

* * *

7 July

In which Jack Friedman is inexplicably unhappy with the generosity of the poultry manager here at the Hot Rod.

For reasons that defy understanding, my father tonight veered and, instead of ordering a grilled chicken club, orders a chef's salad with chicken. It arrives. It is bountiful.

"I think this comes with more chicken than they give you with the sandwich," he says. "Ach! What the hell are they doing?"

* * *

9 July
Obfuscation, thy name is Jack
Scene: Tulsa Jewish Community Center main lobby.
"So, Dad, how was your workout?"
"I'm pooped. Sat in the, uh, the, you know?"
"Whirlpool."
"No . . . yeah. What do you mean?"
"The whirlpool, hot tub."
"You mean the water thing that swirls?"
"Yeah."
"Yeah, with the bubbles, you turn on the thing. Yeah, that's what I said. You know they changed the jets."
"I didn't know."
"What?"
"I didn't know."
"This place just for Jews?"
"No."
"They let other people in?"
"Yeah."
"How many Jews you got in this state?"
"I don't know. Okay, what else did you do?"
"I took a shower."
"That's it?"
"Took two showers. One before the water thing, one after."
"You must be exhausted."
"Not really exhausted, but I'm tired, that's all."
"So why were you sitting out here and not in the waiting area by the gym?"
"Because there was a woman sitting there in one of the chairs and there was another chair. There were three seats, actually, she

was in one, so there were two left . . . You know what I'm talking about? Anyway, I didn't feel like socializing. I felt like she wanted to talk."

"Now I'm exhausted. Hold it! Since when don't YOU feel like socializing?"

"I wanted to sit quietly and take a nap, so I came out here."

"You? I thought you didn't take naps."

"Well, you know what I mean."

* * *

12 July

Jack Friedman at the doctor:

"So let me ask you," he says to Dr. John Schumann. "In Vegas, I had a lot more sex than I am now. A lot of sex. No joke. I met a girl, not right away, but we did. I'm not looking to have sex—that's not my point—but is that why I am the way I am? It's not that I'm horny. I don't mean that. But if it comes up again, should I or should I not back off?"

John started to answer and then just walked out of the examination room and quit the profession, throwing away his entire career.

Our work here is done.

P.S. The nurse came in, put on rubber gloves, and—well, we're off.

"I put those on when I make love," says my father.

She, apparently, is still in the profession. Scarred, but still nursing.

* * *

13 July

In which, while the rest of us try to keep up, it's clear the Hot Rod Casino needs to up its promotion game and then provide therapy for one of its valet attendants.

My father and I arrive at the casino, where he sees a "Win Me" banner on a pontoon boat.

"What the hell is that?" he asks the valet guy. "'Win Me'? What do they mean?"

"It's a pontoon boat, sir. Have you ever been on one? It's a drawing, and you can win it."

"Well, I lived in Vegas for twelve years until my son dragged me to Tulsa, exciting Tulsa. He said I couldn't walk."

The valet attendant seems stunned by the amount of information he's just heard.

"Sir?"

"I'm just joking. So, what, they're giving away a ship now?"

The attendant looks like he wants to form words, he really does, his mouth is open, but no sound is coming out.

We enter the casino, and my father asks, "Hey, Ba, is Patti Page still alive?"

* * *

15 July

In which Jack Friedman talks about age and relationships, and compliments Melissa and my luck in being with her, as only he can.

So the conversation gets around to Melissa's grandmother, "Garny," who is seventy-seven.

"Seventy-seven! Seventy-seven?" asks my father. "I'm older than her grandmother?"

"By a lot."

"No. I don't accept that."

"Of course you don't."

"Seventy-seven? How old's her great-grandmother?"

"She's dead."

"How old would she be?"

"Why would I know that?"

"Okay, so that means Melissa's mom—what's her name again?"

"Cindy."

"Yeah, yeah, I met her. And the husband. What's his name?"

"Steven."

"I know, I know. I met them once."

"More than once."

"I could be Cindy's father. I'm older than Cindy. I'm older than Steven."

"Do they say anything about that?"

"I think they're okay with it."

"Melissa is how old?"

"Forty."

"How'd you get such a child?"

* * *

18 July

In which Jack Friedman wishes not to be burdened anymore by ice cream.

At the Hot Rod Tuesday Night All-You-Can-Eat 2-for-1 Buffet, he has concluded dessert has become too cumbersome and wants to streamline the process.

"Hey, Ba, this time don't get me the cake in the middle with the two ice creams on either side. Just get me the ice cream in a bowl—chocolate on one side, vanilla on the other."

"You want a cone?"

"Nah, I thought about that, but then you have to hold the cone and I'm going to have the coffee and it's, uh, too much to handle."

* * *

22 July

In which Jack Friedman joins us for Chinese food on a Saturday night and, of course, the conversation turns to death generally, and the death of his cousin Bernie specifically, if, in fact, he died.

"This shrimp foo young is the best ever. What's it made of?"

"Shrimp and egg," says Melissa.

"I know, I know, but what's the 'foo' stand for?"

"What's the 'foo' stand for?" asks Melissa. "I don't know."

"I mean, my question's academic. So what did cousin Bernie die of? I still don't know."

"Holy fuck," I mutter. "Dad, I don't know either. You ask this all the time. I didn't know Bernie."

"He was my cousin. We grew up together."

"Jack," says Melissa, "yes, but Barry wasn't born yet."

"Oh, yeah, that's right. But what did he die of?"

"We still don't know."

"Red Meltzer died in his sleep, but Bernie, for the life of me . . . Imagine, you die in your sleep. What happened with Red? You just die . . ."

". . . in your sleep," says I.

"You don't wake up?"

"No."

"You make a noise?"

"I don't know. Probably."

"Wow-wee-wow! Not even a sound. But Bernie, I still don't know. Maybe he didn't die."

"Dad, he died. You weren't close, you hadn't talked for forty years, so maybe that's why nobody got hold of you."

"Okay, so make a phone call. You know Lylah, his wife, died, too, a long time ago. We didn't keep in touch."

"Yeah," I say, "being dead and all."

"No, I don't mean that. I mean, what did she die of?"

"Why would Barry know that?" asks Melissa.

"She was from *Hunger* altogether. But Bernie, he was one of, like, twenty-three guys in my group. Did you see that picture I have? They're all dead."

"We know. We go through this all the time," says Melissa. "The picture was taken in 1932, of course they're all going to be dead. All those people would be, like, 120 now."

"There's just me and Pitsy left, who married Jerry Parker, who's not well. How'd she come to Jerry Parker? She was Mel's girl. They had a big fight, Mel and Jerry. That's why he came back, and next thing I know he's with Pitsy? Anyway, so they moved to New Rochelle from Florida. Something with his foot. Ach, I give up. There's only two of us left. Two!"

"What about your brother Leo?" Melissa asks. "He's left."

"He wasn't in my group of guys."

"He still counts, doesn't he?"

"He's going to be ninety-six, you know, he still shoots. He gave up his license."

"We know," we say together. "We've had this exact conversation four hundred times already."

"I went to the cemetery. When did Cynthia die?"

"The dates were on the stone," says Melissa. "What did it say?"

"Good point. I never thought about reading it."

"Never thought . . . what else do you do there," I ask, "except read the stones?"

"You know Vivian, her mother, was my sister. You ever meet her?"

"Yes, she was my aunt."

"She was a very sickly girl."

* * *

25 July

In which even Freud would say, "Nah, I got nothing."

"Ba, I had a dream, wow-wee-wow!" says my father. "What a dream!"

"About what?"

"Oh, you know."

"Not a clue."

"Wild."

"About Mom?"

"No, no. It was about, oh, you know . . . about, uh, calisthenics."

"Calisthenics? That was my next guess. What happened?"

"I couldn't do them, so I called your brother."

"Why did you call Wayne?"

"Why? I called him."

"And?"

"Nothing. Couldn't get him on the phone, so I left a message and then I woke up."

"That was the dream?"

"Yeah. I think I need a summer comforter. I slept so well and I'm still tired."

* * *

27 July

Jack Friedman on the origin of cities—Broken Arrow, Oklahoma, specifically.

"Broken Arrow? Broken Arrow? What kind of name is that? An Indian came here, broke his arrow, and decided to retire?"

"I'm sure that's exactly what happened."

"No. Seriously. Did the tribe make a deal with the white man that if they let them settle here, they'd break their arrows and not fight anymore?"

"People think I make up these conversations."

"What people?"

"It's a long story."

* * *

28 July

In which Jack Friedman reminds us about priorities.

I call to tell him I would pick him up at two o'clock to take him to the dentist. I can hear the TV on, quite loud.

"Hold on," he says.

"What's the matter?"

"Ach! You caught me right in the middle of something. Let me make the TV lower. Picard's in trouble. Now, what's up, sweetheart?"

* * *

29 July

In which Jack Friedman battles hard fruit.

So, the story goes, my father dropped his dentures in the sink and chipped one of the false teeth. It was fixed. No problem.

I thought.

"Ba, I'm done with apples."

"What do you mean? Why apples?"

"I'm not going to bite down anymore on apples."

"But that's not why the tooth broke."

"I know, I know. But I'm afraid. Well, I'm not afraid, I'm just not going to eat an apple anymore. I know I can, but, you know."

"You could cut up the apple."

"Yeah, but most people, when you think of an apple, you bite down," he says, making a crunching sound and pantomiming the apple.

"You don't even eat apples, do you?"

"That's not the point. I'll eat other fruit—softer fruit. And I know you can eat the apple other ways, but, you know, I'm going to stay away from all hard foods."

"The denture, again, broke when you dropped it."

"So the piece went down the drain?"

"Probably."

"I don't know what the hell I did."

"You dropped your denture and it cracked and the piece probably went down the drain."

"I just don't know what the hell I did."

[Ed. note: My B/P at the moment: 376/178]

"Dad, you can eat what you want."

"I still don't know what the hell I did."

[Ed. note: My left arm is tingling, going numb.]

"Dad, you accidentally broke your denture in the sink. Really. You can eat what you want."

"So the law changed in Oklahoma so they can now use dice?"

"Whoa. Okay, so we're done with apples?"

"Someone told me that."

"I told you that."

"Where did you find out?"

"The news."

"What news?"

"News. News. I don't remember what news."

"What about the buck they charge with each hand?"

"That stays," I remind him.

"Burns me so. Cards they play crap with, nu?"

"I don't know what to tell you."

"Don't misunderstand me about the teeth. They feel great. Your guy did a nice job. No joke. I just won't bite down, that's all. I just can't consume the food that I used to. The quantities."

* * *

30 July

A father's love.

"Have a good colonoscopy." —Jack Friedman to his son, July 30th, 2017

AUGUST

1 August

In which my father worries too much—or not at all.

"Hey, what kind of father are you? You're supposed to call to check on your son's colonoscopy."

"Oh, yeah, that's right. You had that done."

"Yes."
"Yesterday, right? Or Monday?"
"Yesterday was Monday."
"What's today?"
"Tuesday."
"What happened to Monday?"
"I'm fine, thanks for asking."
"Yeah, I was going to call, but I forgot, so I waited for you to call, that's all."
"I think I just pulled my groin trying to follow that."
"What?"
"Nothing."
"So what were they looking for?"
"Cancer."
"Oh."
"'Oh'?"
"Yeah, I know, I know."
"Anyway, no cancer. I'm fine."
"I had one of those."
"I know."
"They do that to check, that's all. So when are you having it done?"
"Yesterday."
"I know, I know. I mean, were they looking for anything in particular?"
"To see if I have cancer."
"Oh."
"Yeah."
"Okay, what else? How's Missy?"
"Fine. Want to go to the buffet tonight?"
"Right. It's Tuesday. Yeah, we can do that. Which casino?"
"The one that has the buffet that we always go to."
"You mean the, uh . . ."
"Yeah, that one."
"Okay."

* * *

2 August

In which Jack Friedman deconstructs Pastor Carlton Pearson. And it's fucking brilliant.

So I run into Carlton, whom I know a little, in the valet area at River Stix Casino tonight, and we talk for a few minutes. When I get back into the car, my father asks who he was. So, briefly, I tell him about Pearson having at one time the largest church in Tulsa, with more than five thousand parishioners, being heir to the Oral Roberts University throne, until he lost his kingdom, as it were, when he decided to tell his congregation one day that God hears the prayers of all and that heaven wasn't just reserved for Christians.

"Maybe," my father says, "he had a dream and God came to him and said, 'Knock it off. There's enough room for everyone.'"

Jack Friedman and Pastor Carlton Pearson

* * *

4 August

In which the English language should just surrender quietly with whatever dignity it has remaining.

As many of you know, nobody traverses his way through a malaprop quite like my father; hence, in terms of casinos, River Spirit became River Stix and Hard Rock became the Hot Rod. Today, he was discussing the town of Broken Arrow, Oklahoma, which, for reasons that defy all understanding of how language and thought flow through the cerebrum of a ninety-year-old man, he referred to as "Buxom Whore."

* * *

5 August

In which no good deed is completely underappreciated.

"Ba, I can't find the earplugs," my father says in a call, "and I'm not buying new ones. That's it. No more doctors."

"Dad, hold on. I'll come over and look."

"You're not going to find them. I looked everywhere."

"But you can't see without your glasses."

"What?"

"Nothing. I'll be over."

"What?"

"Stay there."

"Where am I going? I don't have a car. How much were they?"

"About eighteen hundred dollars."

"Forget it."

"I'll find them."

"You're not going to find them. I give up."

I enter the apartment and find what he is now calling "earrings" in the hamper of dirty clothes.

"What the hell were they doing in there?" he asks.

"You probably took your shirt off and they got attached."

"Were they in the shirt or the hamper itself?"

"The hamper itself."

"They must have fallen off the clothes. What kind of shirt?"

"Does it matter?"

"No, I mean, was it a shirt?"

"Probably a shirt."

"What shirt was I wearing?"

"Dad, way too much time on this. You've got your hearing aids back."

"They probably came off when I took my shirt off."

"I should have thought of that."

"Oh, Ba, thanks for coming over."

"No problem."

"No. You came all the way here."

"Don't worry about it."

"Yeah, that's right. You have a car."

* * *

7 August

Mornings With Jack

A Play in Four Acts

Act One

Medical Care

On the way to getting his reading glasses, he asks, "Hey, Ba, how many dentists are there in Oklahoma?"

Act Two

Penal Reform

Outside my father's apartment, we pass a woman in shorts, chain-smoking, heavily tattooed, with an ankle bracelet, talking on the phone.

"No, I've been good," she says into the phone and then, seeing us, "Hi, there."

"Morning," says my father to her. "Now behave yourself," he adds, "this is a public place."

Act Three
Housing and Urban Development

As we drive by a nice residential area in Tulsa, he asks, "Is this where the Jews live?"

Act Four
At *Dunkirk* (before the movie starts)

"I'm sure the Germans love this picture."

* * *

8 August

Further evidence this is Jack Friedman's world and the rest of us are but bit players.

(Other eateries, take note.)

The fabulous LeAnna, the buffet manager at the Hot Rod who is always so sweet to my father, once again just pulled him out of a long line at the Tuesday Night All-You-Can-Eat 2-for-1 Buffet and escorted him to a table.

Later...

"Does the other casino, the River, uh, you know, have a buffet?"

"Yeah, we've eaten there. You remember?"

"But just for lunch."

"They have the same buffet for dinner too."

"Oh, yeah?"

"Yeah, we've eaten there too."

"I don't remember, but they don't have shrimp. Why don't they have shrimp?"

"I don't know that they don't have shrimp."

"They don't have shrimp, I remember."

"You don't even remember eating there."

"Because I stay away from the meats," he says, cutting into a piece of prime rib. "I don't know what happened to my appetite. Why don't you eat shrimp?"

"I eat shrimp."

"Since when?"

"I don't have a date. Now, do you want shrimp? I'll get you some. Or, I don't know, turkey? You like the turkey here."

"I got, I got," he says, pointing to his plate.

"That's prime rib."

"You know what I mean."

* * *

9 August

Jack Friedman is having his second-ever pedicure around 11 a.m., which means that at around 11:05 a.m., I will once again hear my father tell the parrot joke to a Vietnamese shop owner in Tulsa, Oklahoma, who doesn't speak or understand English. And that he fought in the Philippines.

* * *

11 August

In which we are reminded to never, ever fuck with the paradigm of Jack Friedman's Half & Half.

"Why'd you buy the half-gallon? I like the two quarts that come attached with the plastic holder."

"Two quarts is a half-gallon."

"I know, but I like the two quarts because they last longer and we don't have to run out all the time."

"They last exactly the same because it's the same amount of liquid. Besides, what else do we have to do every third day or so?

We're not that busy. We go to Owl Head and buy Half-and-Half. It takes up half the morning sometimes."

"But I just like the two quarts—they last longer."

"It's the *same* amount of Half-and-Half. It doesn't last longer!"

"Yeah, but the two quarts come together—"

"—making a half-gallon."

"I guess we can do it that way, but why did you buy it this way?"

"Because this is the one I grabbed."

"What store has the two quarts?"

"I'm sure they all do."

"All right, I just like the brand name, you know, the . . ."

"Nestle?"

"Yeah. I don't know. Does that one come with the plastic, you know, thing?"

"Again with the plastic holder. You like the holder? Okay. Do you want the Half-and-Half flavored?"

"I don't care about that."

"But you do care."

"Only if you can get it, you know. The last one you got was wild. Had that taste, something, some flavor. Very good."

Later . . .

In a country losing its moorings daily, we end this workweek with a universal truth, brought to you by Jack Friedman, who "stuck" it to the Hot Rod tonight for $53.

"I could have won more," he says, handing me ten dollars for no particular reason, "if the dealer had won less."

* * *

14 August

In which Jack Friedman responds to a news story that a ninety-year-old man and a ninety-three-year-old woman who met in an exercise class and then married.

"You know, at that age, you're not looking for sex. I mean,

c'mon, how often do you have sex when you're that old? Once a month, once every couple of months? No, you're looking for companionship. Someone to wake up next to."

[Ed. note: This was said while we were behind a truck that was moving excruciatingly slowly. When the driver finally turned left, also maddeningly slowly, my father said, "Enjoy your turn."]

Later...

[Edited for time]

"Dad, there was a water main break outside your building, so you have no water."

"What do you mean?"

"There was a water main break outside your building, so you have no water."

"So no water?"

"No water."

"What kind of break?"

"I don't know. I guess a main pipe broke."

"Broke? How did it break?"

"I don't know."

"It just broke?"

"Yes."

"So it was a pipe?"

"Yes."

"Does the elevator work?"

"I'm sure it does. Doesn't run on water."

"So what are the people doing, sitting in the lobby?"

"I don't know. I'm with you."

"They're probably sitting there."

"I don't know."

"I'll just take my showers outside."

"Outside?"

"Well, you know what I mean, but I'm wondering, it just broke? Has the pipe broken before?"

"I don't know."

"How many houses in the area?"

"I don't know."
"Because there are houses in the area."
"I know."
"They going to buy us dinner?"
"Who?"
"The hotel."
"What hotel?"
"I mean, the apartment."
"Why would they buy you dinner?"
"Because what if I was cooking dinner and I had no water?"
"It broke this morning."
"The whole pipe?"
"I don't know how much of the pipe."
"Is it just my building?"
"No, it's the whole area. It apparently is a major break."
"So, what, they called you?"
"Yes, your neighbor downstairs."
"Does she have water?"
"No. It's the *whole* area."
"You know there are private homes in the area?"
"I know."
"And they don't have water?"
"No."
"So they can't go to the bathroom?"
"They can't flush."
"I know, I know, so how'd she know to call you?"
"Because she knows."
"She probably came upstairs to talk to me before she called you, but I wasn't there."
"Probably."
"Okay, I'll just come to your house if I get thirsty."
"Perfect."
"A water break? Nu? Does the city know?"
"I'm sure they do."

"So why'd they say the pipe was good? I mean, they have to inspect it, right?"

"A great question, that."

* * *

15 August

We arrive at 61 Nails.

"Do you want me to take my shoes and socks off?" my father asks.

"Yes, please," says Amy, our long-suffering pedicurist.

"You sound like the bride on the wedding night," comes the response.

And we're off.

Later...

If you bet the under (+/- 45 seconds) on my father reminding Amy about the war injury resulting in the bum toenail that resulted in the Purple Heart, congratulations.

Later...

My father just *whispered,* "I want to give her five. Okay, five. Five dollars. I want to give her five, okay? I'm going to tip her five."

He played with the massage feature on the chair. "All right, *all right!*" he screamed. "Turn it off!"

Later...

"Where were you," he asks Amy, "when I was in the Army, walking miles and miles and miles? This is World War II. You weren't even born yet."

The pedicure is done. Back in the car, Jack Friedman has questions, a few comments, and then ends with a rhetorical flourish.

"So is Amy married?" he asks.

"I don't know."

"I mean, does she have a husband?"

"Same question."

"Who's the other girl?"

"Diane."

"What does she pay Amy?"

"I don't know."

"By the foot or by the hour?"

"I don't know. 'By the foot'—really?"

"How long they been in business?"

"I don't know."

"Are they making it?"

"Apparently so."

"Who's the guy?"

"That's the brother, I think."

"That's not the brother."

"How do you know that when you just asked who he was?"

"I mean, I don't know. It could be. I think he's the husband, though. He probably takes all the money."

"Why would he take all the money?"

"That's what happens in Asian homes. The women knock their brains out and the men take all the money."

"Okay, let's move on. The casino tonight?"

"Yes. I'm trying to remember what I was wearing when I won all that money last week. I'm not being superstitious."

"No, that's exactly what you're being."

"Well, I'll be playing blackjack, so I'll be sitting down."

P.S. On the wall of 61 Nails, there's a picture of a horse.

"You do the horse's toes, too?" my father asks Amy.

Amy smiles, clearly not understanding.

"I'm just joking."

* * *

17 August

In which Jack Friedman, master car thief, after casing the joint and assessing the difficulties, finds a caper-ending flaw in his plan.

We pass an auto-auction facility on the way to Hot Rod.

"Wow-wee-wow!" he says. "How many cars they got there? They got a million cars!"

"A million, Dad?"

"Maybe not a million, but twenty-five thousand at least."

"Whatever."

"You could steal one, they'd never know it's gone. How would they know?"

"They'd probably find out, but go on."

"Nah, wouldn't work. 'Cause once you got into the car, how could you drive it away with all those cars stacked up like that?"

* * *

18 August

Hand to God, word for word, this just happened.

At the indoor pool at Zarrow Pointe today, Malyn, one of the personal trainers, comes up to me and asks, "So are you trying to get your dad into the retirement center?"

"You know my dad?" I ask.

"Yeah. He has a Purple Heart, right?"

"You know that story?"

"Every day he tells me, and why he can't do all the exercises in the stretch class. Something about his knee, a war injury."

"Oh. My. God."

"Hey, that's a toupee, right?"

* * *

19 August

In which Jack Friedman would be a tough guy to double-date with.

After the pool, I meet my father at the designated spot and find him talking to a woman—I'm figuring early eighties. He spots me.

"Hey, here he is," he says to the woman, "my son. Imagine! Thirty years younger than me and he's got physical problems."

* * *

20 August

Jack Friedman stars in "The Mystery of Bernie and Lylah."

Sunday dinner, and the conversation turns to gym/pool attendance, after a brief discussion of whether "pizza" is an Italian word and if it's legal for a non-Italian to make pizza, which I've just done.

"So, Meliss," he says to Melissa, "you don't go to the gym?"

No answer.

"I mean, you don't like going?"

No answer.

"I mean, why not?"

No answer.

"You don't want to go? What's the matter?"

No answer.

"Hey, honey," I say, "are you going to answer him?"

"Nah, I think I'm going to first wait to see where this line of questioning goes."

"Good thinking."

Moments later: "So what did Bernie and Lylah die of?"

"We don't know," says Melissa.

"Nobody calls to tell me."

"You weren't close," I remind him.

"You know, one time your mother and I went out to California to see them. And we're sitting there, Bernie's there, and then Lylah comes home and goes right into the bedroom. Doesn't say a word. Nu?"

"Maybe she was anxious around people," says Melissa.

"Nah," says my father. "She just wouldn't come out of the bedroom."

I then remind my father that this goes back to a pinochle game they were having when Bernie accused him of cheating. Lylah obviously took Bernie's side, and Jack's wife, my mother, Florence, took his side. After that, the friendship was over.

"I cheated?"

"Apparently so."

"Were we playing for money?"

"How would I know that?"

"I cheated?" he asks again.

"What do you want me to tell you, Dad?"

"What do you mean 'I cheated'?"

"Which word's giving you trouble? Apparently you cheated."

"Cheated? I cheated? I didn't cheat. Cheated? So why did Bernie let us in the house?"

"Well," says Melissa, "apparently he was over it, but Lylah wasn't."

"Yeah," he says, "and now they're both dead. Hey, you know what, this is a different Bernie. This was Bernie Metz, not Newman. Bernie Metz was married to Lylah. Bernie Newman was married to someone else. "

* * *

22 August

Anyone else want to explain to my father who Steven Tyler is and why there's a large chocolate microphone in the casino announcing his upcoming concert?

Sometimes, there's just more day than energy.

* * *

23 August

In which Jack Friedman admires Melissa's dress and reminds her of the importance of accessorizing.

"Hey, baby, that's cut really low. I hope you have a brassiere on. By the way, you look great as a blonde."

Later...

My father is now telling the DIRECTV repairman that the connection broke because he watched "too many dirty-picture movies," how his wife died, about the fifty guys he "ran around with in Vegas," and how he came to "exciting" Tulsa only after his son—"that one," he says, pointing to me—"dragged me out of my house in Vegas where I used to play tennis every day," but it's okay, he adds, because "he," again pointing to me, "means well."

* * *

25 August

In which Jack Friedman receives a notice that the city of Tulsa will once again be working on the water pipes outside his apartment this coming Tuesday, and there will be no water service for about six hours.

"What the hell are they doing on the pipes? They're broken or what?" he asks, handing me the notice.

"They're apparently still broken or need work."

"What the hell happens?"

"I don't know."

"No water? Wow-wee-wow! I mean, I guess you could freeze some water the night before and then use it during the day, but you can't use the bathroom."

"It's not like you'll need survival skills. It's only for a few hours."

"Okay, you can take a shower before they get there, but after that, you're out of luck, baby."

"Or the day before."

"What's with the pipe? One pipe or two? They're that broken? How can pipes go out? What happens to a pipe?"

"Couldn't tell you."

"Is this the city doing this or someone else?"

"City."

"Is it a crack or a break or what?"

"Don't know."

"I mean, my question's academic."

"Of course it is."

"Just like that? Am I going to be charged for water that day?"

"No."

"You sure?"

"You're never charged for water."

"I'm not?"

"No."

"Pipes! Go know."

* * *

26 August

In which Jack Friedman has an out-of-body experience. He thinks.

"Ba," he says as I pick him up to take him to the gym, "I think I'm dying."

"Why?"

"My life flashed before my eyes this morning."

"But I think that only means you're dying if that happens while you're actually dying."

"Okay, so where's your mother? And what the hell did Cynthia die of? And, you know, Normie doesn't have a stone, just a stick. I give up. You know who Cynthia is, right?"

"Yes. She's your sister's daughter."

"My what?"

"Your sister's daughter. Your niece."

"Did you know her?"

"Yes."

"You knew her? How did you know her?"

"She was my second cousin or first cousin once removed."

"Oh, yeah, that's right. So what the hell did she die of?"

"I don't know."

"You know Normie was blind?"

"Yes."

"And there's no stone? Why is there no stone?"

"Because her son, I guess, didn't spring for one."

"So why did He take Mom and not me, and how did I ever wind up in Vegas?"

"God or Normie?"

"What?"

"Nothing."

"I should have stayed in Asbury Park."

"You never lived in Asbury Park."

"I mean Atlantic City. Your mom worked at the MGM."

"Taj Mahal."

"Right. Mr. Trump. You know she sewed a button on his jacket once."

"I know."

"Yeah, he came upstairs and he needed a button sewed on his jacket, so she did it. I had a big place there. Four bedrooms."

"I know."

"I should never have left."

"It was too big."

"What the hell was I going to do with four bedrooms?"

"Exactly."

"So why did I move to Vegas?"

"You wanted to."

"You know, what's-her-name wanted to get married in the worst way. She wanted my car, too. What was her name again? She was from Vermont."

"I'm not telling you again."

"You know the bowling league broke up?"

"I know."

SEPTEMBER

2 September

In which Jack Friedman breaks down the language barrier.

Two women walk into Owl Head wearing matching "Strawberry and Cream Cheese Forever" T-shirts.

"What do those shirts mean?" my father asks them.

"No *inglés*," one says, smiling.
"No, no. I mean what do they mean?"
The woman smiles again.
"Strawberry?" he asks. "You mean strawberry-strawberry?"
The other woman smiles.
"Where did you get them?" he asks.
The women nod.
"The shirts?" he asks again.
"No *inglés*," the second woman says.
"What kind of shirts?" he asks. "Strawberry and cream cheese? Hee-hee."
The women are now hurrying out the door.
"I'm just joking," my father says. "Have a nice day."
They smile.
"Strawberry and cream cheese?" he asks me. "What does that mean?"
"No *inglés*."

* * *

3 September
In which Jack Friedman opines on the rigors of exercise and the importance of rest.
"So, Dad, want to go to the center today?"
"Nah, I think I'm pushing it at the gym."
"Pushing it? You sit in the whirlpool, go to the sauna, and take two showers."
"Yeah, I know, but I think I just want to lie around today."

* * *

5 September
In which Jack Friedman, during a quiet Tuesday Night All-You-Can-Eat 2-for-1 Buffet experience at the Hot Rod Casino, still doubts the events leading up to Leo "Red" Meltzer's death.

"So he died in his sleep, nu?"
"Seems to me the best way to go."
"But how do you die in your sleep?"
"You die in your sleep."
"I understand that. But what happens? You just die?"
"Your heart stops, an aneurysm, probably a lot of things can happen."
"Do you make a sound?"
"How would I know that?"
"Don't get so shook up. Wouldn't Ida have heard him?"
"What did Ida say? Did she hear him?"
"She didn't hear him. Just that he died in his sleep. She couldn't wake him."
"Well, there you go."
"I still don't figure. Something's wrong. Die in your sleep—c'mon?"
"He's dead. It's a great way to die."
"Was he sleeping beforehand?"
"What did Ida say?"
"I should call her. And Bernie Newman, how did he die?"
"Here we go."

* * *

8 September

In which Jack Friedman meets a woman and within minutes distills all the important information needed for a successful relationship.

"Met someone last night. Very nice. Divorced her husband. Not Jewish."

* * *

9 September

In which, on this glorious Saturday, Jack Friedman returns to aging and mortality.

"What a system! They either take you when you're old and your whole body breaks down, or they take you when you're young and give you all these fakakta diseases. The whole thing is screwed up. Ach, I give up."

* * *

12 September

In which Jack Friedman knows women and introduces the latest in cinematic technology.

"How are you?" asks LeAnna as she approaches the table at the Hot Rod buffet.

"Got a half hour, I'll tell you the whole story," my father replies. "Or better yet, wait for the movie. It's in color."

"Hi, Barry."

"Hi, LeAnna."

"That's my son," says my father.

"She knows."

"You know him?"

"Dad, we come here every week."

"I'm his father. So how goes your life?"

"Can't complain," she says.

"That bad, huh? Don't worry. It'll get worse."

"Oh, I have to go," she says. "Sorry. Just got paged."

"Bye, dear. Behave yourself. And if you can't, take my number. Nobody calls! Nobody calls!"

After she leaves: "She wants me."

"LeAnna wants you?"

"Yeah, her, the big one."

"The big one?"

"You know what I mean."

"Why do you think she wants you?"

"She walks me to the front of the line on the buffet. She gives me a chair to sit in. She just came over."

"What other explanation could there be?"

* * *

13 September
In which we have a special guest today at Owl Head, and Jeannette gets thrown under the bus.

An old friend, Rabyne, happened to be in for lunch, so I invited her to join us.

(Everyone, Rabyne; Rabyne, everyone.)

"Rabyne, this is my father, Jack."

"He's my son," my father responds.

"Yeah, Dad, that was pretty much just established."

Anyway, after she orders a Reuben, which my father determines was way too big for her and she wasn't going to finish anyway ("And how the hell can you eat all that?"), he tells her she should take it home.

"Get a bag or something, wrap it up."

Rabyne casually mentions she's half Jewish.

"Which half?" my father asks, as if we didn't know that was coming. "The waist down or the waist up?"

And we're off.

Filling Rabyne in on his life—including showing her a picture of himself when he was twenty-five, which he insisted was taken a few years back, when he lived in Vegas, and two pictures of my mother, in both of which she's a blonde ("She colored her hair in this one," he says, pointing to one), he mentions, after telling her the parrot joke, that he lived in Vegas for ten years until I came and dragged him out of there.

"No, no, I know he meant well. And I was running with a girl from, ah, where the hell was she from? Oh, yeah, Vermont. But she wanted to get married in the worst way. And when I didn't want to marry her, she said she wanted my car."

My mother, Florence Friedman, as a blonde.

* * *

14 September
In which Jack Friedman revisits the birth of Jesus and discovers anti-Semitism in the hospitality trade.

Outside Mondo's sits a Presbyterian church with an enormous parking lot, which, tonight, is filled with cars.

"So what the hell's going on tonight in the church? They praying?"

"It's not the church. It's all the restaurants around. They use the parking lot."

"Isn't tonight a big church night?"

"Thursday? No."

"Oh, I thought there was a big meeting or something. You know, not a service, but a meeting."

"No, I don't think so."

"Maybe they're meeting."

"Fine. They're meeting."

"Why do they have such a big parking lot?"

"I don't know."

"This a big Presbyterian town?"

"Don't know that either."

"So what's the difference between Presbyterians and Catholics, anyway?"

"Well, less guilt, for one thing, and they're usually more liberal, and, as best I can tell, Presbyterians have less focus on the Virgin Mary than Catholics."

"Why? She was Jewish. I mean, they were all Jewish—Jesus and Mary and Joe—and that's why when they went to the hotel, they couldn't get a room, and had to go sleep in the barn."

You gotta love the "Joe."

* * *

15 September

A man—I'm thinking in his eighties—approaches me outside the Jewish Community Center indoor pool, points to my sandals, and says, "I see you're wearing your air-conditioned shoes."

"Yes, I am."

"Say, let me ask you something."

"Go ahead."

"You like Korean food?"

"No, I don't."

"Well, I didn't either, but then I went to this Thai restaurant and it was great."

"Nice."

"I mean, it's okay if you don't. You don't have to like the same food I do. So what are you doing?"

"Reading."

"Well, it's a beautiful day."

"Yes, it is."

Later...

Jack Friedman explains why the Methodists got his grandson.

Jesse, my sister's oldest son, has decided to leave the job where he was making the "big bucks" to become a Methodist minister. All things considered, my father has taken it pretty well.

Tonight, however, some questions arise.

"So, a minister," my father asks. "Where'd he get that from?"

"Heard a calling, I guess."

"A what?"

"Nothing."

"I mean, a pastor. He was making big bucks. They are all making big bucks. Susan, the boys, even Emily [granddaughter]."

"But it's what he wants to do."

"I'm not knocking it, but a minister. Nu?"

"Yeah, how about that?"

"You know why he's becoming a pastor, don't you, and not a priest?"

"This should be good."

"Because they let you marry. Priests can't marry."

"Well, that, and he's not Catholic. He's Methodist."

* * *

19 September

In which Jack Friedman has met the enemy and it is the row of chocolate cookies in the Reasor's Variety Pack.

"I got sick this morning," my father tells me in a call.

"What happened?"

"I know exactly what happened. It was those chocolate cookies, you know, the cookies with the vanilla ones. But the vanilla ones are fine. The chocolate ones crunched. I knew when I bit into one."

"They're supposed to crunch."

"No, you're wrong. The vanilla ones, when you eat them, they're soft. The cream slides off. But the chocolate ones, you bite [he adds the sound effect] and you get the crumbs. No, no, I know exactly what it was. It was those cookies, the chocolate ones. I know it."

"But the vanilla ones are in the same package."

"Yeah, but the cream didn't slide off the chocolate ones."

"I don't think it was the cookies, Dad. I'm going with the milk."

"What are you talking about? I've had that milk for three weeks."

"That's my point."

"I've been putting milk in the cereal for twenty years and I never had problems."

"What can I tell you, Dad? Your streak is over."

"I just won't eat cookies anymore."

"That's a little severe."

"What am I going to do?"

"First check the expiration date of the milk."

"You know, I put it on my cereal every day."

"I'm aware. Could be the Half-and-Half, too."

"No, I just put that in my coffee. It's the cookies, I'm telling you. When I threw up, that's what came out first."

"Maybe the cookies are the victims, innocent bystanders, in the purge?"

"What are you talking about?"

"I have no idea."

* * *

21 September

Just walked my dad into morning Rosh Hashanah services. Hand to God, I swear *he* just whispered, "And we're off."

Later...

Jack Friedman at Rosh Hashanah Services, Part 2:

He is given a white yarmulke as we walk in, as are all who don't have one when entering the synagogue. Jews are an amazing, resourceful people; nevertheless, they have failed to create a fabric for the kippah that can overpower the fibers on my father's hairpiece. As such, the skullcap is unceremoniously evicted from his head many times. Once, a woman behind him taps him on the shoulder to hand it to him, as it had fallen again, and my father says, "Why do I keep losing this damn hat? I'll just hold the thing."

The pages of his prayer book were sticking together, so my father had trouble following the service, especially the Hebrew parts, as if being on the right page would have mattered.

"Jesus Christ," he says loud enough for Maimonides to hear, "what's with these pages? They're impossible."

Two hours into the service, we decide to leave, his nap during the sermon not really the deal-breaker. Surveying the large crowd, my father exclaims, "Look at this. You got the whole mob here. Very nice. Let's come back next week for, uh . . ."

"Yom Kippur."

"Yeah, yeah. I'm not going to fast, though."

* * *

25 September

In which Jack Friedman reviews the film Brad's Status.

"What an odd movie. Lots of shots of him in bed, thinking. And the kid eats potato chips and wants to go to Harvard. And then it ends. Good acting, though."

* * *

29 September

In which Jack Friedman decides on lunch.

"So, Dad, Owl Head for lunch? You want your turkey today?"

"I don't know. What do I want? I like the turkey. They make a great turkey. They put it on the . . . you know."

"The bread."

"Not the bread."

"The croissant."

"The what?"

"Never mind. I know. You know, you had turkey yesterday."
"I did?"
"You have turkey every day."
"I do?"
"Yeah."
"What else they got there?"
"You could have the white cheese, an egg sandwich. You could have a salad?"
"What do you mean?"
"A salad."
"A salad?"
"A salad."
"A salad? You mean lettuce?"
"The very basis of a salad. Yes."
"Nah, salad's a dinner thing."
"What are you talking about?"
"I mean, I don't know. A salad?"
"When we go to Panera, you have a salad. When we go to Jason's, you have a salad."
"That's true."
"Okay, so, a salad?"
"How big do they make it?"
"I don't know."
"I can't eat the whole thing."
"I'll help you finish it."
"You want a salad?"
"I . . . sure."
"What should I have on my salad?"
"I don't know. Okay, you should have a Caesar salad."
"Why?"
"Because I can feel myself getting old."
"What?"
"Nothing. You can get a Caesar with chicken."
"Chicken?"
"Yes, chicken."

"They'll put chicken on it?"
"I promise."
"And coffee."
"Yes."
"Salad? Okay, good idea."
Later...
In which the River Stix Casino pulls a fast one:
Today, my father gets a card in the mail, entitling him to two free buffets for his birthday—his ninety-first birthday, let me add parenthetically, which occurs on October 14th. When he goes to cash in the coupon, however, he is told that because it's September 29th, and not his actual birthday month, the promotion is not valid and won't be until October, a stipulation that doesn't appear on the card.

Seems to me, if you're over ninety, with a birthday in October, if it's fucking June and you have a coupon, they should cut you a little slack on this because, well, you know, you never know.

"Dad, you can't die before Sunday."
"Why?"
"Because we're coming back! And we're going to punish these miserable bastards!"

* * *

30 September
In which Jack Friedman gives sound business advice when seeking a partner.

"I got a client," he says to me on the way to the Yom Kippur service. "I know this young kid. He's in hock up to the balls of his ass and he runs around with girls. Bad scene, baby."

This morning's service, as most are at Congregation B'nai Emunah, was filled with instrumentation and music, harmonies, responsive and joyful singing, clapping, and occasional swaying.

"I thought this was supposed to be a solemn holiday," he says.

"It is. Day of Atonement."

"Then why all this jumpy music? It's all so jumpy."

OCTOBER

1 October

In which, while waiting to be seated at the Hot Rod buffet, Jack Friedman asks a question for the ages.

"What's a Frank Caliendo, and what does he do?"

* * *

3 October

In which Jack Friedman finds the joke lacking.

We begin, though, earlier in the day at a ninety-minute lunch with the stupidly talented photographer Western Doughty in which the mysteries of both women and sons are unraveled over an eighteen-inch double-cheese-and-garlic pizza. Western tells the following joke: "Two guys are talking and one says, 'I got a watch from my new lesbian neighbors.'

"Why did your new lesbian neighbors give you a watch?" the other asks.

"Well, I think they misunderstood me when I said 'I wanna watch.'"

Fast-forward to the Tuesday Night All-You-Can-Eat 2-for-1 Buffet at the Hot Rod.

The joke is retold.

"Now, *that's* funny," my father says. "*That's* funny. But you should have mentioned they were women."

"What are you talking about? Why would I mention that? They're lesbians. Of course they're women."

"But you didn't say that."

"Why would I say that? They're lesbians. It's understood."

"Would still be funnier if you said they were women neighbors, because nobody would know that."

"Nobody except everybody. Lesbians are women."

"Well, yeah, I guess. Okay, tell me the joke again. Who gives who the watch?"

"No. Forget it. You can't have the joke."

* * *

6 October

In which Jack Friedman expects one to keep up.

"Say, Ba, I like the corn flakes—not the chocolate ones, the plain, but now I'm thinking I should get Rice Krispies. But I don't know. What do you think?"

"Gotta go with the corn flakes."

"You know I eat them every morning with the coffee?"

"Yes, I'm aware."

"In Vegas, I mixed them."

"Those were the days, huh?"

"Which are better for you?"

"They're all sugar. Not sure it matters."

"All right, what the hell. Get me the corn flakes. The frosted ones. Plain."

"Problem solved."

"Did you know George Toporoff, my friend from school?"

"Why would I know him?"

"Oh, yeah, that's right, you weren't born. He died anyway."

"What does he have to do with corn flakes?"

"Corn flakes? No. His father was my family doctor. He spelled my name wrong on the birth certificate. Spelled it F-r-e-e-d-m-a-n. This was the father, the doctor. He's gotta be dead, too."

"Yeah, he'd be, like, a hundred and thirty."

"Good-looking man. Both of them. Stuck-up son of a bitch, though, George."

Later . . .

This one may take a while. Get a beverage.

My father gets a text from Joanne Price, wishing him an early happy birthday. Who is Joanne Price, you ask? Doesn't matter, except that she's not Jeannette Willette, his long-suffering girlfriend in Las Vegas.

"Did you see Jeannette sent me a message? A text. What's a text?"

"It wasn't from Jeannette," I say.

"What are you talking about? It's Jeannette. I nearly married her but she wouldn't convert."

"That's not what happened, and that's not who sent you the text."

"Well, then, who sent me the text?"

"Joanne Price from Atlantic City."

"Who's Joanne?"

"I have no idea."

"That's Jeannette. Jeannette Price."

"That's not Jeannette, and Price is not her last name."

"What's her last name?"

"Willette."

"Willette?"

"Joanne Willette. That's what I said."

"No. Jeannette Willette lives in Las Vegas. Joanne Price lives in Atlantic City."

"Then why did Jeannette send me a text?"

"She didn't. Joanne sent you the text."

"Who's Joanne Willette?"

"Price!"

"I'm confused because they both have the same last name."

"But they don't. One is Price. One is Willette."

"I meant the first name."

"But one is Joanne, the other is Jeannette."

"I know that."

"Joanne is the one who wrote you."

"Jeannette?"

"Joanne!"

"I knew her in Vegas."

"You knew Jeannette in Vegas."

"You know, she wanted to get married but I wouldn't convert."

"I thought she wouldn't convert."

"She was from Vermont. Now there's something wrong with her leg. But she sent me a text."

"Joanne sent you the text!"

"Who's Joanne?"

"I don't know!"

"Oh, I know who she is. We had an affair, hot and heavy. She wrote me? What did she say?"

"'Happy birthday.'"

"How did she know it was my birthday next week?"

"You must have told her."

"I told her?"

"Who else would have told her?"

"You mean you can send a text and not know where the person is?"

"Yeah."

"I want to write her back. I want to text her back."

"What could go wrong there?"

"What?"

"Nothing."

"Show me how."

The tutorial finished, he sends her four texts. One says "I"; one says "R"; one says nothing but has six returns, so it's a block of white; and one says, "It's nice writing you."

We continue.

"How does she know they're from me?"

"Because they'll come in the same message thread that she sent her original message."

"But what if someone else writes her?"

"She'll know."

"What did she say, again?"

"'Happy birthday.'"

"Why didn't I ever get married again?"

"Well, Joanne wouldn't marry you, and you didn't want to marry Jeannette."

"Nah, that wasn't it. With Joanne, it was hot and heavy. But she was married and wouldn't leave her husband."

"That'll do it."

"She was a beautiful blonde. She was a waitress. Her husband was a handyman and her mother-in-law was a former Miss New Jersey a million years ago. But she died."

* * *

7 October

Florence Friedman's birthday. His wife. My mother. She would have been eighty-seven. That's all for today.

* * *

10 October

In which Jack Friedman makes his move.

LeAnna, our favorite hostess here at the Hot Rod Tuesday Night All-You-Can-Eat 2-for-1 Buffet, stops by our table to talk about family. I'm figuring LeAnna is in her late forties, early fifties.

"How goes your life?" asks my father.

"It's fine, Jack, but I miss my kids. I can't get them to come visit."

"How many do you have?"

"Three."

"Well, this one here," he says, pointing to me, "kidnapped me from Vegas."

"Oh, stop it. You like being here."

"He's all right. He means well. So you got a husband?"

"Not anymore."

"Well, there's a lot of that going around. Why don't you get married again?"

"Got to wait for the right one to come along, Jack."

"How about me? I'm pushing ninety-one."

* * *

11 October
In which the dinner conversation breaks orbit.

I found out tonight that after World War II, my father, his injuries notwithstanding, injuries that could have killed him—hence the Purple Heart—spent the next ten years living in the Philippines before moving to Vegas and subsequently was kidnapped by "this one here," pointing to me across the table, "who brought me to exciting Tulsa." The couple to whom he tells this story—at the next table—were in their mid-seventies, I'd guess. Their check comes; the woman picks it up.

"You let her buy?" my father asks the man. "What? She doesn't trust you with the checkbook?"

"We're dating," he answers.

"Dating? Not married?"

"No. Dating."

"So you're not married?"

"Not married."

"Not married? My wife died," my father says.

"Oh, sorry," the man says.

"I'm pushing ninety-two." (He turns ninety-one in three days.)

In the most troubling development, as the couple is leaving, my father says, "Behave yourself. And if you can't, take my number."

To both of them.

* * *

14 October
In which Jack Friedman, on his ninety-first birthday, describes my sister Susan's family to Melissa, with Susan and Chris, one of her sons, sitting there at the birthday dinner.

"You should see the mob they have. They all live at home and are all big eaters."

* * *

20 October
In which Jack Friedman sees a man in a dashiki ordering a pizza.

"What the hell is that? Is that the outfit for the Middle Eastern Army?"

"Yes, that's exactly right," the man says.

* * *

21 October
In which Jack Friedman, ninety-one, reminds us that your better relationships come with a healthy work ethic and clear expectations.

At the Tulsa Jewish Community Center, he sidles up to a woman who's working the front desk and asks, "So what's your function here besides watching the door? I mean, what do you do all day?"

At the River Silk Casino ninety minutes later, he says to his favorite valet attendant, "Give me a kiss and tell me you love me."

* * *

24 October

Jack and Florence Friedman

Before kids, suburbia, housecoats, toupees, convertible Cadillacs, cancers that came and went and came again, a trip to Italy (where, on a boat in Salerno, she looked at him and mouthed the words "We made it"), and before they were Mom and Dad, they were Jack and Florence, and sixty-four years ago tomorrow, October 25th, 1953, they got married.

"What happened? I was sixteen two weeks ago."

Later...

In which Jack Friedman takes on the TSA.

"You're telling me," he says to me, "I can't fly from state to state without a passport because the Oklahoma license isn't good anymore?"

"More or less, yes. Oklahoma officials didn't want to comply with federal regulations, and after the feds gave them extension after extension, the feds said, 'Fine, don't upgrade your license. Now your people can't fly without a passport, even domestically.'"

"What kind of state you got here?"

A great question, that.

* * *

25 October

In which Jack Friedman celebrates his sixty-fourth wedding anniversary in his own inimitable style.

"Hey, Dad, happy anniversary," I say.

"What are you talking about?"

"Your anniversary. Yours and Mom's."

"Your mother?"

"Yeah. Today's your anniversary."

"Today? Oh, yeah, yeah."

"You forgot."

"No, no."

"Yeah, yeah. That's all right. You're ninety-one."

"No, I thought about it—just not today. I did a couple of months ago."

"Stop. I'm tearing up."

* * *

26 October

In which Jack Friedman introduces a new member of his childhood group, to go with Bernie, Bucky, George, Jerry, Gene, Mel, Milton, Morris, and the two Marvins—Cherpakov and Kraftchin. Ladies and gentlemen, please say hello to Al "Blue Eyes."

"Dad, tell me about Al 'Blue Eyes.'"

"Oh, Al. He died early."

Later . . .

For reasons that continue to defy understanding, Jack Friedman, ninety-one and computer-challenged, is still doing accounting work. One of his clients is an old friend of his, a Yugoslavian doctor, Petar Jovanovic, who has lived in New York City for the past thirty years. Lately, I have been helping my father with this work. I know nothing about preparing taxes, but I can download an accounting program, so I'm Arthur Andersen in this relationship—and I've noticed that he has been making errors lately the size of the Bronx, which is where Petar lives.

"You know," I tell him on the phone, "you've been spelling Petar's name wrong for thirty years."

"What do you mean?"

"It's P-e-t-a-r, and you've been spelling it P-e-t-e-r."

"Yeah. That's how I spell it."

"But that's not his name."

"Doesn't matter on the return."

"What do you mean it doesn't matter? It's his name."

"They don't care."

"Maybe he does."

"Nah, he doesn't know what the hell's going on."

"Well, he mentioned it."

"Who mentioned it?"

"Who? Petar."

"You know, it's pronounced Pay-ter."

"Yes, I'm aware."

"He doesn't look at the return."

"He doesn't look at his own return? Of course he does. Dad, I'm serious, you have to spell the man's name right."

"All right, maybe so. Anyway, did you ever get the two grand for the return we did? You electrified it, right?"

"You mean did I file it electronically? Yes."

"No, as a matter of fact, I didn't get the money. I think I'll call and remind him."

"Well, give him some time. He just got it last week. What do you think?"

"Wait a week."

"Okay, good idea."

An hour later, he calls back.

"I called Peter [Petar]."

"Of course you did."

"I didn't bring up the money."

"You didn't?"

"Not at all."
"Nothing?"
"Not a word."
"Nicely done."
"We had a nice talk. I asked how he was doing, blah, blah, blah, mentioned the quarterly estimate, how he had to get it in by the end of October, unlike my bill for the two grand, which was due anytime."
"Subtle. Very subtle."

* * *

28 October

In which Jack Friedman, playing hurt, insists on completing his appointed rounds. Such as they are.

"Barry, I fell," he says as I arrive at his apartment.
"How bad?"
"Well, I didn't fall, I tripped. It was more of a ski."
"A ski?"
"Yeah, you know, a ski," he says, and then takes the position a non-skier would take when skiing.
"Are you okay?"
"Yeah, it wasn't so much a fall. It was the floor."
"The floor?"
"Yeah, the carpet. My slippers."
"Got it. Carpet and slippers."
"What?"
"Nothing."
"Listen, I need to go to Costco or the Dollar Store. I need some sprays."
"Sprays? What kind of sprays?"
"Well, not for the hair. I got those. For the room."

* * *

29 October

In which Jack Friedman meets my friend Michael Doane, who flew in from Paris.

"When did you get here?" my father asks.

"Yesterday. And the first thing I did was throw up," says Michael.

"Oh, I thought you were here on business."

* * *

31 October

In which I warned you gals that if you didn't make it to Tulsa, you could lose him.

Our good friend LeAnna, the sweetest hostess in all the land, here at the Hot Rod, comes up to me at the buffet tonight and asks, "Would you mind if I took your dad to a movie? He's so sweet and he's lonely. I'm off Mondays."

"He'll love it. He'll ask you to marry him."

"I don't want to marry him."

"Damn."

"You just want to get rid of him."

"Oh, sure. It sounds good. Seriously, he really will enjoy it."

I plan to leave the table so she can come over and ask him out. I do. I see her sit down. They start talking. When I arrive back at the table, he's got a piece of paper and a pen waiting for me.

"Write down my number and my hotel. The woman came over and asked me to the movies."

"You mean your apartment?"

"What do you mean?"

"Never mind. I'll write it down."

"Should I take her to dinner, too?"

"Yes."

"Where? Modi's?"

"Mondo's."

"Yeah, yeah. You know she's got a car, too. She's going to pick me up. Did you write the number down?"

"Yes."

"Let me see."

I show him.

"That's my number?"

"Yeah."

"Who the hell can read your writing?"

"Dad, don't worry. She'll be there."

"Should I get her number?"

"No."

"Why not?"

"She'll be more comfortable, trust me."

"What if there's an emergency?"

"Like what?"

"What if I have to go to Alaska?"

"I'll break it to her gently."

"She's going to pick me up. She's got two kids, nineteen and eighteen. No husband, I don't think. Divorced or dead."

NOVEMBER

4 November

In which Jack Friedman discusses the white meats on a Saturday afternoon.

When my father is not eating at the Hot Rod Tuesday Night All-You-Can-Eat 2-for-1 Buffet or at Owl Head, he is home eating turkey, which he calls chicken, and Muenster cheese on dark rye, which I buy at the deli at Reasor's.

And we begin.

"Dad," I say, getting back in the car at Reasor's and handing him the package, "here you go. I got you chicken this time instead of turkey."

"What's this?"

"I bought you chicken this time, instead of turkey."

"What do you mean?"

"I got you actual chicken instead of turkey. You eat turkey, call it chicken, so I thought I'd buy you chicken and see if you like it. So, tell me which one you like better."

"Better? What do you mean? Between the chicken and the turkey?"

"Yeah."

"You know I got bread? I don't need bread. I love the wheat bread."

"I thought you liked the rye."

"Yeah, the wheat."

"Okay. The wheat bread or the rye bread?"

"The dark one you bought."

"It's a dark rye, not wheat."

"I like the combination, that's all. So you bought what?"

"Chicken."

"I know, I know."

"No, you don't know, because I just bought it—that's what I'm telling you."

"You always buy it."

"No, I buy turkey."

"It's the same."

"No, one's turkey, one's chicken."

"Yeah, but they're both, what do you call it, uh, you know—"

"Fowl."

"Fowl, yeah, so that's all right. I like it. It's a good snack—the white meats."

"Let me try this again: You've been eating turkey. This package contains chicken. Let me know if you like it, okay, because I'm not sure."

"I needed cheese, you know."

"I got the cheese."

"Oh, you got the cheese?"

"Yes."

"The . . .?"

"Muenster."
"Yes."
"It's a great combination, the chicken and the cheese."
"You mean the turkey? You haven't had the chicken yet."
"Yeah, yeah, I know. I need cream soda, by the way. Oh, is that good! What is that?"
"Cream soda?"
"Yeah."
"It's cream soda."
"Yeah, very good."
"I didn't know you needed any."
"That's okay, I got a full bottle of Coke."
"I'm exhausted."
"What?"
"Nothing."

* * *

7 November

In which a triumphant Jack Friedman returns to the buffet.

As usual, we arrive at the Hot Rod Tuesday 2-for-1 and, as usual, I send him ahead to get seated, which, because LeAnna is so consistently wonderful, he does. The line is quite long, though, so it takes me a while to get through; nevertheless, he calls me to tell me he's been seated, even though he can see me, and I can see him, through the glass partition.

"Just come in. You'll see me."
"I see you now."
"All right, goodbye."

Seconds later, he calls again.

"Okay, I'm seated."
"Didn't we just have this conversation?"
"All right, goodbye."

When I arrive at the table, I see him in his customary blue

windbreaker (with matching sweatpants) and a tall glass of lemonade in front of him.

"Where you been?" he asks.

"It was crowded. You saw me standing in line."

"Oh, yeah, that's right. Anyway, they seated me."

"Did they, now? Lemonade?"

"Yeah, she brought it."

"Who did?"

"You know, what's her name?"

"LeAnna?"

"Yeah, yeah, the one I went out with last night."

"Very nice. Okay, you ready to eat?"

"Hold it. Let's wait for my girlfriend."

And so it begins.

* * *

10 November

In which Jack Friedman learns the true identity of his ophthalmologist.

For two years, my father has gone to see Dr. Jamal Siddiqui, a wonderful and patient man and an excellent doctor. At an appointment today, my father asks if he could hurt his eyes looking at dirty pictures and whether his injuries during the war could have affected his eyesight.

"What kind of name is Jamal Siddiqui?" he asks me as we're leaving. "Italian?"

"I believe he's from Lebanon."

"Lebanon?"

"Lebanon."

"All the way over there?"

"Yeah."

"He Jewish?"

"Oh, this is going to be fun. His family, I believe, is Muslim."

"Muslim?"

"Muslim."

"Oh, I thought he was Italian."

"Siddiqui is not really an Italian name, Dad."

"Well, you know what I mean."

* * *

13 November

In which the important thing in life is to make rank.

"So Sol made colonel in the Army," he says to me on the way to Owl Head. "He was a doctor."

"Who's Sol?"

"A friend of mine. These are the guys I ran with. There was me and Sol and Jerry and Morris and Milty and Mel and Gene Tannenbaum, who changed his name to Tanner."

"Why?"

"He thought it sounded too Jewish. Good-looking guy, Gene."

"But who's Sol? You never mentioned him."

"He had an older brother."

"Okay."

"Anyway, he died."

"Sol?"

"Yeah."

"When?"

"Oh, about thirty years ago. But how about that? He made colonel."

* * *

14 November

In which we are reminded, if such a reminder were necessary, that nobody sums up a life like Jack Friedman.

My father on the wife of one of his clients:

"Oh, Deanna. Very zaftig. You know, very, uh—what's the

word? Vivacious. She wanted to open up a nude restaurant. No joke. Nude. Can you imagine? Anyway, she died. But she was a spender."

* * *

16 November
    What's in a name?
    My father and I are at Owl Head today and there's a big box of cups Aaron and Joe are giving away that have the Old School insignia—the actual name of the restaurant.
    Says my father, "Old School Bagel Cafe? Cafe? What kind of cafe? I didn't know that was the name. Since when?"

* * *

18 November
    In which Jack Friedman's secret financial empire is revealed.
    "Maybe I should buy a car," he says.
    "You don't want a car."
    "Why not?"
    "Because I'm with you most of the time and I drive you everywhere, so it's crazy to buy a car. It's too expensive. Just the insurance alone."
    "How much?"
    "About three hundred a month."
    "Why so much?"
    "Because you're ninety-one with three accidents in the last eighteen months."
    "I'll lie about my age."
    "What could possibly go wrong there? Besides, you'd use it to go to Panera twice a week by yourself. That's nuts."
    "What do I care? I got plenty of money."
    "You really don't."
    "You don't know what I have."

"I know exactly what you have. I pay your bills."

"Not *that* money. I have other money. In Vegas."

"What other money in Vegas?"

"I got money there. I'm in a partnership with a couple of guys."

"You're in a what with who?"

"A partnership with some guys."

"A partnership? Doing what?"

"Don't worry about it. It's a partnership. And they know if I die where the money goes."

"The guys in your partnership know this?"

"Yes!"

"Tell me again. What does your partnership do?"

"It's just some guys, that's all."

* * *

19 November

In which Jack Friedman adds to the legend of Thanksgiving.

Yesterday, at a lovely pre-Thanksgiving dinner at the home of my dear friends Mike and Jan, my father, after asking, as he usually does on such occasions, if the bird gave up its life willingly, asked, "So why do we eat turkey on Thanksgiving, anyway?"

A number of possible answers were discussed, including myths about the Pilgrims and/or how, perhaps, the turkey was brought by the Indian tribes invited to that meal, none of which satisfied my father's curiosity.

"Oh," he said, "I thought it was because they didn't have cows and couldn't have steak."

* * *

20 November

Jack Friedman is at Tulsa International Airport, waiting for his flight to Los Angeles to see his son, Wayne, his daughter-in-law, Hope, and his granddaughter Francesca.

He calls. I'm in Denver on the way to Medford, Oregon, to see my daughter. I put him on the plane before I left.

"Hey, Dad, how you feeling?"

"Oh, yeah, I ate. I think I'm going to call Bernie and tell him I'm at the airport."

"Bernie? You mean Wayne, your son."

"What did I say?"

"No, no, my mistake. You had it right. Yes. Bernie. Of course, Bernie. Give Bernie a hug for me, and his wife, Lylah."

* * *

27 November

In which Jack Friedman's ways are mysterious.

He tells Melissa, who has picked him up at the airport, "When Barry gets back, have him call my cell once. I won't pick up. But this way, I'll know he's back. That will be the signal. Remember. Tell him to let the phone ring once and I won't answer. Okay?"

And then he gave her twenty dollars.

* * *

30 November

Jack Friedman, in his own inimitable style, shares his thoughts on sexual harassment in the workplace in general and morning newsmen in particular.

"Say, Ba, have you been following the news? They're firing all these emcees for playing with the girls. I mean, what the hell are these guys doing?"

DECEMBER

1 December
In which Jack Friedman wants to talk about ducks and dinner.
We drive by a park.
"Why are there so many ducks?" he asks.
"I don't know."
"Is it because they feed them?"
"I'm sure food does attract the hungry ones."
"Can you shoot one?"
"Do you want to shoot one?"
"No, but I'm sure there are guys who do and then take it home for dinner."
"I don't think you can shoot a duck in a city park."
"I know. I know. Can these ducks fly?"
"They all can."
"How far?"
"I don't know. Away from the people shooting at them, I imagine."
"What time you coming tonight?"
"Six thirty."
"Then we're going to have pizza with Bernie, and then the casino."
"Ed, not Bernie."
"Why do I get them confused?"
"I don't know."
"And what did Bernie die of?"
"I don't know."
"I heard he died. That's all."
Later...
Enter the Meltzer Boys:
Tonight Jack Friedman enters the car with a $24 invoice from the Yankef-Leibish Family Circle, which guarantees burial plots for my brother, my sister, and me.
"You know what these things cost?" he asks, handing me the bill. "Hundreds. So I figured what the hell? Eight bucks a year, even if you don't use it."

"Thanks."

"No, it's no joke. There's a plot for all of us. Now, you know, one thing, though. If you ever get married, Melissa can't get in, because she's not Jewish. Only Jews allowed."

"How are they going to know?"

"No, no, no. You gotta be Jewish. Ach, you're right. We could bluff. No big deal. You ever been out there?"

"Yeah."

"Your mother's there, you know."

"I'm aware."

"And so is, oh, what's his name? He was married to Cynthia. Herbie?"

"Norm."

"Normie, yes! He went blind, you know?"

"I know."

"What happened? He lost his sight? How does that happen?"

"I don't know. You lose your sight."

"Blind? Nu? And there's just a stick there. No gravestone."

"I think that's because his son didn't spring for one. We've talked about this."

"What?"

"Never mind."

"And what the hell did Cynthia die of?"

"Oh, Jesus, here we go."

"They're all gone. I ran with, like, nineteen guys. All gone, except Mel and me, but he's in California. He takes naps. I give up. All the Meltzer boys from Rockaway are gone."

* * *

3 December

In which Jack Friedman discovers Jews are everywhere.

"Must be a lot of Jews in Tulsa, Ba."

"Why do you say that?"

"Well, we've been driving around and there are a lot of houses without Christmas lights up."

"You're exactly right."

* * *

12 December

In which Jack Friedman makes his grocery list.

"Hey, Ba, I need the world. Milk, juice, cereal, Half-and-Half, and two-sided tape."

"Two-sided tape?"

"Yeah, you know, for the hair."

Later...

"So what are we doing tomorrow, Ba?"

"Well, I'll have to see you early because I have lunch with the mayor."

"Of Tulsa?"

"Yeah."

"Why does he want to talk to you?"

"I'm sure it's a question he's asking himself right now."

"Think he'll offer you a job?"

"I don't think so."

"You could do something, couldn't you?"

"Not really."

"Something in city government?"

"No. He's not offering me a job, Dad."

"Is he a Republican or Democrat?"

"Republican."

"How can you talk to a Republican?"

"Now, that's funny."

"You know this is a solid Republican state."

"Really? Hadn't heard."

"So you're meeting with a bunch of people?"

"No. Just him and me. We do it every six months or so."

"Really? You? What do you talk about?"

"Politics."
"Local politics?"
"Usually."
"Well, tell him to fix the goddamn lights in town, would ya?"

* * *

16 December
In which Jack Friedman discusses legs and hoops.
The day begins. He enters the car for our morning trip to Owl Head.
"Why do my legs still work, Ba?"
"Why do your legs work?"
"I mean, shouldn't I be in a wheelchair or a walker?"
"I don't know that you should be. Many people your age are."
"No, I'm just saying. I'm ninety-one."
"I know."
"Ninety-one? Is it because I played so much tennis?"
"Oh, that reminds me. You like basketball, don't you? We can go to a game. University of Tulsa."
"Is that pro or college?"
"College. You want to go?"
"Nah."
"No? I thought you liked basketball."
"I don't know. I don't like watching. I like playing."
[Author's note: spit take]
"You like playing? When did you ever play basketball?"
"In Vegas."
"You never played basketball in Vegas. Cut it out."
"You don't know. Sometimes, we didn't play tennis and we played basketball instead. Someone had a ball and we played."
"Someone had a ball? Five ninety-year-old guys?"
"We weren't very good at it."
"Imagine that."
"Anyway, basketball is boring. All they do is put it in the

basket. And when did it get so physical? It's a very physical sport. You know it's a black sport now. At least what I see on television."

"They don't telecast the white guys."

"What?"

"Nothing."

"And why did you come and drag me out of Vegas, anyway? I could still walk. I'm going back. I'm not going to buy. I'm going to rent."

* * *

17 December

In which the word of the day reveals itself early and often.

"Hey, Ba, I need some granulated sugar."

"Why?"

"You know, the granulated sugar. It comes in a bag, not too big. I need a small bag of the granulated sugar."

"You don't use sugar."

"But the granulated sugar is good to have around."

"Why do you need it?"

"No, but I eat the cereal every morning and I need the granulated sugar for the, uh, you know, the flakes. That's all."

"You eat Frosted Flakes. You want to put sugar on that?"

"Well, also the coffee. I want to have some granulated sugar for the coffee."

"You put, like, four Sweet'N Lows in your coffee. Just add a fifth. You want to add sugar to the Sweet'N Low already in your coffee? That doesn't sound good."

"But I can't get the goddamn thing sweet enough. That's why I want the granulated sugar—a small bag, not a big one. It's because I'm drinking decaf."

* * *

18 December

In which Jack Friedman does not dwell on death.

"You'll never guess who I got a call from today, Ba."

"Couldn't guess."

"You remember Don Abraham?"

"Yeah, your old partner."

"Well, he died, so it wasn't him who called me."

"That's a relief."

"But his wife called and said, 'Is this Jack Friedman?' I said, 'Yeah.' She said, 'You're the only one in the office still alive. Don's dead, Melinda's dead. What are you still doing alive? What are you, like, a hundred and two?'

"I told her, 'No, ninety-one.' So what's up, sweetheart?" he goes on, turning his attention to me. "We're going to the casino tonight?"

* * *

19 December

In which Jack Friedman . . . I can't even begin.

Here goes.

We're at the Tuesday Night All-You-Can-Eat 2-for-1 Buffet at the Hot Rod Casino when LeAnna, the sweetest hostess in all the land, seats my father early, as she usually does, while I wait in line to pay.

"You know, we've been out twice," he says after I sit down.

"I'm aware."

"Hi, Jack. Hi, Barry," she says, now at the table.

"Hey, hi."

"Oh, I'm so excited," says LeAnna, "my mom's coming into town on Friday."

"That's wonderful," I say.

"Yeah, she's got incredible energy. Eight brothers and me."

"How many children does that make?" asks my father, the accountant.

"Nine," she says.

"Oh, yeah, that's right," he says.

"And she's only ninety-five pounds," says LeAnna.

"Ninety-five pounds?" asks my father. "Ninety-five pounds? You're joking. Does she know about the size of you?"

Yes, he did.

Best part of the story is when LeAnna, without missing a beat, replies, "There are bigger ones than me."

(*LeAnna has approved this message.)

* * *

22 December

In which Jack Friedman, ninety-one, and Gregory Moss, eleven, have a conversation in the car.

"Hey, Grandpa, when's your birthday?"

"October fourteenth. I was ninety-one."

"You think you'll make ninety-two?"

"I think I'll make ninety-six. My older brother is ninety-six. He's going to be ninety-seven in July. I had another brother who died who was four years older than me. He was the most successful. He was in the Air Corps in World War II. He was a mechanic and then he married an English girl."

* * *

23 December

In which Jack Friedman gushes.

"Ba," my father said not ten minutes ago, "I want to thank you for all you do for me. You did a lot of work this week."

* * *

27 December

In which Jack Friedman makes special financial demands.

"Hey, Ba, when you go into the bank today to make a deposit, ask them: If you have a bowl of coins, will they take it and deposit it? That's all."

"An actual bowl?"

"Yeah, you know, a bowl with quarters, dimes. Probably have over a hundred bucks in there, so what the hell?"

"Thing is, Dad, I don't think the U.S. banking system has recovered from your bottle of pennies yet. But I'll ask."

"What the hell happened to my bottle, anyway?"

"Damn it! I was nearly out."

"What?"

"Nothing."

* * *

28 December

In which Jack Friedman issues a new dietary edict.

"I don't know what it is, Ba. I have no appetite anymore and all I can eat is shrimp."

That he said it at Owl Head, eating a toasted croissant with a scrambled egg and drinking decaf with four Sweet'N Lows and five different-flavored dairy creamers just adds to the disconnect and the charm.

* * *

29 December

In which Jack Friedman gets wrong every aspect of his niece's husband but insists it's all part of the plan.

"Now, Kate's husband, Eli."

"Elon."

"What?"

"His name is Elon. You called him Eli."

"Why did I think it was Eli?"

"God himself probably doesn't know."

"Well, I call him Eli."
"It's probably why he doesn't talk to you."
"Anyway, he's a doctor, right?"
"Yes."
"But we can't see him, right?"
"Right."
"Because he sees dogs."
"Dogs? No. He's a child psychiatrist."
"That's what I meant."

* * *

30 December

Fun at Owl Head with Jack Friedman and Rebecca Joskey:

Dear friend Rebecca suffers from hearing loss. Making matters worse, today, she tells me, her hearing aids were not working particularly well. Enter Jack Friedman, who also suffers from hearing loss. He also doesn't listen, isn't interested in most things people say, rarely pays attention to the events at hand, and has no short-term memory.

Here's just a snippet.

"So you two fooling around?" asks my father, pointing to me.

"What?" Rebecca asks.

"You know," says my father.

"Going around?" she asks.

"What?" asks my father.

"We're friends," says Rebecca.

"You know him?"

"Yes."

"We're friends, Dad," I repeat.

"What's your name, dear?"

"What?" asks Rebecca.

"There's a lot of that going around," says my father.

"He wants to know your name," I say to Rebecca.

"Rebecca."

"What?" asks my father.

"Rebecca," she says.

"Good to meet you."

"You've met, like, six times, Dad."

"I don't remember. So I was attacking this girl in an—"

"—Dad, you can't tell that joke," I say.

"What joke? Don't listen to him. You don't know what joke I'm going to tell. He doesn't know what joke I'm going to tell," he adds to Rebecca.

"What?" asks Rebecca.

"I came from Vegas. He came and grabbed me. So how goes your life?"

"Fine."

"What's that?"

"Fine."

"What's your name again, dear?"

"Rebecca."

"Say it again, I'm sorry."

"Rebecca."

"Rebecca," I say.

"I heard, I heard," he says.

"Good to see you again," says Rebecca.

"I'm Jack. I'm the father."

* * *

31 December

How's your New Year's Eve going?

four
2018

JANUARY

2 JANUARY

In which a smooth Jack Friedman once again shows you rubes how it's done with the ladies.

The patient and wonderful LeAnna joins us intermittently for dinner at the Tuesday Night Hot Rod All-You-Can-Eat 2-for-1 Buffet, and the conversation usually gets around to the next time she and my father will have dinner. Mondo's is discussed, Charleston's is discussed, but then my father drops this suggestion.

Listen and learn, gents.

"What if I just bring over a chicken and you cook it?"

* * *

5 January

In which Jack Friedman resumes his conversation with and about death.

"I didn't know what's-his-name died this year."

"Who?"

"The actor. Well, not the actor. The guy who, you know . . . you've seen him. Oh, you know."

"I don't."

"C'mon. He was the guy with the other guy and he died, but I didn't know this guy died, too."

"I'm going to take a shot here. Jerry Lewis?"

"Yes. I didn't know he died. He died?"

"He died."

"When did he die?"

"Recently."

"Is Lana Turner still alive?"

"No."

"When did she die?"

"I don't know. Why would I know that?"

"She was gorgeous."

"Okay."

"And the other one died too."

"Yes, she did. Whoever we're talking about."

"And how did Bernie Newman die?"

* * *

6 January

Jack Friedman to Melissa's brother Shawn:

"Are you wearing an earring?"

"Yes."

"Does it help your hearing?"

"No."

"Seriously, do those things help your hearing? You know, increase the volume?"

"No."

"Because I thought they did. I have them, too," he says, referring to his hearing aids.

* * *

9 January

In which he may get a few facts wrong, but nobody nails the obscure Jamie Farr reference quite like Jack Friedman.

"So, Ba, last night, Leona—"

"LeAnna."

"What'd I say?"

"Doesn't matter. Where did you go to dinner?"

"We were going to go to Charlemagne's."

"You mean Charleston's?"

"Yeah, yeah, but we went to Modi's instead."

"Mondo's."

"Mondo's. Very nice. They all thought I was your father there."

"You are my father."

"You know what I mean."

"Sure."

Just then, LeAnna—this being the Hot Rod Tuesday Night All-You-Can-Eat 2-for-1 Buffet—ushered us to our table ahead of others standing in line.

"Thank you, dear," says my father. "May your harem never know the horrors of stretch marks."

* * *

12 January

And we continue today's culinary theme with Jack Friedman.

Tonight's episode: The importance of moisture.

"Now, this is a good pie," he says of the fourteen-inch cheese from NYC Pizza in Tulsa, Oklahoma. "It's moist."

"Moist?"

"Wet."

"You mean you like the amount of sauce on it."

"The what?"

"The tomato sauce."

"No, it just has more moisture than the other pie, that's all. It's good here. NYC? What's that?"

"New York City."

"I know, I know. I was just asking if they were from New York?"

"The father is."

"What happened? They throw him out?"

"I don't know."

"It's moist. It's very good. And it comes with a fork and knife. Very refined."

"You can get a fork and knife anywhere."

"No. You know why the Italians made the pizza pie?"

"This should be good. Why?"

"They didn't have utensils."

"The Italians didn't have utensils?"

"Well, they had them. You know what I mean."

Jack and Barry Friedman and a pizza sign

* * *

13 January

In which a father's love is a powerful thing, Part the Infinity.

Running into David Blatt at Owl Head this morning, my father points to me and says, "My sperm made that."

* * *

17 January

Aunt Marilyn died today. She was ninety-three. We got close the past few years on the trips I took down to Delray Beach with my father. I used to tease her about her e-Machine and she would say, "Barry, what do I care? I don't know how to do anything on this. I play solitaire, I check email, then I turn it off." And she always made sure she had gumdrops and cans of Diet Coke at the house before I got there. She and Leo, as most ninety-year-olds do, screamed a lot at each other, at the world, and then she would dismiss him and his argument by backhanding her hand at him in the air and he'd start whistling some tune in his head.

The first seventy years were wonderful.

I heard her scream at John McCain during the 2008 debate, Mitt Romney in 2012, and Donald Trump in 2016.

You can take the liberal Jew out of New York, but you can't take the liberal Jew out of the liberal Jew.

She hated the NRA and loved Dwyane Wade.

My father, Marilyn's brother-in-law, said, as he usually does on such occasions, that she wasn't cut short, had a life. But then he stopped, thought about all those no longer with us, and added, "Ba, we're dissipating."

* * *

19 January

In which Jack Friedman likes what he likes.

"Ba, that Half-and-Half you bought, the Mudslide, whatever it's called. It's the best I've ever had. Wow-wee-wow! Where did you get it?"

"Reasor's."

"It's fantastic. The coffee comes out great. Perfect. Oh, I have to get more. It's called Mudslide. Where did you get it?"

"Reasor's."

"Oh, I didn't open up the other one you bought—the red one you bought [White Chocolate Peppermint Bark]—but I don't care about that one. This one, the Mudslide, I have to buy more. I want to buy two."

"Okay, we'll get you more."

"Where'd you find it, again?"

"Reasor's."

"Oh. I love it so. Mudslide. I have to remember the name."

"Shouldn't be a problem."

"Reasor's, right?"

"Reasor's."

"Fantastic. The best thing I've ever tasted. Mudslide. You know which one I'm talking about?"

"Yeah, I think so. Mudslide."

Later . . .

For reasons that defy understanding, my father wanted Burger King tonight. But not too much.

"Get me something small, Ba."

I decide to get him a kids' meal. It comes with a "Sherlock Gnomes" plastic toy.

"Look, Dad, you got a prize."

"What the hell is it?"

"Sherlock Holmes, more or less," I say, figuring I would not have enough energy if I lived 1,500 years to explain the "Gnomes" business.

"What does it do?"

"What does it do? It doesn't do anything."

"I mean, what is it?"

"It's a Sherlock Holmes plastic meal toy."

"Why?"

"Why? I don't know why. It's a toy. They give them away to kids."

"Does it do anything?"

"What do you want it to do?"

"I just don't know what the hell it is. Here, let me see it."

I hand him the bag that contains "Sherlock."

"So it doesn't do anything?"

"For the love of Christ, it's a toy. It's for kids. It doesn't do anything."

"Kids?"

"Kids."

"You mean kids?"

"Kids."

I take the gnome back from him.

"What are you doing?"

"Giving it back to them at the register."

"Why?"

"Because you're ninety-one, that's why. Do you want it?"

"Well, wait, maybe I'll give it away."

"To whom?"

"A neighbor."

"You have four-year-old neighbors?"

"There must be someone."

"What? You're going to ask around?"

"There must be someone."

"There's not."

"What the hell does it do, anyway?"

"Again he asks me. I'm giving it back to them."

"You sure there's nobody we can give this to?"

"Never been more sure of anything in my life."

"All right, give it back to them. What the hell? I don't even know what it does."

* * *

21 January

Jack Friedman, while nursing a small injury, talks about pancakes and politics.

Joe at Owl Head, as he is wont to do, made my father pancakes and eggs this morning.

"Who the hell ordered this?" he asks as the plate is placed in front of him.

"It's a surprise," I say. "Joe said he'd make this for you."

"Joe?"

"The owner."

"You mean the big guy or Owen?"

"Aaron . . . No, it's the other guy."

"Why?"

"He likes you. I asked and he said he'd be happy to. He just does this for you, you know?"

"Too much. How many eggs is this?"

"I don't know. Two, three, I guess."

"More, has to be more."

"What difference does it make? It's a nice gesture."

He tastes them.

"Too hot."

"Blow on them."

"And a pancake? He makes pancakes? I'm glad he made one, because I can't eat the way I used to."

"He made them for you before."

"Oh, that's right, but too much before."

He tastes the pancake.

"Too hot."

"Blow on it."

"You want some? I can't finish all this. Why did he make so much? And why is everything so hot?"

"Why . . . I'm thinking a 'thank you' is coming at some point."

"What?"

"Nothing."

"Everything is so goddamn hot. You know I had cereal this morning, the flakes."

"I know."

"So, let me ask, the things you write in the . . . the *Voice*, are they political?"

"Why don't you read them and find out?"

"You know, they're in the lobby of my apartment. A big stack."

"I know."

"I mean, do you pick them out, the topics, or do they pick them for you?"

"I pick. You know, again, you could read one or two."

"Read. I . . . you know. You take me out all the time. Who has time?"

"That's why you don't read me—I take you out too much?"

(He brings a napkin to his face, pulls it away, looks at it.)

"Is my nose bleeding?"

"No."

"I think it's bleeding."

"It's not bleeding."

"What do you know?"

* * *

22 January

The art was not so much my father stealing packets of Sweet'N Low from Owl Head today, but rather when I saw him do it and said, "What are you doing stealing from our friends?" and he said, "You're right, you're right," and then he reached into his pocket and gave me . . . half of what he had pinched.

* * *

27 January

In which we now know why, when the time comes, there won't be an open casket.

Scene: My father's apartment. On the bed, probably fifty shirts, still on hangers.

"Dad, what are you doing?"

"Going through some shirts, that's all. You know how many I got? And, frankly, these don't fit anymore. I think I'm gaining weight. I'm not active anymore since I stopped playing tennis."

"Here we go."

"No, I'm very serious. They're tight. I got a gut. It's your fault, taking me to these buffets."

"My fault?"

"Nah, I'm not active anymore. I used to go out, play ball, run around. Should we throw these out?"

"Nah, we'll take them to Goodwill or someplace like that."

"I haven't gone through the pockets. If they find money in them, will they call me?"

"I'm sure of it."

"Will I eventually see people in my shirts walking around?"

"A frightening thought, that."

"What?"

"Nothing."

"I'm keeping the suit, though."

"Why?"

"'Cause I may need a suit. Why, you don't think I should keep the suit?"

"You can keep the suit."

"I don't know. What do I need a suit for? I don't need a suit."

"Then don't keep the suit."

"Yeah, but you've gotta have a suit."

"Then keep the suit."

"I'll keep the suit. What the hell? I may need a suit."

"Exactly."

"I may get married again."

"Good reason to keep the suit."

"But maybe I won't get married in the suit."

"You can decide, you know, when you meet someone."

"I don't wear suits anymore, you know."

"You never wore suits."

"Yeah, but I had dress shirts, but I don't wear those anymore since I retired. But the suit I think I'll keep. I had a lot of dress shirts."

"Yes, you did. You know, a lot of men keep suits, so when they die, they can be buried in them. You want to be buried in a suit?"

"No, no suit. I want to be buried stark naked."

* * *

28 January

In which, with this one line, Jack Friedman breaks the internet today.

Cleaning out my father's bedroom closet earlier today, with him supervising every move, I came across, count 'em, five boxes of toupees on the top shelf, underneath some old comforters and pillows, to which he said, "Oh, look! Hair!"

* * *

January Supplemental

In which it happens.

The year started the way the past few have, with me preparing to write another letter to Jim at Zarrow Pointe at the Tulsa Jewish Community Retirement Center, petitioning to get my father an apartment.

"So when am I getting into the Hebrew Home?" my father had begun asking.

"The what?"

"The Hebrew Home? It's mostly Jewish, right?"

"Well, founded by Jews."

"Who's this Zorro?"

"Zarrow?"

"Am I getting in, or what?"

"It'll happen."

"I'll probably be dead by then."

Maybe not—a strange thing happened. I was about to send Jim my annual letter about why my father needed the "Hebrew Home" and why it needed him, when Jim called to tell me that he would take care of it.

This was promising.

A few days later, I was swimming at the Hebrew Home indoor pool—Jim had given me access to use the facility years before—lapping the eighty- and ninety-year-old residents in the shallow end when I noticed he was standing over me.

"Your dad's in," Jim said.

"How'd you know where to find me?"

"You're not that hard to find. Anyway, he's in."

"What happened?"

"I petitioned the board personally, and your father was approved unanimously."

"Aren't all the residents approved unanimously?"

"No—first time I've seen it."

"Holy fuck, this is good news. He'll love the 'unanimous' part."

"When do you want him to take occupancy?"

"Let's do it on February fifteenth."

"Can it happen that fast?" he asked.

"I'll make it happen that fast. Hey, you know this will change his life."

To be continued...

about the author

Barry is the author of *Jacob Fishman's Marriages, Funny You Should Mention It, Road Comic, Four Days and Year Later,* and *The Joke Was on Me, Jack Sh*t: Volume One Voluptuous Bagels and Other Concerns of Jack Friedman*, the first in his three-volume collection of life with his nonagenarian father.

Barry is an essayist, reporter, standup comedian, and political columnist. His work has appeared in *Esquire*, where he has co-hosted "The Politics Blog with Charles P. Pierce" (Pierce in fact gave him the name "Friedman of the Plains"), *The Progressive Populist, Inside Media, The Las Vegas Review-Journal*, and the *AAPG Explorer*, a magazine for petroleum geologists, which is mostly noteworthy because he knows little about petroleum geology and has hurt himself pumping his own gas.

Barry was also "Fletcher Cronie #1 or #2" (there is still some debate) in "Weird Al" Yankovic's *UHF*.

Barry hates being referred to in the third person.

also by barry friedman

Jack Sh*t Volume One: Voluptuous Bagels and Other Concerns of Jack Friedman

Jacob Fishman's Marriages

Four Days and a Year Later

The Joke Was on Me

www.ingramcontent.com/pod-product-compliance
Lightning Source LLC
Chambersburg PA
CBHW022026050526
44107CB00118B/1293/J